Viable Values

Viable Values

A Study of Life as the Root and Reward of Morality

TARA SMITH

ROWMAN & LITTLEFIELD PUBLISHERS, INC.
Lanham • Boulder • New York • Toronto • Oxford

ROWMAN & LITTLEFIELD PUBLISHERS, INC.

Published in the United States of America
by Rowman & Littlefield Publishers, Inc.
A wholly owned subsidiary of The Rowman & Littlefield Publishing Group, Inc.
4501 Forbes Boulevard, Suite 200, Lanham, Maryland 20706
www.rowmanlittlefield.com

PO Box 317
Oxford
OX2 9RU, UK

Copyright © 2000 by Rowman & Littlefield

British Library Cataloguing in Publication Information Available

Library of Congress Cataloging-in-Publication Data

Smith, Tara, 1961–
    Viable values : a study of life as the root and reward of morality / Tara Smith.
        p.   cm.
    Includes bibliographical references and index.
    ISBN 0-8476-9760-6 (cloth : alk. paper)—ISBN 0-8476-9761-4
(pbk. : alk. paper)
    1. Ethics.   2. Life—Moral and ethical aspects.   I. Title.
BJ1012.S525   2000
171'.9—dc21   99-045671

Printed in the United States of America

♾ ™ The paper used in this publication meets the minimum requirements of
American National Standard for Information Sciences—Permanence of Paper for
Printed Library Materials, ANSI/NISO Z39.48–1992.

Contents

Acknowledgments

I extend my sincere gratitude to the many individuals and institutions who have, in various ways, supported my work on this project.

Much of the preliminary writing was completed in the summer of 1996 as a visiting fellow at the Social Philosophy & Policy Center at Bowling Green State University. The center's hospitality in tending to every detail that might facilitate visitors' research created an ideal working environment.

The University of Texas Research Institute awarded me a special research grant in the spring of 1996 and a faculty research grant in the fall of 1997. The former funded a terrific research assistant in Cooper Henson.

I am grateful to several people who commented on drafts of portions of this book: Harry Binswanger, Harry Dolan, Bob Kane, Doug Browning, Steve Rogers, Ann Ciccolella, John Paulus, and Sue Ann Hill. Among many others who helped clarify my understanding of specific issues treated in this book, I especially thank Darryl Wright, Jay Garing, and Brandy Rogers. Thanks also to Marc Baer for preparing the index.

Some of the material in this book makes use of previously published articles. Chapter three is a revised version of "Intrinsic Value: Look—Say Ethics," *Journal of Value Inquiry* 32 (1998): 539–53, which appears here with kind permission of Kluwer Academic Publishers. A portion of chapter six draws on "Reconsidering Zero-Sum Value: It's How You Play the Game," *Journal of Social Philosophy* 28, no. 2 (Fall 1997): 128–39, which appears here with permission of Blackwell Publishers.

1

Introduction

E thics has been "in" over the last few years. Between best-sellers on virtues and moral responsibility, calls from conservatives and communitarians for a return to values in education and community life, a burgeoning industry of university courses devoted to business ethics, medical ethics, legal ethics, engineering ethics, and so on, and hospitals hiring moral philosophers to advise them on patient care, ethics has enjoyed a prominent profile.[1]

So why aren't people more moral? The spotlight on ethics has not been matched by an obvious strengthening of the practice of morality. If anything, much of this attention to ethics is in response to perceived immorality. Hand-wringing about the declining condition of our culture's morality is tiresomely familiar. We hear and observe that standards are slipping; people's regard for the moral ramifications of their actions seems increasingly lax, when not altogether absent. One need not deny the existence of sincere, well-meaning people to observe an abundance of corner cutting, a widespread cynicism toward morality that excuses all manner of infractions, modest and monumental. The person of upstanding moral character seems an endangered species.

Obviously, individuals differ about exactly what constitutes moral behavior. Yet even people of disparate convictions concerning the contents of morality's demands would likely agree that the surge in overt attention to ethics is having little positive effect; it is often designed as "PR" to soothe a disgruntled constituency (voters, consumers, investors) and often consumed for purposes of self-congratulation more than changing one's ways. Typically, people do not lament that their own particular moral code (Catholic or Muslim or Utilitarian, for instance) is losing out to the increased practice of some alternative code as much as the impression that ethics per se is in a free fall. Indeed, the fact that people of divergent moral beliefs are dissatisfied with our moral condition may testify to the depth of morality's decay.

The reason that people are not "more moral," I submit, is fairly simple: We have been given no good reason why we should be. The problem rests not with "the crooked timber of humanity," people's imperfect or corrupt nature.[2] Nor is it a matter of deficient self-discipline, a lack of resolve. Rather, theorists have yet to provide a compelling, logical explanation of what morality requires and why it requires it. Traditional explanations cannot withstand scrutiny. Utilitarianism is besieged with counterexamples, prompting revisions that dilute its very utilitarian character; Kantianism seems coldly indifferent to human experience and employs a distorted conception of reason. Religious morals rely on dictates of authority and faith that are not corroborated by observable evidence and that are paralyzed, logically, on encountering the inconvenient fact of competing faiths issuing competing moral directives. In short, until a better explanation of why we should be moral is provided, resistance to morality is understandable. We cannot expect moral conduct as long as people remain uncertain about its value.

In this book, I address the most fundamental grounds of moral obligation. What is it that instills moral prescriptions with their authority? If it is proper to be moral, why is that? What is the explanation of that fact?

Thus, my subject is metaethics rather than normative ethics. My immediate concern is not as much with the question of how to be moral as it is with why one should be moral. While I would dispute many prevailing ideas of what morality demands, these disputes are derivative from differences over the foundational facts that generate moral obligation. The source of moral authority is logically prior to the contents of moral prescriptions, for we cannot determine how to be moral until we understand the purpose of being moral. Thus, a rational moral theory must begin with this metaethical issue.[3]

In particular, I wish to examine Ayn Rand's thesis that values and morality are grounded in the requirements of human life. It is only in relation to the goal of living that we can distinguish objects as good or bad, Rand argues. All genuine values are such by virtue of their contribution to this end. Morality is intended to guide a person toward the achievement of values; thus, the identification of values serves as the basis for the further identification of actions as morally right or wrong. Only with a secure understanding of value and corollary notions of what is good and bad for human beings can we determine what people should and should not do. The heart of the book is an elaboration and analysis of Rand's view.

OVERVIEW

The first part of the book concentrates on existing treatments of the question of why we should be moral. I address the legitimacy of the question itself since it has often been challenged. I then critique some of philosophers' most influential explanations of moral authority. None of these, I argue, delivers a convincing case for moral obligation.

In the second part of the book, I develop Rand's proposal that the quest for life is the foundation of values and morality. First, I spell out the central reasoning for this conclusion. Next, I elaborate on the sense in which the reward of morality is a flourishing life. Finally, I consider the theory's egoistic implications for normative guidance.

Rand's account is distinctive in several significant respects. First of all, values are neither intrinsic "givens" that we simply find nor subjective constructs that our thoughts or desires manufacture. Rather, a value reflects a relationship between a particular thing and a particular person. Something is valuable if it advances an individual's life.

This entails that values are objective. Facts are as genuine—as factual—in morality as in the hardest of sciences. Claims that a certain object is good or bad or that a certain action is right or wrong are true or false, depending on the relation in which those objects or actions stand to the person in question. Just as certain nutrients or exercise can be ascertained to promote a person's health, certain ends and actions will be moral insofar as they advance a person's life. Morality's objectivity resides in this relationship.

Rand's theory is naturalistic insofar as morality is grounded in facts of human nature. The mandate for morality stems from the conditional character of human life: the fact that human beings have certain needs and that living depends on actions that fulfill those needs. A moral code designed to sustain man's life will steer him toward life-promoting actions and away from life-destructive ones.

At the same time, Rand's theory is also thoroughly functional. Morality is an instrument of practical guidance; it is a means to the end of a person's life and flourishing. On her account, morality is wholly driven, from its inception to each of its particular prescriptions, by a practical mission. The account is teleological insofar as moral action aims at a telos. This end is not imposed from without but must be sought by individuals. Embracing the goal of one's life is what gives a person reason to abide by moral prescriptions, and the means of attaining one's life are what establish the content of all moral prescriptions.

Rand's account of morality thus defies easy classification within the usual categories. According to Rand, values are objective without being intrinsic and relational without being subjective. Morality is naturalistic without being an externally imposed, unchosen duty and is functional without being arbitrary. Morality unites practicality with realism.

This much offers an image of the book's basic trajectory. Let me now offer a slightly more specific breakdown of what lies ahead.

Chapter two focuses on traditional treatments of the question "Why be moral?" Since the very posing of this question has sometimes provoked hostile resistance, I address the major arguments of its foes. Essentially, opponents maintain that no reasons for moral action could provide a satisfactory answer to the question of why we should be moral: Moral reasons would beg the question, while nonmoral reasons cannot warrant truly *moral* action. These critics contend that the demand for a reason to be moral is incoherent; an action's moral rightness supplies the reason to perform that action.

I argue that, in fact, the rejection of "nonmoral" reasons for moral action itself begs the question since it assumes that morality is inherently authoritative. It also assumes that we already know the actions that morality demands. Yet that is part of what the probing of morality's foundations challenges. We cannot know how to be moral until we have identified what morality is for.

I then turn to three influential historical accounts of morality's authority: Intuitionism, Contractarianism, and Rationalism. Intuitionists believe that human beings enjoy direct, unmediated awareness of right and wrong. Relying on conscience rather than any particular method of discovery, the simple recognition of one's duties allegedly carries all the reason for being moral that one needs. By examining the nature of intuitions, the grounds of intuitions' authority, the fact that moral truths are not self-evident, and the notorious problem of conflicting intuitions, I demonstrate Intuitionism's failure. Perhaps most important, because objectivity is a function of the method by which a person reaches conclusions and because Intuitionism disavows any specific method of uncovering moral truths, I show how Intuitionism could not offer the objective moral verdicts that it claims to.

Contractarians maintain that moral obligation is a product of human agreement; essentially, a person should be moral because he has agreed to be moral. After tracing Contractarianism's apparent strengths, I detail its shortcomings, proceeding from some familiar criticisms to more fundamental difficulties. Contractarianism faces serious questions concerning relativism, the status of those who do not agree to the moral contract, and the precise origin of obligation. To the extent that Contractarianism appeals to reason or interest to explain why one's agreement obligates, it abandons its distinctive contractarian character.

Still worse, Contractarianism's response to the notorious free-rider problem reveals defective conceptions of the nature of interest and of the nature of morality. Contractarianism portrays morality as wholly social: Morality is a solution to the "problem" posed by other people, and people (through their agreement) provide the solution. This fails to recognize the full stakes of individuals' actions regardless of whether they are in society with others and thus misses the deeper need for morality.

Rationalists believe that the rational and the moral go hand in hand; a person should be moral because rationality requires it. Rationalism's appeal rests in its seemingly straightforward logic and its corresponding rigor, broad reach, and neutrality. Moral obligation is set above the contingencies of individuals' circumstances.

The question of why a lapse of rationality should be seen as a lapse of morality, however, invites us to explore the authority of reason; this is where my critique focuses. I consider the basic nature of rational action, what constitutes a full-fledged justification of action, and the rationality of a person's ends. The ultimate sanction of reason, I find, is conformity to reality. That is, reason essentially consists of tracing facts, and the reason to adhere to reason is the desire to identify facts relevant to one's purposes. This is the most effective means of achieving one's purposes. Rationalism, however, divorces reason from the practical incentive that underwrites its authority. Thus, I explain how Rationalism's failure as an account of morality stems not from reason's deficiencies but from its impoverished conception of what reason is.

Even if these theories do in fact fail, many believe that certain things' intrinsic value provides the anchor for firm moral conclusions. Thus, chapter three considers another widely claimed foundation for morality: intrinsic value.

Here, I proceed in three stages. First, I examine exactly what intrinsic value refers to, distilling two importantly different strains: something that is good in itself and something that is sought for its own sake. Evidence for the "sought for its own sake" type of intrinsic value is far more readily available than evidence for the "good in itself" type, but the sheer fact that something is sought for its own sake does nothing to prove claims that it is good *in itself.* Yet the latter is what advocates of intrinsic value typically seek as their shield against subjectivism.

Second, I consider the evidence presented for intrinsic value, critiquing advocates' appeals to things such as organic unity and the quality of the observer's experience and G. E. Moore's "isolation method." All such accounts reduce to the claim that intrinsic value is self-evident. In fact, it is not. The failure of these accounts reveals the latent subjectivism in the embrace of intrinsic value. Although advocates of intrinsic value tend to believe in objective value, I explain how assignments of intrinsic value are invariably subjective.

Third, I consider the argument that seems the most sensible basis for belief in intrinsic value: the reasoning that intrinsic value is necessary to plug what would otherwise be an infinite regress of values. Some things must have intrinsic value, the contention is, in order for anything else to have value. This argument suffers from three fatal flaws, however. It moves the question of the grounds of value rather than providing those grounds, it fails to recognize that intrinsic value and instrumental value are not the only types of value, and it relies on an equivocation over the meaning of instrumental value.

With chapter four, the book turns from the failings of reigning theories to the presentation of a positive alternative. This chapter sets out the argument for the book's core thesis: that morality depends on a proper understanding of the concept of values and that values depend on the alternative of life or death.

First, I elaborate Rand's argument for morality's basis in life. The principal claim is that life makes the concept of value both possible and necessary. By contrasting living organisms with inanimate objects as well as with imagined immortal beings, we see that values arise only where life is at stake. The alternative of life or death is crucial to the phenomenon of values. The conditional nature of life—the fact that an organism's life depends on its taking certain actions—means that an organism must act to gain values that sustain its life.

Because of value's conception in the demands of life, I explain, life is the goal and the standard of value. This realization provides the basis for a normative code that offers more specific guidance for leading our lives. The good, in essence, is that which advances a person's life; the bad is that which damages it.

In the second part of chapter four, I spell out the most significant implication of this metaethical view: value's objectivity. Whether a given thing promotes a person's life is a matter of fact. Objectivity does not imply that values are always easily identified but, rather, that since only certain actions will satisfy needs and propel a person's life, the valid attribution of value reflects a factual relationship. Something's being a value reflects its position relative to the end of an individual's life. This distinguishes Rand's view from that of Rationalists, Intuitionists, and intrinsic value advocates, who regard value as simply given or found, and from Contractarians and subjectivists, who regard value as an artifice. Here, I also explain the difference between certain things that are valuable for all human beings and others ("optional" values) that may legitimately vary from person to person.

Next, I explain how this basis for value bridges the notorious fact–value gap. Values are inextricably grounded in facts. If a person wishes to live, various things become valuable to him on the basis of their effects on that end. The point is not that we can deduce values from facts but that inductive generalizations about the effects of various events on human life supply the factual grounds for ascriptions of value. Certain facts acquire value in relation to a person's aim of maintaining his life.

In the final part of this chapter, I address several plausible objections to this account of morality's foundations. Answering these further clarifies various aspects of Rand's theory.

Chapter five amplifies on the end of morality, arguing that the life aimed at is not minimal subsistence but flourishing. The first part of the chapter elaborates on the character of flourishing. Flourishing refers not to a separate outcome of moral conduct but to the process of living in a life-promoting manner. The requirements of flourishing are dictated by the requirements of life, and flourishing is measured by the standard of life.

In the second part of chapter five, I explain why flourishing is morality's proper aim. In particular, I address the suspicion of equivocation between life and flourishing and the corollary objection that their requirements are not interchangeable. To dispel this concern, I demonstrate that life and flourishing actually reflect two perspectives on a single phenomenon. The "difference" between life and flourishing is built on exaggerated distinctions between quantity and quality of life and between needs and wants. Explaining the extent to which these are often differences of degree rather than of kind paves the way for understanding flourishing as a condition of life rather than an independent objective. It is no more appropriate, for the purposes of specifying life's requirements, to interpret "life" as something less than a flourishing life than it would be for a biologist specifying a duck's life's requirements to employ the model of a lame duck.

Further, I argue that human beings *need* to flourish. Because life depends on actions and actions are volitional, a person's will to live is critical. The feelings associated with flourishing help sustain a person's motivation to engage in life-furthering actions. Insofar as the fact (as opposed to the feeling) of flourishing involves growth and strength, it is also essential to life. In a further sense, flourishing just *is* the end of life.

In the final part of chapter five, I explain how flourishing can be measured objectively. Against familiar refrains that "different things make different people happy," I show that resistance to this proposal typically rests on confusing a person's feeling as if he is flourishing with the fact of flourishing. Since flourishing is essentially living in a "pro-life" way, the same standards that determine what furthers a person's life determine whether a person is flourishing.

The egoistic inclination of this theory is fairly apparent. Many of its concrete prescriptions will be antithetical to conventional views of moral obligations. Since some might seize on this as reason to dismiss the theory, in chapter six I seek to clarify the egoistic character of the normative theory that emerges from these metaethical foundations. Without attempting to spell out its specific prescriptions, I argue that principled egoism is required for living and flourishing.

In the first part of chapter six, I explain the propriety of egoism as a logical implication of chapter four's argument that life makes the pursuit of values necessary. I cite several pockets of egoistic practices in ordinary life as testimony to the need for egoism. Further, I explain that the inveterate image of egoism as posing a "me or you" choice mistakenly narrows egoism's guidance to a single issue: how to deal with others. Yet morality is not primarily social; it is not *about* how to respond to other people. The fundamental fact that necessitates egoism holds regardless of other people's presence: Individuals flourish by acting for their own benefit. A moral code aimed at promoting individuals' well-being must thus be egoistic.

The second part of the chapter elaborates on the nature of self-interest. Disentangling egoism from hedonism, materialism, and subjectivism, I emphasize egoism's spiritual dimension and the demands that it makes of a person. Self-interest refers to a person's psychological well-being as much as to his physical well-being. Moreover, self-interest is not advanced by rabid consumption or wanton indulgence of appetites. A person's well-being is, at core, a matter of how he leads his life rather than of how much he acquires. Far from the slack rejection of standards that people frequently associate with selfishness, advancing one's interest requires considerable foresight and discipline. Egoism is not only *for* a person; it also demands a great deal from a person.

In particular, I explain an egoist's need to adhere to principles. Piecemeal determinations of how to act, insulated from the larger perspective of an action's full effects on all of one's values, are a poor means of advancing one's interest. Only principles can adequately account for the vast scope and interwoven components of an individual's interest. Moral principles' authority is thus grounded in their practicality.

A striking feature of this portrait of self-interest is that ill-begotten gains are not truly gains. That is, circumventing moral principles—which are designed to advance a person's life—is not in one's interest. I probe some examples to show how, despite initial appearances, the violation of proper principles works against a person's interest.

In the third part of chapter six, I explore the most provocative implications of this account. First, I argue that the pursuit of interest is not a zero-sum game. Proper egoism is not predatory, with one person's gains coming at others' expense. The keys to appreciating this are the contextual character of values, the fact that values are made rather than found, and the fact that a failure to gain something cannot be equated with a loss.

Second, I argue that rational interests cannot conflict. Careful identification of exactly what is in a person's interest and of exactly what constitutes a conflict are pivotal to appreciating this. If value were subjective, conflicts would be rife, as interest would simply reflect individuals' desires, which certainly could conflict. Since desires are not definitive of interests, however, conflicts between desires cannot be accepted as conflicts between interests. Conflicting claims to something are not necessarily valid, and the fact that a person thinks that something is in his interest does not guarantee that it actually is. I test this no-conflicts thesis by considering some hard cases.

This preview should have illuminated the book's title. The values defended here are "viable" in two senses. On one level, my contention is that these are the only values that can withstand critical scrutiny. Only the account of values provided here truly substantiates moral obligations. On another level, these values are viable by virtue of being rooted in the literal requirements of human life. Values are intelligible only in relation to living organisms; life mandates the achievement of (life-sustaining) values. Thus, *life* is the source of value.

As for the subtitle, life is the root of morality insofar as the alternative of life or death is what makes the phenomenon of value possible. Correspondingly, life makes morality—guidance for the achievement of values—necessary. Life is the reward of morality insofar as a person's own life is the proper end of moral action. A person should be moral for the sake of maintaining and enhancing his own existence.

ETHICS AS ALLY

Earlier, in commenting on the state of morality in our culture, I claimed that moral theorists have failed to provide a convincing rationale for compliance with morality. Lacking such a rationale, even those who take morality seriously tend to view morality as a burden. One must grit one's teeth to conform to its strictures, but strictures they are, hampering the pursuit of one's interest. Moral decisions are routinely framed as a contest between self-interest and duty, or between what a person would like to do and what the voice of conscience tells him he must do.[4] Morality requires resignation to such perpetual conflicts.

Without consciously identifying it in these terms, the result is that many people come to regard ethics as a necessary evil. They consider morality of grave but somewhat murky authority, an impediment to the unrestrained pursuit of their happiness. If only one were liberated from the straitjacket of moral demands (alleged duties to sacrifice for others, for instance, or to be honest although it "costs" you), one could capitalize on all of one's opportunities and lead a thoroughly rewarding life. Morality, in short, is seen as the rival to full-blown enjoyment of life.

As long as this image of ethics remains unchallenged, we can expect no progress in the practice of morality. Rand's theory, however, explodes this image. Rand offers a fundamental reconceptualization of our relationship to morality. Ethics is not a bitter wind in one's face, stinging a person with injunctions to act against his interest, but a breeze at one's back, aiding a person toward the achievement of life-enhancing values. Morality is not a burden to be resented or scrimped on, complied with only grudgingly. If Rand's theory of the nature of morality is correct, cutting moral corners amounts to cutting one's own throat. Far from being a necessary evil, ethics is a necessary ally, an indispensable tool for living. To the extent that a moral code accurately identifies a life-promoting course, morality is a tremendous benefactor.

The conception of ethics as a necessary evil is further reflected in the widespread belief that you cannot teach ethics. Many scoff at efforts to require formal moral instruction (those "Ethics for Engineers" courses), dismissing as silly the expectation that a course in moral philosophy could alter a person's character.

Doubtless, there is truth in this. As long as individuals possess free will, all the lecturing in the world will not eradicate a person's ability to engage in immorality. No one can remold another person into a consistently right-choosing agent. Yet the same applies to anything that we teach a person; it is for the student, ultimately, to decide whether to apply what he has learned in leading his life. The contention that you cannot teach ethics thus suggests something more than recognition of individuals' autonomy.

In fact, it suggests that we have no reason to be moral. Its animating premise seems to be that you either care about morality or you do not, but reason cannot argue you into it. For if it could, ethics would be teachable. The belief that ethics is unteachable treats morality as a set of pointless duties devoid of practical benefits, for again, if morality's demands served some practical purpose, that certainly could be taught. If immorality brought bad consequences, for example, we could point those out.

The deeper truth here, then, is that one cannot teach an *irrational* moral code. One cannot provide sound or persuasive reasons for people's doing things that they have no good reason to do. As long as irrational moral codes are advocated, ethics will not be teachable. The fact that irrational ethics cannot be taught does not entail that ethics cannot be taught, however. It is only the currency of mistaken codes and of the conception of ethics as a necessary evil that prevents our teaching—and learning—how properly to lead our lives.

The solution to our moral malaise rests not in recovering bygone ways. It lies in discovering the life-and-death stakes that necessitate morality. Thus the need for viable values.

NOTES

1. Among the specifics I have in mind are William Bennett's *The Book of Virtues* and Hillary Clinton's *It Takes a Village.* Other signs of ethics' trendiness: corporations have been developing ethics training seminars; in the mid-1990s, National Endowment for the Humanities chair Sheldon Hackney initiated a "national conversation" about values; "family values" have become a theme of political campaigns; President Bill Clinton launched a nationwide voluntarism initiative in 1997 with bipartisan support; "give something back" has become a mantra; and my pharmacy (I recently noticed) posts a "Code of Ethics" behind the cash register.

2. A phrase taken from Kant's *Idee zu einer allgemeinen Geschichte in weltbürgerlicher Absicht* (1784)—"out of the crooked timber of humanity no straight thing was ever made"—and recently used as the title of a collection of essays by Isaiah Berlin, *The Crooked Timber of Humanity,* ed. Henry Hardy (New York: Knopf, 1991).

3. Consequently, I do not regard clarifying the grounds of morality as useful simply as a means of strengthening devotion to principles that most people already recognize. Also, throughout I use "morality" and "ethics" interchangeably.

4. The "or" is exclusive; I am not equating these two sets of alternatives.

2

Why Be Moral?

At the base of ethics rests a simple question: Why? Why be moral? When people debate the right way to live, contesting everything from abortion and cloning to capital punishment and assisted suicide; when they argue the merits of pride and humility, justice and forgiveness, Donald Trump and Mother Theresa; or when they strive to specify the role of intentions and the conditions of responsibility, a serious question looms in the background: Why does the answer to such questions matter? If we were one day to resolve our differences and agree on *the* moral way to live, why should anyone care? What hinges on our correctly answering these questions?

It is widely taken for granted that moral judgments are a special class, carrying a unique gravity. It is one thing to observe that a person is a weak tennis partner or a middling poet; it is another to claim that he is dishonest or disloyal. Why should that be? Do we have good reasons for assigning this special weight to moral evaluations?

The history of ethics has offered periodic engagements with this question. Occasionally, "Why be moral?" has been squarely confronted, as in Socrates' exchanges with Thrasymachus and Glaucon in the *Republic*.[1] Often, the answer is implicit in a particular theory of *how* to be moral (e.g., we should obey God's commandments so as to avoid his punishments). Still other times, the question has been dismissed as sophomoric, revealing a defective understanding of the nature of morality or an unwillingness to adopt "the moral point of view."[2] The one claim we can safely make is that philosophers have forged no consensus around a single answer.

Yet the question is vital to a rational moral theory. We never know how to do something until we know what it is that we are trying to do. How to construct a building depends on what it is that one is trying to build (a

13

home? a school? a factory?). How to craft a drama depends on what the playwright is trying to convey. How to raise a child depends on the qualities that the parent wishes to inculcate. The same applies for morality. We cannot know how to live unless we know why we should attempt to live according to *any* particular rhyme or reason—until we know what it is that we are trying to accomplish.

If morality is concerned with prescribing how a person should lead his life, "Why be moral?" poses a metaquestion: Why suppose that a person should lead his life in one way as opposed to another? Answering this question will actually serve two critical purposes: It provides the goal toward which normative guidance should be directed, and it clarifies the stakes of morality. That is, discovering the source of the moral "ought" illuminates the force of the moral "ought." Knowing why we should take morality seriously, what hangs in the balance, also tells us how seriously to take it.

At one level, this entire book investigates why we should be moral. Before presenting what I consider the proper explanation, however, it is instructive to consider some historical treatments of the question. Exposing the serious inadequacies of prominent moral theories will both underscore the centrality of the question and drive home the need for a better answer.

In this chapter, then, I take up two main tasks. First, I will consider the charge that the question "Why be moral?" is misconceived, arguing that the issue is not merely legitimate but crucial to any acceptable moral theory. Second, I will identify the deficiencies of the most influential answers that previous ethicists have supplied, showing that none provides adequate justification for morality's authority. In the course of the latter (particularly in assessing Rationalism), I will consider the nature of justification itself, which will begin to illuminate what sort of explanation might constitute a satisfactory answer to "Why be moral?".

Before proceeding to these tasks, a couple of preliminaries are important.

First, we must be open to the possibility that no justification of morality is attainable. That may sound obvious since a justification is exactly what "Why be moral?" seeks. Yet it is worth emphasizing because of the difficulty in sincerely surrendering the assumption of moral obligation. Even when we think that we are challenging basic assumptions about morality's demands, we tend to retain, subconsciously, entrenched beliefs about its authority. The tenacity of these assumptions may be especially strong among ethicists, who are usually committed to taking (at least some version of) morality quite seriously. Unless one is willing to relinquish such assumptions, however, our discussion will be an artificial exercise in gerrymandering preset conclusions rather than an honest inquiry into morality's foundations. The fact that certain moral conventions have been long or widely accepted carries no guarantee that they can withstand rational scrutiny. In order to arrive at a sound defense of morality, all prior suppositions about morality's authority must be on the table. Any reader unwilling to suspend such suppositions is warned: Continued reading will be a waste of time.

Second, we must surrender assumptions about the contents of morality, concerning what sorts of actions it commands. Rigid commitment to particular normative doctrines will restrict the viable explanations of morality's grounds. Dogmas about the directives of morality inevitably affect whether and what sort of justification is possible. *What* you are trying to justify determines the kinds of justifications that might succeed. If one is precommitted to particular virtues or vices (e.g., certain that adultery must turn out to be always wrong or forgiveness to be always right), one is seeking a rationalization for one's existing beliefs rather than a justification of true beliefs. Such is not my project; it is not what is needed to provide the foundation of morality.

Can we really do this? Some might protest that these prerequisites are impossible. However much we might like to, we cannot begin shorn of *all* presuppositions concerning the fact or content of moral authority. Such suppositions seem to be the leverage that enables us to evaluate various theories. If we were truly to shed such assumptions, we would have shaved away the very subject. What would be left to discuss, having dropped beliefs about morality's authority and prescriptions?

The answer is straightforward. We are investigating the *concept* of morality. Given that people have long discriminated between "moral" and "immoral" behavior, we are probing whether sound reasons exist for drawing such distinctions. One need not accept particular conventions of etiquette in order to investigate whether sound reasons underlie those conventions. One need not be religious to understand the idea of religious authority. One can investigate the occurrence of miracles without precommitment to their existence. Similarly, one need not accept the authority of morality in order to investigate whether its alleged authority is genuine.

We should also notice a serious error in the idea that presuppositions about morality's authority and content are necessary in order to evaluate proposed theories of morality's authority. This reflects a mistaken view of standards of assessment. We do not judge an idea simply by the yardstick of accepted beliefs since those might themselves be mistaken. If evaluations were bound by accepted beliefs, how would new ideas ever come to be accepted? The objection implies that the only way to prove morality's authority is by taking it for granted from the outset. This stance, apart from its patent circularity, misses the point of an inquiry into morality's foundations.

Obviously, we must accept the general subject matter of morality to ensure that a coherent inquiry can proceed. But that requires agreement only on the basic category, on the fact that certain decisions and actions are often reputed to be moral or immoral. We must know what people have *thought* that morality commands. There is no need, however, to concede that it actually commands any of those sorts of actions—which is simply another way of saying that one need not import any assumptions to the effect that morality is binding or that any particular moral directives are justified.

In sum, the prerequisites are perfectly attainable. And they are necessary if the inquiry is to be objectively fruitful.

A MISCONCEIVED QUESTION?

While the request for the basis of morality's authority seems innocent enough, it has precipitated remarkable hostility. Many ethicists preempt its serious consideration by assuming its incoherence.[3] They maintain that the question is misconceived. This is supposedly revealed as soon as one considers possible answers. If a moral reason for behaving morally is given, that does beg the question. The authority of moral grounds for acting in certain ways is exactly what is being challenged. The alternative seemingly fares no better, however: A nonmoral reason for being moral would not provide an explanation of why one should be *moral.* Such a rationale for adherence to moral demands would subordinate morality to whatever type of consideration it is that allegedly explains why a person should do as morality commands (e.g., for social harmony, self-interest, or peaceful sleep). But this misconstrues the nature of morality's claim on us. Moral behavior, many contend, requires a purely moral motive; it is not performed for the sake of any extraneous considerations. To the extent that one appeals to such factors to "justify" morality, it is no longer morality that one is justifying. As F. H. Bradley put it, if we look upon morality only as good for something else, we have not really seen her.[4]

The inference usually drawn is that the request for morality's grounds is confused. One can find no further reasons to comply with morality beyond the recognition that morality demands it.

This position is encountered far more often as a casual aside—passing observation of a truism—than as the conclusion of a systematic analysis of the issue. Still, to give it its due, we should consider the specific claims of a couple of authors who have directly addressed the issue.

John Hospers contends that "we should be moral, simply because it's right." Once a person accepts that an act is right, its rightness supplies the reason for performing the act. "Isn't it enough simply that the act is the right one to perform? Perhaps the rightness of the act isn't enough to *cause* us to perform the act . . . but doesn't the rightness provide a sufficient *reason* for performing the act?"[5]

In defense of his position, Hospers clarifies: "We are not merely asking 'Why should we perform right actions?' and giving the tautological reply, 'Because they're right.' We are asking, 'Why should we do this act rather than other acts we might have done instead?' and we are answering, 'Because it's the right act.' "[6]

Hospers then goes on the offensive, charging the question with incoherence. The questioner is demanding a self-interested reason for moral action. "But the situation is *ex hypothesi* one in which the act required of him is contrary to his interest. Of course it is impossible to give him a reason *in accordance with his interest* for acting *contrary to his interest*. . . . It is a self-contradictory request," comparable to looking for square circles.[7]

Stephen Toulmin similarly dismisses the question, emphasizing the limits of logic in providing a basis of morality. "There is no more general 'reason' to be given [for an action] beyond one which relates the action to an accepted social practice." Any attempt to use facts to justify a practice or moral code would be guilty of the naturalistic fallacy. We cannot travel "outside" competing practices to assess them and discover which is *really* right. In ethics, "the range of decisions for which it makes sense to talk of a 'moral justification' is limited; again there is a point up to which morality can take you, but beyond which it cannot go." Toulmin concludes that "the final decision is personal."[8]

Thus, like Hospers, Toulmin regards "Why be moral?" as a confused question. "Why ought one to do what is right?," he holds, is on a par with "Why are all scarlet things red?" "Since the notions of 'right' and of 'obligation' originate in the same situations and serve similar purposes, it is a self-contradiction . . . to suggest that we 'ought' to do anything but what is 'right.' " The proper response to "Why ought one to do what is right?" is "What else 'ought' one to do?"[9]

In sketching the boundaries of an explanation of morality's basis, both Hospers and Toulmin comment on the philosopher's responsibility. Hospers remarks that the philosopher can only move people who "are willing to hear rational arguments." Toulmin maintains that it is not the philosopher's job to provide "the case for morality" or to make you want to do what you ought to do. "It is absurd and paradoxical . . . to suppose that we need to produce a 'reasoned argument' capable of convincing the 'wholly unreasonable.' " While this, allegedly, is what his opponents demand, Toulmin insists that "we do not prescribe logic as a treatment for lunacy."[10]

The proper response to these arguments is fairly simple. The logic of the question naturally depends on the interpretation of the question. If we are seeking moral reasons for compliance with morality, the only possible answers will be circular; "Why be moral?" *would* be comparable to asking "Why are scarlet things red?" Thus, I concede that "moral reasons" for being moral could not provide a satisfactory justification. Nonmoral reasons, however, cannot be dismissed so easily.[11]

The claim that appeal to nonmoral reasons for being moral would inappropriately subordinate morality rests on a major assumption: that morality's authority is autonomous or self-contained, not derived from any extramoral facts. The "subordination" of morality to such facts would be objectionable only if morality's authority were already held as independent of such nonmoral underpinnings. But whether that is so is precisely what is in question. It is the grounds of moral authority that we are attempting to identify. To insist that morality is inherently authoritative begs the question, presuming that morality's grounds can be found only within morality.

More broadly, Toulmin's and Hospers's dismissals of "Why be moral?" treat the question too superficially, failing truly to engage it. One could reject the request for a reason to be moral as self-contradictory only if one took for granted that we already know what we ought to do. But again, my project is not to rationalize common beliefs about how to be moral. Honest moral theory must purge such assumptions. A large part of the point of asking "Why?" is to determine what, in fact, morality demands of us. Indeed, the disparities in people's views on moral matters testify to the need to identify the grounds beneath these competing views.

While it is true that once one accepts the authority of morality it would be silly to inquire as to why one should do as it prescribes, "Why be moral?" asks why a person should recognize morality's authority in the first place. From the "moral point of view," a person should do what morality dictates; the further question being raised is "Why should a person adopt that point of view?"[12] Toulmin's and Hospers's discussions, however, leave this deeper question completely unexplored. Why regard some acts as right? What accounts for their being right? Why does it ever make sense to think that someone ought, morally, to do something? Usually, a person ought to do something so as to further some objective. You ought to change the air conditioning filter if you want to keep the air clean; you ought to floss your teeth if you want to prevent gum disease. If the moral sphere is different, such that reasons need not be tied to purposes, we need an explanation of the basis of its special status.

The reason for Toulmin's and Hospers's neglect of these questions, again, is that they take the content of morality for granted. More specifically, they assume that morality is antithetical to self-interest. Toulmin portrays self-love and a sense of right as direct antagonists.[13] Hospers, we saw, glibly asserts that moral demands are *ex hypothesi* contrary to a person's interest. Granting this assumption about the contents of moral prescriptions, however, entirely misses the point. Why does morality demand self-sacrifice? We cannot know any of morality's demands until we know what it is that morality seeks to accomplish. *This* is why building morality on an answer to "Why be moral?" is imperative.

Notice that Toulmin cloaks himself in the banner of rationality without having earned it by having provided an argument for allegiance to morality. His contention that philosophers need not convince "the unreasonable" leapfrogs past argument by misrepresenting what those who ask "Why be moral?" are seeking. The question simply requests a logical explanation of moral authority. That is precisely what those rushing to reject the question have not supplied. Labeling one's opponents unreasonable does not relieve one of the burden of answering the question. Those who challenge the grounds of morality can be dismissed as unreasonable only after the reasons for moral obligation have been demonstrated.

In sum, if we assume that morality demands self-sacrifice and that the only satisfactory answer to "Why be moral?" would appeal to self-interest, then "Why be moral?" is a question that cannot be answered. But we can—and should—question those assumptions. *Is* the only adequate answer one that appeals to self-interest? *Does* morality demand self-sacrifice? We cannot rule egoism out at the outset any more than we can rule it in. We cannot resolve any of these issues, however, without forthrightly tackling them.

Refusal to consider "Why be moral?" amounts to stubborn dogmatism: "You just should be moral." The feebleness of this familiar refrain may explain why so many people feel ambivalence toward morality and why even those who try to follow it often do so with reservation or resentment. The resistance stems from a lack of conviction as to why they truly should adhere to moral strictures. As long as such uncertainty remains, we can hardly expect greater devotion to moral living. This is all the more reason to pursue morality's demands to their roots.

HISTORICAL ANSWERS

While many have scorned "Why be moral?", others have answered it, more or less directly. One could tease presuppositions about the source of moral authority from any prescriptive moral code, of course, but I will consider three schools of thought that have addressed the issue head-on: Intuitionism, Contractarianism, and Rationalism.

I focus on these three primarily on the grounds of their influence and fundamentality. In various forms, Intuitionism, Contractarianism, and Rationalism continue to be widely held today. Their influence, both in the past and the present, is a function of their fundamentality. By digging fairly near the root of the question of moral authority, one or another of this trio actually stands beneath many other moral theories not treated here. That is, several other schools are variations on more basic positions staked out by these three alternatives. Utilitarianism, for example, is often defended on the essentially Contractarian reasoning that social utility is agreed to be the most worthy end of our actions. Other times, Utilitarianism is defended as reflecting the inherent value of the social good, which is intuitively obvious (Intuitionism).[14] Egoism is sometimes advocated through the methods of Contractarianism, sometimes by appeal to pure rationality (Rationalism). Altruism also often relies on Rationalist arguments about the universalizability of actions. Natural Law theory sometimes seems simply a species of Intuitionism.[15]

In short, since we do not have space to explore all possible answers to "Why be moral?," reviewing these three should offer a clear window on the basic options. Since each has its appeal, it is important to understand their shortcomings. Recognizing the failures of these major accounts of morality's authority will expose the need to reopen the question and find a better answer.[16]

INTUITIONISM

One response to "Why be moral?" comes from Intuitionism. The influential eighteenth-century bishop Joseph Butler is the father of Intuitionism, and it has been ardently embraced into this century, most famously by H. A. Prichard, W. D. Ross, and, on the issue of what things are good, G. E. Moore. (Moore remained a utilitarian on the question of which actions are right.)[17]

Today, one encounters more implicit than explicit Intuitionism. Fewer people will label themselves card-carrying Intuitionists than will reach for intuition as the default defense of their convictions. Yet Intuitionism retains a sizeable contingent of open devotees. Rawls's widely invoked procedure of seeking reflective equilibrium, recommending that we check conjectural principles against our considered judgments, has quietly revived the respectability of intuitions among many philosophers.[18] T. K. Seung observes a "new vogue" for normative Intuitionism. Such prominent ethicists as Bernard Williams, Robert Audi, Lawrence Blum, and Jonathan Dancy have all professed their allegiance.[19]

The core thesis of Intuitionism is that human beings possess direct knowledge of right and wrong. Prichard maintains that "the sense of obligation to do, or of the rightness of, an action of a particular kind is absolutely underivative or immediate." We do not come to appreciate an obligation by a process of nonmoral thinking, tracing intermediate premises or argument. Rather, this appreciation is an activity of "moral thinking," a unique and irreducible kind. Our apprehension of actions' morality is immediate "in precisely the sense in which a mathematical apprehension is immediate," Prichard explains. Our sense of the rightness of an act is not a conclusion from our appreciation of the goodness of it or of anything else. Indeed, the belief that certain acts are duties is not arrived at by argument at all.[20]

Butler located the seat of this moral knowledge in a particular faculty: conscience. Just as we possess eyes with which to see and ears with which to hear, we possess conscience to distinguish right from wrong. Conscience is a "superior principle of reflection," "the faculty which surveys, approves or disapproves, the several affections of our mind and actions." We know that we possess this faculty simply by observation of our own experience and that of others. Butler writes,

> [A]llowing the inward feeling, shame, a man can as little doubt whether it was given him to prevent his doing shameful actions, as he can doubt whether his eyes were given him to guide his steps. And as to these inward feelings themselves—that they are real, that man has in his nature passions and affections, can no more be questioned than that he has external senses.[21]

Correspondingly, Intuitionists contend that moral truths are self-evident.[22] Another early Intuitionist, Samuel Clarke, spoke of moral knowledge as awareness of our obligation to act in conformity with the universe's "eternal fitnesses." Our obligations to obey God or to promote the general welfare, for instance,

> are so notoriously plain and self-evident, that nothing but the extremest stupidity of mind, corruption of manners, or perverseness of spirit, can possibly make any man entertain the least doubt concerning them. For a man endued with reason, to deny the truth of these things; is the very same thing, as if a man that has the use of his sight, should at the same time that he beholds the sun, deny that there is any such thing as light in the world.[23]

Since moral judgments are not conclusions of argument, moral truth cannot be logically demonstrated. We have no method, procedure, or device (such as the categorical imperative or principle of utility) by which to decipher morality's dictates. Intuitionists are committed to a plurality of potentially conflicting first principles as well as to the absence of any particular method for prioritizing these principles.[24] Yet the moral realm still admits of truth. The lack of a method is no defect, according to the Intuitionists; it simply reflects the nature of moral phenomena. Ross, speaking of claims that certain actions are morally obligatory, posited that "the moral order expressed in these propositions is just as much part of the fundamental nature of the universe . . . as is the spatial or numerical structure expressed in the axioms of geometry or arithmetic."[25] In other words, moral distinctions are valid, and we *can* have moral knowledge; we simply cannot defend claims of knowledge by appeal to rational argument. We "just know" right from wrong.

The answer to "Why be moral?" is thus given by conscience. Basically, the Intuitionists contend that once a person recognizes the specific moral obligations that conscience alerts him to (e.g., to be fair in judging a certain person or not to cheat on a test), he knows all he needs to concerning why he should act as morality demands. It is a confusion to seek some additional answer on top of that. In holding that every particular moral obligation is self-evident, the Intuitionist is claiming that the reason to be moral is self-evident.

Should a person wonder why he is obligated to follow his conscience, Butler would remind him that he has no guide besides conscience to consult. Why open your eyes, when you want to see something? Why eat, when you are hungry? Conscience simply *is* the faculty for guiding our actions. We are naturally constructed to recognize moral obligations. Butler contends that the question of conscience's authority

> carries its own answer along with it. Your obligation to obey this law is its being a law of your nature. That your conscience approves of and attests to such a course of action is itself alone an obligation. Conscience does not only offer itself to show us the way we should walk in, but it likewise carries its own authority with it.[26]

Thus, conscience is bedrock, as basic a ground for morality as probing could uncover. As Ross summed up the Intuitionist view, "We have no more direct way of access to the facts about rightness and goodness and about what things are right or good, than by thinking about them; the moral convictions of thoughtful and well-educated people are the data of ethics just as sense perceptions are the data of a natural science."[27]

Intuitionism is thus something of an antitheory. It does not offer a justification of morality as much as the contention that no justification is needed. As such, it is closely akin to the view that "Why be moral?" is a misguided question.

The Case for Intuitionism

The nature of the Intuitionist doctrine entails that it cannot be defended in the customary ways, for one cannot directly argue for the validity of obligations that are allegedly self-evident. If the denial of some self-evident obligation is comparable to denying the evidence before one's senses, no further assemblage of premises and inferences can hope to provide a compelling case for that obligation. The person who refuses to acknowledge the evidence before his senses is no more likely to assent to claims that are further steps removed from, and thus less obviously true than, the evidence of his senses. Since the Intuitionist holds that obligations are self-evident, all he can do to support this thesis is point. When persistent pointing to the alleged self-evidence of specific obligations fails, Intuitionism's most promising avenue of defense lies in arguing against alternative views.

To do that, the Intuitionist might allege widespread consensus on moral issues and contend that this is not the result of everyone's being convinced by the same arguments. Many people around the world accept a version of the Golden Rule, he might argue, yet this is not because all its practitioners have read the same books or been persuaded by the same syllogisms. People in various cultures show deep respect for the sanctity of human life (albeit in sometimes exotically disparate forms), but this, again, is not due to their concurrence on a particular rationale for such respect.

Further, the Intuitionist might contend, arguments often make people no *more* sure of actions' moral status. When a person is convinced that courage and integrity are admirable and that cowardice and hypocrisy are not, or that truth telling and just judging are good and that wife beating and child molesting are bad, discovery of some flaw in a particular argument for these beliefs is unlikely to jostle a person's confidence in them. People's moral beliefs seem largely immune to the fortunes of Kantian, utilitarian, or other arguments supporting those beliefs.

What all of this allegedly demonstrates is the irrelevance of argument to moral knowledge. Argument is not the basis of people's moral beliefs, and people attach no additional certainty to their moral convictions on account of arguments. Conscience is sufficient. The directives of conscience explain the tremendous overlap in people's moral views despite the absence of shared logical routes to those views.

In effect, the best defense of Intuitionism amounts to a challenge to their opponents to "put up or shut up." If one denies that intuitions distinguish right and wrong, one must demonstrate the stronger alternative that actually does. Until such a rational explanation of morality is provided, the Intuitionist contends, Intuitionism offers the most plausible account of moral obligation.[28]

Critique

The path to intuitions as the base of morality is not so smooth, however. Intuitionism suffers from several serious problems.

First, we might reasonably inquire, what exactly *is* an intuition? One rarely encounters clear statements of their nature. If an intuition is a thought, why employ a term suggesting that it is anything less than that? If it is a particular type of thought, what type? If an intuition is an emotion or feeling. what distinguishes intuitions from ill-founded feelings? And what prevents Intuitionism from collapsing into Emotivism?

Are intuitions desires? Hunches? Stubborn convictions that a person refuses to surrender? The point is, we cannot be sure whether we have such things, let alone what role they play in providing moral guidance, until we know precisely what intuitions are. One suspects that the absence of definition, keeping intuitions afloat as a hazy "something" between a thought and a feeling, may hide the fact that there are no such things. Without a forthright explanation of what intuitions are, Intuitionism's affinity with mysticism is hard to deny.[29]

Further, suppose (generously) that we pinned down what intuitions refer to and found that we do experience intuitions about moral matters. Why should we follow those intuitions? Why accept what intuitions incline us to believe as true? Are they infallible? Intuitionists have differed on this question. But whether allegedly fallible or infallible, more needs to be said to demonstrate intuitions' authority.[30]

The Intuitionist might reply that he has already answered this: Conscience shows the authority of intuitions. We should not focus on the definition of intuitions or on the source of their authority but on the self-evidence of our obligations. *This* is what is crucial to the Intuitionist stance.

This contention runs smack into the wall of reality, however. Moral truths are not self-evident. To see this, we should consider Intuitionism's two pivotal concepts: conscience and self-evidence.

Is conscience a valid concept? Certainly, people can reflect on their motives, desires, and actions. Prospectively and retrospectively, we can evaluate the merits of alternative actions, approving of some and disapproving of others. To the extent that "conscience" refers to these activities, it designates a genuine phenomenon. If "conscience" is meant to designate a distinct mental faculty, however, it is not a valid concept, for we do not have adequate grounds to accept the existence of such a faculty.

Human beings are endowed with reason. Among the things that we can reason *about* is morality, deliberating over what we should do and should not do, engaging in self-censure or self-approval for what we have done. But this hardly warrants the conclusion that we possess a unique faculty of specifically moral reflection.[31]

Moreover, the ability to reason about moral matters bears none of the characteristics that Intuitionists attribute to it. It is certainly not universally employed. When the capacity is employed, it is not always rationally employed. And people do not unfailingly converge on the same answers to moral questions. Nor does moral knowledge arrive unbidden, with obvious moral truths simply making themselves known, if only we open our "moral eyes."

The ability to think about moral matters does not operate automatically. Whether a person thinks about morality is up to him. Further, the rationality of his reflection depends on the principles that he employs, the information that he considers, and his own decisions in every stage of thinking. The logic of his conclusions depends on the inferences that he draws. A mistake at any step could invalidate his conclusion. We possess no infallible equipment that, if utilized, unerringly homes in on moral truth. Similarly, we are not born with innate ideas revealing moral truths (any more than we possess innate ideas about anything else). If moral knowledge were imprinted on everyone's mind from birth, we would find far more uniformity in people's moral opinions.

The other concept in Intuitionism that demands some scrutiny is "self-evident." Self-evidence concerns our means of awareness of something, the manner by which we come to know it. The self-evident is, literally, that which is evident by itself, without reference to other facts, information, or knowledge. Self-evidence is not a function of how simple or complex an alleged fact is nor of how widely believed it is. What is self-evident is readily available to the senses.[32]

What should we make of the proposal that moral truths are self-evident? Let us test it by a few examples of claims that many regard as true: It is wrong to cheat; it is wrong to engage in extramarital affairs; it is wrong to have an abortion, to murder, to engage in homosexual acts, to be dishonest or disloyal, to be unjust or ungrateful, to be proud or to refuse to forgive.

Are these self-evident truths?

What is most obvious about these claims is that not everyone accepts them. (I certainly do not subscribe to all of them.) What is allegedly self-evident is not self-evident to all. Obviously, this is a difficult fact for the Intuitionists to explain.

Seemingly, to defend their position, Intuitionists would have to assert that half the world's population is suffering from a defective conscience—impaired abilities to appreciate the self-evident. Apart from its implausibility, such an amendment would effectively void Intuitionism's contention that we all "just know" right from wrong and would seriously undercut the value of conscience.[33]

Equally significant, note that even those moral beliefs winning the widest consensus are not self-evident and are not held as self-evident by many people who profess strong beliefs about them. Rather, their purported truth is built on more basic propositions, such as the belief that dishonesty thwarts another person's ability to achieve his goals or that marital infidelity causes pain or corrodes trust. Certain features *make* an action right or wrong; an action might be wrong because it is based on an evil intention or carries malignant effects on social utility; an intention might be evil because it cannot be universalized or disobeys the will of God.

Morality is a much more sophisticated phenomenon than could be explained by self-evident truths. Important as these are at the base of any knowledge, conclusions about the morality of actions reflect higher-level integrations of knowledge. The suggestion that morality could be self-evident arises from a gross oversimplification of the function of morality. Any action's being morally good or bad rests on other facts about that action. Obviously, this is exactly what orthodox Intuitionists deny, and a full defense of it must await the argument for moral obligation that I will present in chapter four. Yet even without that, we have ample reason to reject Intuitionism's claim that moral truth is self-evident.

To this stage, we have set aside serious questions about the meaning of intuitions and the authority of intuitions. Now, suppose that the Intuitionists simply did not think very deeply about the meaning of conscience or self-evidence and thus did not realize the problems with their reliance on these concepts. Even if we set aside these problems as well, one would still have compelling reason to reject Intuitionism. Recall the Intuitionist's reasoning against opposing theories: Arguments do not lead people to their moral convictions about justice, honesty, child abuse, and so on; thus, it must be intuitions that explain them.

Notice two things. First, a lesson from elementary logic: There is a crucial difference between what leads people to a firmly held conviction and what, if anything, justifies that conviction. The fact that many people share a particular moral belief does not entail its truth. Nor does it show that their grounds for believing it are sound. Why people believe what they do—however many believe it, however tightly they cling to it—is irrelevant to the truth of what they believe and to the logic of their method. Even if people do hold many of their moral beliefs as a matter of intuition, that does not show that intuition is in fact the objective basis for moral truths.

Second, the Intuitionists' assertion of the irrelevance of argument is plausible only as long as the examples invoked are carefully selected, restricting the discussion to relatively uncontroversial cases. Fewer people will dispute the immorality of child abuse or wife beating than of abortion or homosexuality. In fact, people often have sincere, deep-felt disagreement about moral issues. One need only remind oneself of the examples I mentioned earlier or a few of the raging controversies reported regularly in the press to recognize that moral truth is not evident to all. These disputes cannot be dismissed with the glib contention that some people are not trying hard enough to "see" the truth.

The absence of self-evident moral truths becomes glaring when we consider the frequent fact of conflicting intuitions. This is the notorious, single most crippling obstacle to Intuitionism. When two individuals' intuitions about what is right in a given case stand directly at odds or when a person's own intuitions pull in opposing directions (e.g., "I should hold this person to the rules," "I should be merciful"), what is an Intuitionist to do? Ross writes that when more than one of his prima facie duties seems incumbent on him, he

> must study the situation as fully as I can until I form the considered opinion (it is never more) that in the circumstances one of them is more incumbent than any other; then I am bound to think that to do this *prima facie* duty is my duty *sans phrase* in the situation.[34]

How should one study the situation more fully? What should one attend to, to "form the opinion" of which duty is paramount? No particulars are offered. Engage in further "moral thinking," and the answer will emerge.

Essentially, when it is not immediately apparent what morality demands, Intuitionism instructs you to "think harder."

That is ridiculously unsatisfactory.

As if sensing this inadequacy, both Ross and Prichard refine their claims. Prichard writes that appreciation of an obligation is possible only for a "developed moral being." Ross contends that "the verdicts of the moral consciousness of the best people are the foundation on which [we] must build."[35]

These qualifications hardly strengthen their position, however. To rescue Intuitionism from the fact that moral obligations are not self-evident, Prichard and Ross rein in the class of people to whom obligations allegedly are self-evident. When a dispute arises, we must consult the moral experts. Who are the experts? We have nothing other than intuitions to tell us.

The problem here is not the belief that some people may be better than others at discriminating right from wrong. Sustained, thoughtful practice can sharpen one's skills in recognizing the moral salience of actions, such that, over time, some people might become better at moral discrimination. The problem is that no *basis* is given for the alleged propriety of certain intuitions. Intuitionism offers no grounds for the "proper" adjudication of conflicting intuitions.

Part of the appeal of Intuitionism is no doubt in its claim to offer objective moral knowledge. Many will cheer its commitment to moral truth. Yet while Intuitionism aspires to objectivity, it does not deliver it.

Objectivity concerns the manner in which a conclusion is reached. When a basketball referee calls a foul on the basis of what he observes and the relevant rules, his action is objective; when a referee calls a foul in order to hurt the team that he wants to see lose, he is not being objective. If jurors base a verdict on their scrupulous, logical weighing of all the evidence and testimony heard in court, their verdict is objective; if jurors base a verdict on irrelevant characteristics, such as the defendant's race, it is not objective.

The only way to determine whether a conclusion (or decision or action) is objective is to examine the method by which it was reached. Intuitionism, however, expressly disavows methods. Intuitionism provides no explanation of how to distinguish a properly functioning conscience from a defective one. It prescribes no procedures to be followed in order to arrive at moral knowledge. Rather, it proclaims, such knowledge results from immediate apprehension; we enjoy direct, unfiltered insight into right and wrong.

By eschewing any methods by which to uncover moral truth, Intuitionism forfeits the possibility that any of its claims could be objective. The claim that certain truths are self-evident is objective *when* it is applied to truths that are, indeed, self-evident. But affirming the self-evidence of beliefs that are not is anything but. By endorsing certain beliefs in the absence of proof, Intuitionism detaches itself from the moorings of objectivity.

All this underscores the antiphilosophical character of Intuitionism that I alluded to earlier. Intuitionism refuses to provide reasons to support its assertions of moral propriety. As one commentator has observed, Intuitionism completely fails to explain what distinguishes the claim "I know it by intuition" from the claim "I believe it."[36] Consequently, Intuitionism's account of morality—of how to be moral as well as of why a person should be moral—is completely arbitrary.

CONTRACTARIANISM

Contractarianism offers a very different answer to "Why be moral?" Although better known as a theory of political obligation, many have embraced Contractarianism as the explanation of moral authority. Its core thesis is that obligation is a product of human agreement. "Contractarian moral theories hold that an action, practice, law or social structure is morally permissible just in case it, or principles to which it conforms, would be (or has been) agreed to by the members of society under certain specified conditions."[37] Moral responsibilities result from our own deliberate actions. Essentially, you should be moral because you have agreed to be moral.

Advocates have defended variations on this thesis, differing over such issues as whether the agreement is explicit or tacit, whether the contract is actual (one that a person did make) or hypothetical (one that a person would make if he were acting fully rationally), how individually or socially oriented the contractors are, and how direct the rewards of compliance.[38] Regardless of the details, Contractarians agree on the principal rationale driving such a contract. People voluntarily place restrictions around themselves only because they believe that they will be better off as a result. In Hobbes's classic model, individuals trade freedom for security since a lawless, amoral society precludes "industry . . . cultivation of the earth . . . navigation . . . commodious building . . . arts . . . letters . . . society."[39] It makes sense to agree to restrictions in order to enhance one's own well-being.

Self-interest allegedly motivates people's initial agreement to the contract as well as their subsequent compliance with it. It is only because keeping one's agreement can further one's interest and breaking it can hurt it that agreement creates obligation. Hobbes makes no effort to disguise this, writing that obligation arises from fear of evil consequence. Indeed, it is fear of death that inclines men to peace.[40]

The most prominent contemporary Contractarian, David Gauthier, offers morals by agreement (the title of his influential book), "a contractarian rationale for distinguishing what one may and may not do. Moral principles are introduced as the objects of fully voluntary *ex ante* agreements among rational persons."[41]

Gauthier vehemently rejects intuitions as the base of morality, casting Contractarianism as a development of Rationalism. Like Kant, Gauthier contends that in order to be rational, a person must be moral. But a rational morality turns out to be Contractarian.

Further, Gauthier sees contract-based morality as constraining a person's pursuit of self-interest in ways that turn out to be more truly advantageous for that person. And by fleshing out the excessively abstract image of persons prevalent in prior Contractarian theories, Gauthier seeks to enlarge our understanding of the kind of self-interest that generates morality.[42]

The Case for Contractarianism

Contractarianism carries an undeniable commonsense appeal. The same kernel that makes Contractarianism attractive as a political theory also nurtures the moral theory, namely, the idea that if a person agrees to do something, it is completely fair to hold him to his word. Consent is a sufficient warrant for obligation. "If you said you would, you should" seems such a basic rule of social relations that it is difficult to analyze or defend. (Children tend to grasp this idea fairly early, holding adults uncomfortably accountable for broken promises.)

Contractarianism also benefits from its simplicity. Compared to Intuitionism, it is plain and straightforward, positing no special faculties or "self-evident" truths that turn out to be very difficult to decipher. Familiar with promise making, people can easily understand the terms of Contractarianism.

Moreover, Contractarianism carries a democratic air that many find congenial. Rather than providing self-sufficient grounds for moral obligation, it defers to what people want. Contractarian morality is not "imposed" from without; a person is obligated only if he has agreed to be. The implicit message that no one has to do anything that he doesn't want to (or hasn't agreed to) suits a taste for autonomy.

Beyond this level of general appeal, Contractarianism's supporters might cite more specific lines of defense. Advocates would defend Contractarianism largely on the ground of its realism. This takes two main forms.

First, they would argue, Contractarianism accepts people as they are. It recognizes the wide diversity of people's values, goals, tastes, and desires and makes peace with this plurality by allowing individuals to pursue their different ideals. As long as a person's pursuits respect the agreed-upon moral rules, a person may do as he likes. Contractarianism is thus a tolerant ethic that can seem a realistic concession to the difficulty of substantiating the belief that some values are superior to others. Through the tangled strands of people's divergent ends, Contractarianism seeks a common thread from which to weave morality. The thread that it finds is self-interest. Thus, it constructs morality, seen as a set of basic rules of conduct necessary to maintain the order requisite for people to pursue their ends, accordingly.

This is the second aspect of Contractarianism's alleged realism. Many believe that it is human nature to be self-interested. One need not subscribe to hard-core psychological egoism to consider self-interest a widespread and tenacious motivation.[43] Thus, Contractarianism "speaks to people where they will listen." By resting moral obligation on self-interest, it touches a responsive chord and supplies the motivation that "Why be moral?" demands. Contractarianism bridges the is–ought gap by deriving morality from what people want. You ought to be moral (comply with the contract), it advises, because that will give you what you seek.

In presenting this rationale for morality, some would argue, Contractarianism offers the bonus of justifying morality to those least inclined to accept it. It does not call on the "angelic" aspects of our natures, a readiness to sacrifice for others. Rather, Contractarianism addresses more base desires. This is apparently yet a further reflection of its clear-eyed realism.

Others might cite a further aspect of human psychology to defend Contractarianism: widespread feelings of reciprocity. Generally, when a person agrees to something, he feels a greater commitment to do it than he would if he had not. Even if he later regrets having agreed, because he did agree, he sees himself as obligated to follow through. Perhaps because we can easily imagine being on the short end of broken agreements, the idea that one should keep agreements resonates rather naturally for people. Contractarianism's account of the grounds of obligation taps this feature of human psychology as well.

In short, its advocates would maintain, Contractarianism offers an account of morality's foundations that dovetails with human psychology and offers compelling motivation. If people truly are better off living under moral rules than they would be in an amoral free-for-all, this is a potent incentive to be moral.

Critique

There have been many criticisms of Contractarianism in the philosophical literature, and it will be instructive to review several. I will begin with some of the more familiar and build to those that are more fundamental. Some of the latter depend, in order to be fully appreciated, on a proper understanding of morality's base, which I have not yet presented. Nonetheless, I think we will be able to appreciate the ample evidence of Contractarianism's failure.

One common objection concerns Contractarianism's relativism. Are there any constraints on what rules might be adopted in the obligation-creating contract? Is *any* code valid, as long as people agree to it, such that whatever is agreed to binds? If so, we can envision some rather unsavory terms. Without extracontractual considerations reining in the code that is adopted, we have no grounds for condemning all manner of horrendous things that a given group of people might agree to. Obviously, this prospect alone is not a refutation of Contractarianism. The invocation of certain obligations that a particular contract might not recognize begs the question until the true basis of moral prescriptions is established. Nonetheless, Contractarianism's relativist implications reasonably create suspicion.

A related objection zeroes in on precisely what generates the obligation. Why is one's contract binding? What, exactly, performs the obligation-conferring work? Is it the fact that a person gave his word? How could words by themselves bind? Is it the fact of creating expectations through one's words? Yet we sometimes create expectations without creating obligations, as when we announce plans or intentions ("I'll see you there," "I'm going to apply for the job"). Having invited you to dinner, I may create expectations that are subsequently disappointed when the meal or the conversation does not measure up. No obligation has been violated, however.

Is it, then, the fact that in making the moral contract, I specifically *prom-*

ise, not merely creating expectations but implicitly adding "count on me" or "I hereby recognize that I am bound to you to do this"?

Why, however, do those intentions do the trick? Are we empowered to situate ourselves within or outside of morality at will? If we are, then it seems that we should be able to relieve ourselves from moral obligations by similar pronouncements. "I take it back" would be sufficient to excuse a person from an agreement-generated obligation. That, clearly, would eviscerate moral authority. If the Contractarian holds that agreement is sufficient to take on a moral obligation but not to cast one off, he must demonstrate why assuming and shedding obligations stand in different relations to a person's choice.

If we assume a preexisting obligation to live up to one's word, we face the obvious question, What is the basis of that obligation? If, in order for a contract to be binding, we must presuppose certain precontractual obligations, then contract is not the most basic answer to "Why be moral?" The reach for some extracontractual prop that supports the obligation to keep one's word amounts to an admission that agreement is not the fundamental source of moral obligation.

One sign of Contractarianism's apparent need for an external crutch is the fact that people usually resist recognizing the legitimacy of contracts made under duress. Valid contracts must be made under fair conditions. If so, the same would apply to the original contract creating moral obligation. The problem is, how are these antecedent standards of fairness justified? Whence their moral authority?

The problem can be framed as a dilemma. The initial situation in which the morality-creating contract is made either does or does not include moral constraints. If it does not, then any obligations agreed to in that situation will have no moral force because nothing requires a person to keep his word. Whatever allegedly obligates a person from this amoral situation remains mysterious. If the initial situation does include moral constraints, on the other hand, then it is not a truly Contractarian foundation. Moral obligation precedes the making of the contract.

Notice yet a third shortcoming: Contractarianism offers a purely social portrait of morality, for it attempts to explain only obligations between one person and others. Self-regarding behavior is omitted altogether. If moral prescriptions also govern self-regarding behavior (as I will argue they do), however, then Contractarianism is only a partial account of morality's roots. It is incomplete—at best, providing the foundation for *some* of morality.

A further difficulty is that Contractarianism has no means of obligating those who have not signed on to the contract. Its "net" is narrowed to actual contractors, affording no basis for criticizing those who did not agree to the contract and who do not respect its terms. This seems a grave failing, given the customary conviction that everyone should be moral. At this stage, of course, we must be open to the possibility that that conviction is mistaken, but accounts such as Contractarianism typically attempt to explain how morality binds everyone, not only a smaller set of volunteers. Contractarianism does not usually present itself as a theory of moral obligation for some people rather than for all.

The typical Contractarian maneuver to quiet this objection has been to adopt Hypothetical Contractarianism, maintaining that morality arises not from an agreement actually made but from a hypothetical contract that it would be rational for people to agree to. This modification addresses two issues at once: The alleged rationality of the hypothetical contract explains the generation of obligation for everyone, and it provides a bulwark against relativism. One is obligated because this is what rationality demands. If rationality does dictate a particular contract, then the antirelativists' worries about Contractarianism endorsing any code that a given group of people happen to fancy dissolve.

Unfortunately for the Contractarian, this solution creates its own problems. Hypothetical Contractarianism faces difficult questions. Why is anyone bound by a hypothetical contract? Why is a person bound by something that he has not actually agreed to? A person is not bound by a promise that he has not made, even if he should have made such a promise; a person is not liable for a bet that he meant to place, if he never placed it. Indeed, as Ronald Dworkin points out, a hypothetical contract is not only not a binding contract; it is no contract at all.[44]

A Contractarian is likely to reply that compliance with these terms best advances a person's interest and is the most reasonable course. That may be. But notice what has taken place. To cite either interest or reason as the ground of one's obligation is to depart from Contractarianism. The imposition of conditions restricting the contents of obligations or explaining the obligation to adhere to a contract, regardless of the character of those conditions, is impossible *from within the confines of Contractarianism.* To the extent that any external constraints limit the terms that can be agreed to or justify a person's obligation to comply, one has fundamentally changed the nature of the account and abandoned Contractarianism. Fortifying Contractarianism by importing extra-Contractarian elements by which to establish obligation reveals that mutual agreement is not the ultimate foundation of moral obligation.

The upshot is that Contractarianism cannot originate moral obligation while remaining truly Contractarian. A contract is either incomplete as the basis for ethics, not sufficient to generate obligation, or it is irrelevant, for if rationality or self-interest plays the pivotal role in explaining obligations, the contract becomes unnecessary.

These excursions beyond agreement proper lead us to the more fundamental problems with Contractarianism. Many object to the egoism operative in Contractarianism. If people agree to moral restrictions to promote their own interest, Contractarianism is not a theory of *morality,* some protest; it misses the distinctive character of moral "shoulds." Contractarianism is merely a strategy for promoting self-interest.

The problem for Contractarianism is not simply that its inherent egoism will be unsavory to some. The self-interested motivation behind the contract also spawns the notorious free-rider problem. Having made a contract, why should a person live up to it? Particularly when he can get away with breaking it?

If the contract is entered into for self-interested reasons, then when it seems in a person's interest to defy morality (as it will when he believes that he can avoid detection), he has no reason to be moral. When self-interest calls for shirking moral obligations, one should shirk. Since self-interest sometimes counsels immorality, however, Contractarianism is an unstable basis for moral obligation.

This is a potentially disastrous problem for Contractarianism because it undermines cooperation and its corollary benefits. Once people realize that it can be in their interest to violate the contract, they will do so. Realizing that others are doing the same, the trust that was a principal value of the contract—its medium of security—has been punctured. Cooperation will unravel.

The lesson usually drawn is that we cannot ground morality on self-interest. Self-interest will invariably advise against consistent compliance with the moral contract.

Dubious Conceptions of Morality and Interest

In fact, this is the wrong lesson to draw. The free-rider problem is premised on a mistaken conception of the basic nature of morality and on a mistaken conception of how a person could best promote his interest. Contractarianism itself largely shares these misconceptions.

The free rider assumes that morality stands opposed to a person's interest and that he maximizes his interest by defying morality. It is only if morality is conceived as constraining a person's interests that departures from morality could be expected to leave a person better off. Indeed, the more of a burden morality is, the more of a sacrifice that compliance presents, the keener the incentive to cheat.[45] Thus, morality is viewed as a second-best path to promoting one's interest. Compliance is a regrettable concession, reluctantly made. The free-rider scenario also suggests that self-interest is best served without any systematic code of instruction (since no alternative code is cited as a stronger route to self-interest). The implication is that a person can best promote his interest when, liberated from morality, he does whatever he pleases.

It is important to recognize that if this portrait of morality is correct and morality represents a necessary evil, the free rider's logic is impeccable: Morality should be skirted whenever possible. To the extent that a Contractarian accepts this portrait of a person's situation vis-à-vis morality, it accepts the free rider's notions of morality and interest.

Consider Hobbes's response to the free-rider problem. A person cannot be sure that it will be to his benefit to disobey, Hobbes wrote. It might turn out that compliance will be in his interest since events sometimes turn out in unexpected ways. Moreover, a person needs allies. Particularly in our naturally antagonistic condition of war, "there is no man [who] can hope by his own strength, or wit, to defend himself from destruction, without the help of confederates." Yet in breaking the contract, a person would be foolishly isolating himself from others whose friendship and support he needs. Thus, the best strategy is consistent cooperation.[46]

In its essence, this response is representative. Since self-interest animates the contract and subsequent obligation, any Contractarian must maintain that compliance better serves self-interest. The Contractarian will contend that a closer examination of how interest is best promoted shows that noncompliance is not truly in a person's interest. While the free rider thinks that he is effectively advancing his interest by cheating, in fact he is not.

Notice that in addressing the free-rider objection, Contractarianism does not dispute the idea that a person might better serve his interest by departing from moral rules *because of the nature of interest* or because of the more specific nature of the immoral actions. Contractarianism does not invoke an objective standard of human well-being to claim that it is ill-served by immorality; it does not contend that only disciplined adherence to a particular code of actions could enhance a person's well-being. Rather, it appeals to the likelihood of violations being discovered— implying that, undiscovered, such violations would be in a person's interest. Hobbes's second argument, that a person should not risk alienating potential allies by cheating, similarly treats interest as best realized when a person is free to do whatever he likes. Once a person is released from concern for others, his interest could be easily had.[47] The counsel to abide by the moral contract, despite this, suggests that sacrificing the gains that a person could reap from immorality is simply a safer bet. The ideal scenario, however, would be one in which regular defiance of morality goes undetected.

The success of this response depends on a convincing account of interest. Contractarians would have to identify the core and the standard of human beings' interest in order to establish that deviations from the contract are truly contrary to a person's interest. Contractarians are in no position to provide such an account, however, for Contractarians are not typically objectivists about interest. Indeed, their theory achieves its broad appeal by eschewing the exclusivity that an objective account of interest would entail.[48] A subjective account of interest cannot underwrite criticism of any decision to deviate from the contract for egoistic reasons, however. Without an objective account of interest, the Contractarian has no way of condemning deviation from the contract on self-interested grounds. If a person believes that it is in his interest to cheat, the subjective Contractarian has no explanation of why it is not (and, thus, of why the person should not).

Some Contractarians might wish to embrace an objective conception of interest at this stage and invoke it to argue against free riders' cheating. This would face two insurmountable obstacles, however.

First, whether interest is objective is not a matter of taste or fiat; an objective notion of interest cannot simply be plucked out of the air. Interest's objectivity depends on an explanation of what interest is, along with an account of the standards appropriate to measure it.

Second, this grab for objectivity would resurrect a problem we have already noticed. The more heavily the defense of Contractarianism depends on the nature of interest, the smaller the role of agreement. Relying on an amplified account of interest to defend the logic of abiding by the contract leads one to wonder what work the contract performs. Appeals to interest suggest that it is actually egoism that serves as the foundation for moral obligation, in which case the contract is a dispensable layer of distraction.[49]

In short, to prevent the deterioration of allegiance to the contract that the free-rider objection exposes as sensible, Contractarianism must uphold a rugged portrait of interest, demonstrating that allegiance to the contract is, in truth, the best route to promote self-interest. To the extent it does that, however, it loses its distinctive Contractarian character.

Finally, we can glimpse what is perhaps the most fundamental flaw in Contractarianism: its own lack of fundamentality in tackling the roots of morality.

Contractarianism's treatment of moral authority is too superficial. This is because it is too social, fixated with others' attitudes and actions. According to Contractarianism, the main problem to be overcome by morality is other people. It is the threat that others pose that inclines us to make peace and construct rules of morality. And it is the prospect of transgressions being found out by others that advises strict adherence to the contract. Absent other people, evidently, the concept of morality would not arise.

For the Contractarians, society defines morality; what a group of people wants determines morality's prescriptions.[50] By assuming that whatever people agree to is the basis for moral obligation, however, Contractarianism fails to recognize the more primitive, natural *need* for acting in certain ways and not others. By supposing that morality is an optional arrangement, contingent only on the desires of a group of individuals, it fails to identify the full stakes of our actions. This indifference is reflected in the fact that Contractarianism pays little attention to the contents of a moral code. Once it is decided that a number of people desire certain restrictions, whatever they devise will do. Their wants are the sole arbiter of what morality demands. Contractarianism implies that if people did not agree to a code of behavior, one would have no reason to be moral. This, I will argue in chapter four, is false.

The Contractarian might reply that he has noted the consequences of trying to do without morality, in the memorable terms of Hobbes's depiction of amoral life as nasty, brutish, and short. But this response will not suffice. It does not delve to the core of morality's role. What guides the Contractarians' rejection of certain states of affairs as unacceptable? Essentially, their unpleasantness. It is a nuisance to have to lock one's doors or arm oneself on a journey, Hobbes wrote. We do not *like* living that way. The contract is an attempt to secure a more agreeable, more comfortable existence.[51]

This is mere hedonism, however, disguised by the fact that it reports conditions that most people consider tolerable. It does not represent what all men *need,* what life itself requires. That, I will argue, is what necessitates a moral code. One could believe that social consensus is enough to chart morality only if one held that nothing deeper in reality, outside of people's preferences, was at stake. In fact, I will contend, the roots of moral obligation are not "whatever bargain we happen to strike, to achieve whatever condition we happen to like," but the unalterable facts of human needs.

By leaving the power to construct morality to a group's will, any moral code that Contractarianism supports is as fickle as popular taste. Being so inconstant, Contractarianism fails to deliver a moral code that fulfills the function of morality. The full vindication of this criticism awaits chapter four. But we can safely conclude that under the weight of all the serious difficulties we have surveyed—concerning the precise generator of obligation, Contractarianism's relativism, its exclusively social image of morality, its narrow net (the range of people bound by it), the free rider, and the role of reason and/or interest in propping up the authority of the contract as well as these questions about morality's function—Contractarianism collapses. It does not provide a satisfactory explanation of why anyone should be moral.

RATIONALISM

The final prominent position on the ground of morality that we will consider is given by the Rationalists. While their explanations of exactly how morality exerts authority can be rather intricate (e.g., Alan Gewirth's derivation of the Principle of Generic Consistency), Rationalism's essence is simple: We should be moral because rationality requires it. Morality and reason go hand in hand. Doing the right thing is doing the rational thing.

The paradigmatic Rationalist is Kant.[52] In the *Foundations of the Metaphysics of Morals,* Kant contends that "all moral concepts have their seat and origin entirely a priori in reason." Moral laws hold for every rational being as such. Kant's central concept of duty reflects the notion that there are certain things that a person simply must do. Must do, why? Must do qua rational being. It is our rationality that obligates us.[53]

Kant's categorical imperative is authoritative not because of a person's desires or preferences concerning the anticipated consequences of alternative actions. The test of any action is its maxim's rational universalizability, whether reason sanctions its universal employment. If my maxim cannot become a universal law, "it must be rejected, not because of any disadvantage accruing to myself or even to others, but because it cannot enter as a principle into a possible enactment of universal law, and reason extorts from me an immediate respect for such legislation. . . . The renunciation of all interest is the specific mark of the categorical imperative, distinguishing it from the hypothetical."[54]

Rationalism is further reflected in Kant's conception of the nature of moral authority. Morality is its own reward, Kant holds.[55] His opposition to suicide vividly reflects this premise: Suicide would destroy morality in the subject of morality. "It is not necessary that whilst I live I should live happily; but it is necessary that so long as I live I should live honorably." Suicide is contrary to duty because it annuls the condition of all other duties.[56] The implication is that morality is not to serve individuals but that individuals are to serve morality. Our happiness is secondary because rationality is the paramount concern. Morality is an objectively necessary end, an end of pure reason. "Rational nature exists as an end in itself."[57]

Gewirth, one of the most respected contemporary Rationalists, provides an elaborate attempt to tease moral obligation out of a person's conception of himself as an agent. Gewirth maintains that a rational analysis of the concept of action is sufficient to demonstrate the "supreme principle of morality," the anchor for all moral judgments. He argues that any agent, by virtue of being an agent, must admit, on pain of contradiction, that he ought to act in certain determinate ways. Reason will lead him to recognize the Principle of Generic Consistency (PGC), the precept holding that every agent ought to act in accord with the generic rights of his recipients as well as of himself. When an agent violates this principle, his action is irrational.[58]

Plenty of critical analyses of Kant, Gewirth, and other Rationalists are available for anyone wishing to pursue the details of these arguments more closely. Considering Rationalism by its essence, however, should allow a just verdict on its success in providing the basis of moral authority. Beneath the finer points of Kant's formulations of the categorical imperative and Gewirth's derivation of the PGC, the defining Rationalist doctrine holds, again, that the moral is the rational; what is right is right because rationality demands it.

The Case for Rationalism

The general appeal of the Rationalist stance, I think, is fourfold. Its apparent logic, rigor, reach, and neutrality can all seem grounds to embrace it. Let me briefly explain each.

First, consider the logic of Rationalism. "Why be moral?" begs for a rational response. To ask "Why?" is to ask for reasons.[59] Once one accepts that we can meaningfully pose the question, we are already engaged in a rational enterprise, presupposing reason's standards for evaluating answers. Thus, the proposal that the moral *is* the rational seems the strongest answer conceivable, exactly the sort of thing we were looking for. Given a commitment to rationality, if one could show that morality's demands coincide with rationality's demands, the Rationalist line seems the most satisfactory explanation of morality's grounds possible. If rationality commands morality, then one's regard for reason will dictate an equally strong respect for morality.

The second element of Rationalism's appeal is its rigor or firmness. Rationalism posits a necessity that many consider integral to genuine obligations. On this view, we are bound by morality, like it or not; a person cannot opt out at will. (Contrast Contractarianism's "easy come, easy go" policy according to which a person stands under morality's demands if he signs up for morality but not if he does not or if he backs out.) For Rationalism, moral obligations are given, inescapable, nonoptional facts. The belief that reason is the basis of obligations seemingly locks in their unyielding character. To be immoral is to be irrational, and no one can have *reason* to be irrational.

Third, and closely related, the broad reach of the Rationalist position can also seem to weigh in its favor. Because it roots morality in our rational faculty, morality's demands apply to everyone. Obligation is not contingent on the disparate ends of particular individuals. Not only those who happen to fear eternal damnation, social ostracism, or a restless sleep fall under morality's authority. The Rationalist basis for obligations catches everyone, including would-be immoralists.[60] (Again, the contrast with Contractarianism, which binds only those who agree to morality's rules, is striking.)

Finally, Rationalism carries an aura of neutrality. If moral obligation can be grounded in the demands of reason, many think, it is devoid of bias. It carries no contamination from a precommitment to arguable values. Reason is impartial; thus, Rationalism seems clean, pure, above partisan agendas. Indeed, this is what enables Rationalist obligation to apply to everyone.[61]

Critique

While I believe that morality and rationality *are* tightly linked, Rationalism does not provide an adequate explanation of why anyone should follow morality. For it relies on a distorted conception of reason. This is its central, fatal defect. Most of our assessment of Rationalism, consequently, will focus on the nature of reason and justification. Once these are properly understood, the elements of Rationalism's appeal quickly evaporate.

We can begin by noticing a familiar objection to the formalism in Rationalist ethics. How can Rationalism generate normative prescriptions? Useful moral theory must offer substantive directions, guiding people to and away from various types of actions. Yet if reason is "pure" in the ways suggested by Rationalists, they have no grounds from which to generate such directions.

Rationality is a procedure of tracing logical relationships. Thus, it requires material—information, premises, observations, facts—whose relationships it attempts to trace. We can only draw inferences from claims that *say* something. In short, the complaint is, reason alone is too devoid of content to be able to offer substantive instruction.

A different angle on this problem might be clarifying. Why is an intellectual error a moral lapse? Whence the assimilation of issues of morality and rationality? Rationalists do not regard any intellectual lapse as a moral breach. If a person makes a mistake in balancing his checkbook, expanding a recipe, or following a map, it is not a moral failing. Yet this highlights the difficulty: How can we determine which lapses are? On what basis can we sift immoral irrationality from amoral irrationality? To answer, Rationalism must import some normative ingredients beyond rationality itself. It must rely on nonneutral values in order to give credence to the claim that the moral is the rational. The appeal to rationality inevitably hides some other ideals.

Why Be Rational?

Since this objection charges that reason is not sufficient to ground morality, it invites us to inspect reason more closely. Moreover, quite apart from this particular objection, the Rationalist position will prove only as compelling as one finds rationality. Even if we accepted that a certain course would be the rational course, why should that impress us? Whence the obligation to be rational?

A Rationalist might immediately reply that "Why be rational?" is an incoherent question. A reason to be rational could provide justification only if we already assume that we should do what we have reason to do. In other words, to require a reason to be rational is already to be relying on standards imposed by rationality, namely, the need for reasons. Thus, the Rationalist might contend, we cannot ask "Why be rational?" in search of a rational justification of morality. The belief that immorality is irrational is enough.

The question cannot be dodged so easily, however. The propriety of rationality cannot simply be taken for granted. Heaven knows that it is not, either in theory or in practice, by most people. Alternatives to reason are widely embraced—for example, reliance on faith, astrology, emotion, tradition, popularity, or authority. Dogmatic insistence on the "obvious" propriety of reason ignores the fact of these competing methods of thinking and acting. To understand whether it makes sense to act rationally, we must first understand what rational action is.

What Is Rational Action?

Consider several simple instances of people doing things for reasons—the person who consulted the map because he was lost, bought the book because his friend recommended it, Fed Ex'ed the application to ensure meeting the deadline, studied Italian because he was going to Milan, took the course to fulfill the humanities requirement, apologized because he regretted what he had done, applied to Syracuse because it has a strong lacrosse team, switched carriers to save on his phone bill, or bought the car because it was a bargain.

In all these cases, the person's action would actually be rational only if he had certain beliefs and ends. In most of these cases, the relevant beliefs and ends are so obvious as to hardly seem worth mentioning, but they are nonetheless vital to the rationality of the action. Certainly it makes sense to buy a book on a friend's recommendation only if you trust his judgment in such matters and if you wish to read that sort of book; it makes sense to Fed Ex an application only if you want to meet the deadline and you believe that this will assist your doing so; it makes sense to study Italian only if you believe that this will enhance your experience in some way and you wish to so enhance it.

The important point for us is that purposes are crucial to rational action. The world teems with facts, but it does not present us with natural reasons.

Facts become reasons relative to a person's purposes. Reasons for action are facts that bear on the achievement of a person's goals. They indicate that a certain course of action is likely to carry a positive or negative impact on one's goals. A reason for action reflects a link of facts to an individual's objectives.

We cannot assess the rationality of any action until we know what it is intended to accomplish. Was the manager's decision to change pitchers rational? Was the company's decision to hire Heath or to promote Peters? Would it be rational for Megan to attend that school, buy that car, or marry that man? In each case, the answer depends (among other things) on what the person is after.

Until a person identifies his purpose, he cannot know which information to heed and which to discard, what connections to look for, what types of inferences to draw, or what weight to assign different facts. Consider the case of a baseball manager's decision to remove a pitcher. In doing so, he is aware of all sorts of information: the score; the inning; the strength of the bullpen (relief pitchers); the pitcher's customary pattern of tiring; the fact that the pitcher is from Japan, has three children, is just off the disabled list, is batting .108, and so on. Which of these should weigh in his decision? The answer will depend on the manager's primary aim: Is he trying to preserve a lead? Give some experience to a new relief pitcher? Save a tired arm for an upcoming game? Quiet his critics in the press? Send a message about multicultural athletics? Identifying an objective is essential to understanding what rationality demands.

Correspondingly, rationality is contextual insofar as the exact rational course varies for different individuals in different situations. The decision to buy a particular car might be rational when's one's primary objective is aesthetic and irrational when one's objective is economic. The decision to accept a certain job might be rational when one's primary objective is maximizing income and irrational when one's primary objective is maximizing free time. Thus, the same facts may be reasons for different individuals to perform different actions, depending on their ends. What is reason for Tom to enroll at University Y (its strong engineering program) can be reason for Bill not to enroll there (since engineering's strength has come at the expense of art history, which is what Bill wants to study). What constitutes a rational action, again, depends on an individual's ends and the relevant facts of his circumstances.

A couple of clarifications may be helpful. First, because reasons for action are tied to a person's ends, it is tempting to suppose that desire is needed for reasons for action. But this is potentially misleading since ends are easily confused with desires.[62] Given customary connotations of "desire," we must distinguish between felt desire—the palpable psychological experience, at a given moment, of wanting something—and a person's more considered projects, ambitions, or ends. The latter do not always manifest themselves by the former. Ends do not make their presence felt around the clock. Yet the absence of the felt desire—for example, at 3 p.m. today—does not mean that the person surrenders the end. The fact that I do not feel like calling the doctor today, for example, does not mean that I have no reason to; the fact that I don't feel like having this argument with a friend does not mean that I should not have it; the fact that I do wish to write this book does not mean that I feel like working on it every hour of every day.

The lesson is simply that experiencing a particular desire at a given moment is not necessary to having a reason to act in a particular way. A person can have a reason for action without a palpable yearning to perform that action at the moment but not without having an end that it serves.

Second, a mental state is not a reason. Often, when attempting to explain a person's behavior or to determine what a person should do, citing his end or desire may seem to supply a reason for action. Particularly if the other components of the explanation are already known, insofar as the end or desire is the missing piece, it could seem the reason. ("Why did he send flowers?" "He wanted to show his appreciation." "Why did he apply to Syracuse?" "He wants to play lacrosse.") Yet in fact, an end or desire can be only part of an explanation of an action's rationality. Beliefs about flowers' ability to convey gratitude or about the likelihood and value of playing lacrosse at Syracuse also play a role in these cases. While nothing can be a reason without an end, that does not convert the end (or the desire for some end) into a reason for action. It simply means that an end is a condition for any fact's constituting a reason.

Some might object that my emphasis on ends confuses justification with motivation. In "Does Moral Philosophy Rest on a Mistake?," Prichard emphasizes the distinction between what we want to do and what we are obligated to do. Stephen Darwall speaks for many when he differentiates normative or justifying reasons from motivating or explaining reasons.[63] My emphasis on the role of a person's purposes in justifying an action might illuminate the motivation to perform an action—why a person would be inclined to do something—these critics would contend, but that is not the same as supplying a justification. Justification represents a fact as to what a person ought to do; motivation concerns merely whether the agent wants to act in a certain manner.

In fact, the confusion rests in the objection. The distinction invoked does not show what such objectors claim.

The distinction between explanation and justification is certainly valid. What leads a person to act in a given case (the explanation of his action) may or may not actually be rational (a justification of his action). Further,

it is certainly fair to distinguish between whether a person wants to do
something and whether he should.

It does not follow, however, that "shoulds" are independent of purposes. We cannot sever justification from motivation. A person can have
no genuine reason for action without having some end that will be served
by the action. Motivations or ends (I am using the two interchangeably)
are conceptually distinct from reasons, yet ends remain indispensable conditions of reasons. The fact that there is a difference between the two does
not show that there can be a rational action without an end. New Year's
Eve is distinct from New Year's Day, but it still depends on their being a
New Year's Day. "Husband" is a distinct concept from "marriage," yet it
depends on the existence of marriage. In short, I have not meant to equate
an end with a reason but rather to insist on ends' necessity for reasons.

Notice that the strict separation of justification from motivation—of the
"facts" of what a person should do from what he wishes to do—stems
from a particular image of reason. The implicit idea is that reason is inherently authoritative, relying on no relation to anything outside of it to command our obedience. In effect, this presents reason as being authoritative
for no reason. Reason's authority is self-contained, and any association
with a person's wants or goals taints it. Appeals to such goals in explanations of what *renders* reason authoritative are dismissed as defiling reason's stature.

I have argued that this is false. If a person has no objective that is affected by his acting in a certain manner, we have no basis warranting the
claim that he ought to act in that manner. Without ends that stand to be
affected, it is impossible to decipher what it would mean to say that "rationally, he should act in that way."

Notice, further, that the more one insists on a separation of motivation
from justification, as Rationalists defending the "pure" reason of morality
do, the more elusive the union of morality and motivation will prove. The
question "Why be moral?" will inevitably be unanswerable. If one treats
moral obligation as unshakable—irrevocably given by "reason" independently of human purposes—it will be impossible to generate rational allegiance to morality. If one already accepts that one should act morally,
without basis, then nothing could truly explain why someone should. Attempts at such explanations are made moot.[64]

Justification of Action

A reason for action, again, is a fact indicating that a particular action will
affect a person's ends. Since our ultimate interest is in reasons to be moral
and morality carries overriding authority, we need to know not merely
what it is to have *a* reason for action but also what it is to have a decisive

reason. So let us now turn to the higher-level question: What constitutes a justification of an action?[65]

"Justification" is sometimes used weakly to mean simply *a* reason. I will use "justification" exclusively in a stronger sense to refer to the conclusive reason to do something. The question of what constitutes justification thus becomes, What is needed to arrive at such a conclusive reason? The answer, for starters, is: lots of information.

The fact that a certain action will promote a person's end is sometimes outweighed by other facts that provide reasons to not perform that action. Fairly often, some facts support a person's performing a particular action while other facts counsel against it. A positive letter of recommendation will normally be a reason to hire a job applicant but must be considered alongside other aspects of the applicant's record as well as competing applicants' records. Studying a language may facilitate one's visit to a foreign country but exact considerable time and energy from other projects; cheaper phone service might save money but bring the aggravations of inferior quality.

The rationality of a person's action is a function of its relation to all his ends as well as to the available means of pursuing those ends. We cannot determine whether it is rational to hire a person, learn a language, or patronize a particular company until we know what the agent seeks to accomplish and what resources (such as time, money, personnel, equipment, and expertise) and what alternatives are available. Moreover, given that a person holds a variety of ends, the impact of an action on one end must be evaluated in light of its likely impact on other ends. Rationality demands that we attempt to advance one goal without damaging others. It is particularly crucial not to endanger one's higher ends in the process of pursuing lesser ends.

As some recent exegeses of Aristotle's and Aquinas's accounts of rational agency have emphasized, a rational agent must keep his eye on his broad good, his life as a whole, rather than on only some narrow aspect of that end. A fully rational action is not just end directed but ultimate end directed.[66]

One useful yardstick for assessing actions' justification is adherence to a person's priorities. Greater goods should never suffer for lesser ones. It would be self-defeating to act in a way that advances one end by damaging a more important end. It would be irrational, for example, to indulge the appetite for a wild night of drinking on the day before one's medical exams when acquiring one's medical degree is one's more important end. It would be irrational to gamble savings that a person had painstakingly accumulated for fifteen years in order to start his own business so as to quiet the friend who is goading him to bet on a ball game.

Something's being a higher end does not mean that it should be treated as a person's only end. I am not proposing that a person must always tend directly and exclusively to his highest ends. Such a policy would have the effect of eradicating all lesser ends.[67] The point is simply that a person should take no action in pursuit of any goal that is likely to hinder other ends that he prizes more highly.

Further, a single action will often carry a variety of effects, more or less significant, subtle, and immediate, on one end or on several ends as well as on one's means of promoting one's ends. The justification of an action must take all this into account. Rationality requires that a person appreciate the interrelationships among his various ends, the ways in which some enhance or detract from others, and the conditions necessary for the achievement of any of them.

The pursuit of any end, therefore, whatever its ranking within the hierarchy of a person's values, must be conducted in light of the requirements of all his values. To ignore the full ramifications of an action would pretend that actions' effects are neatly confined to insulated compartments. Since mentally containing an action's effects does nothing to restrict its actual effects, however, the rational evaluation of any action cannot be detached from the larger picture of all that may be affected by it. To arrive at the conclusive reason that justification represents, one must assess *all* relevant factors—all of one's ends, all effects of alternative possible actions on those ends, as well as effects on one's ongoing capacity to advance them.

A justification, in short, tells you what you should do, all things considered. What you should do is what you have most reason to do. If a reason for action is a fact that indicates that the action will promote one or some of a person's ends, a justification is a more sophisticated, more encompassing, and thus more definitive judgment that offers sufficient reason to act. It represents the conclusion, after weighing all the pros and cons, all the direct and indirect ramifications on other ends as well as on means, based on the fullest available knowledge, that this action best promotes the person's ends. (By "promote," I mean to include defensive actions that are sometimes necessary to protect ends from threats.)

The Rationality of Ends

So far, I have emphasized that reasons depend on purposes and that an action can be rational only in relation to particular ends. But this leaves the question: What if a person's ends are not rational? Doesn't justification require that ends themselves be rational?

Looking into the rationality of ends will lead to the core of rationality's claim on us and to a fuller explanation of why one should be rational.

Not all ends are rational. Perhaps the man traveling to Milan should finish preparing his sales pitch before dabbling in Italian, perhaps the boy

aspiring to a college lacrosse career should face up to his athletic inept-
ness, perhaps the man seizing a car bargain should not be buying a car at
all, given the one he bought last week and his other considerable bills.
How can we justify the rationality of an end? A justification typically
defends one action by its relation to something else. A baseball manager
might justify switching pitchers to rest a pitcher's arm; a baseball commis-
sioner might justify suspending a player by the rules of league; a company
might justify its policy of awarding bonuses by the intention to encourage
a particular type of work; a parent might justify his disciplinary tactics by
the latest findings of child psychologists.

Obviously, people can challenge those grounds themselves, questioning
the wisdom of a rule or the propriety of a psychologist's recommendation.
How are those defended? By appeal to still further ends that are meant to
be served by *their* adoption. (For example, a particular league rule might
be intended to foster team parity or the image of the game, and a particular
disciplinary strategy might be intended to cultivate children's independence.) Yet again, of course, one can question the propriety of those ends:
What justifies the justifying factors? If one thing is always justified in
terms of another, the propriety of those prior grounds can be challenged.
Looming in the background is the question, How far down can justification
go?[68]

All reasoning must stop somewhere. Reason skeptics would seize on
this to charge that the limits of justification, the necessity of a terminus in
tracing means and ends, reveal justification to be, at root, arbitrary. In the
final analysis, they contend, what is considered rational is simply a matter
of where a given person chooses to halt the chain of ends that he will supply in support of other ends. But this means that reason is subjective. Since
different people will halt their explanations at different depths, embracing
different ends as foundational, what constitutes a rational justification of
any belief or action is a matter of personal preference. Reason is hardly as
rational—as impartial or objective—as its advocates maintain.[69]

In fact, this portrait is seriously mistaken.

The fact that ends are indispensable to rational action and that people
may choose their most basic ends does not mean that rationality is compatible with any end that a person might embrace. Ends are not all mutually
compatible. The pursuit of certain ends will undermine the realization of
others. Crucially, ends are not all compatible with the requirements of reality. While a person can choose not to adopt certain ends, he cannot escape the consequences. *This* is the bedrock sanction of reason. It is anything but a matter of personal preference.

Obviously, a person can forgo certain ends without catastrophic results.
People sometimes lead happy lives without cigarettes, chocolate, cable
television, or the *New York Times*. Other ends carry more momentous ram-

ifications, and the achievement of these is more critical to one's life. If a person leaves an eye infection untreated, he may go blind. If he takes certain drugs, he may impair his ability to think and inflict lasting damage on his brain and nervous system. If he forgoes food and water for a certain duration, he will die.

The point is that, at the deepest reaches in the chain of ends, reason still governs one's options. More exactly, reality governs one's options—for a person's choices about what ends to pursue do not alter the nature of the universe in which he acts. The ability to choose ends does not carry with it the ability to remake reality according to one's will. We cannot dictate the means necessary to achieve our aims. At whatever level of ends one is considering—ambitious and long range or modest and short range— whether we are speaking about launching a career, managing a conglomerate, landing a man on Mars, or seeking a bus ticket, a meal, or a magazine—it always makes sense to inquire into what a person must do in order to achieve his ends. This question "makes sense" insofar as reality sets the conditions for our attainment of our ends. If a person sincerely seeks something, he must realistically identify the means of achieving it.

Consider again the skeptics' objection. They contend that the fact that the rationality of any action depends on ends shows that we must resort to something external to reason to explain reason's authority. That, allegedly, indelibly stains the entire enterprise of rationality as arbitrary.

The first hint that this analysis is askew arises from the suspicion that if it is necessary to identify ends in order to have reasons, there can be no error in doing so. What are one's alternatives? Is this not simply the nature of rationality?

In reply, the skeptic would insist that that may be but that this nonetheless exposes the limited authority and not-fully-rational character of rationality. This response, however, clues us into the heart of the skeptics' error.

The fact that a train of ends comes to a stop does not mean that all rational justification (and, by implication, any attempted justification of morality) is infected by an extrarational element that precludes the rationality of reason. Rather, it simply reflects the fact that a person's ends are not the sole determinants of what is rational. While I have stressed that purposes are necessary to identify a rational course of action, this does not entail that purposes by themselves provide the reason to be rational. Imagine a person who has adopted certain purposes. Why should he adhere to rationality in order to achieve those purposes rather than to the counsel of a witch doctor, faith healer, or astrologer? Because of reality—the unchangeable facts that make certain actions further his purposes and other actions hinder them. It is reality that demands: *Given* your ends, you must be rational if you are to achieve them. Correspondingly, it is reality that provides the gauge for distinguishing rational from irrational ends. Let me explain this a little further.

The case for reason ultimately stems from the nature of reality. It is a reflection of Francis Bacon's dictum that nature, to be commanded, must be obeyed. At bottom, the only "reason" to obey reason is the aim of conforming to reality, which means: guiding one's judgments and actions by the way things really are. *That* makes sense because reality (by which I mean all that exists) has a definite nature that is independent of individuals' thoughts and wishes. (Notice that certain colloquialisms reflect this: "But you've got to be realistic," "Get a grip on reality," "Get real.") Indeed, we define serious mental illness precisely by a person's having lost touch with reality. The mind-independence of reality means that if we wish to achieve any ends, we must identify the nature of the relevant aspects of reality and act accordingly. If I want to live, for example, I must eat, so I must find or make food or find a job or create a product or offer a service that I can trade with others in order to obtain food. If I want to open a profitable business, I must acquire startup money and knowledge of the relevant field as well as knowledge of good business practices in general. Even if I want to kill myself, I must learn which techniques are effective; only certain drugs or weapons will do the trick.[70]

Even if one recognizes this much, it is not difficult to see how a person might be tempted by the skeptics' contention that rationality's relationship to ends renders reason subjective. I have maintained that rationality is contextual; what it is rational to do will vary for different individuals, depending largely on their particular purposes. This may seem to preempt objective assessments of those purposes. If ends are necessary for assessments of rationality, by what ends could we evaluate people's ends? It would be arbitrary to employ our own ends as the basis of such an evaluation since they are, after all, *our* ends and not those of the people in question. Yet if we simply rely on those persons' own ends, we allow the very subjectivism that undermines rationality's rationality.

Framed as a dispute over whose ends should govern evaluations of ends' rationality, this does seem a hopeless dilemma. But this is a mistaken way of framing the issue. In truth, the question we face is not *whose* ends determine the rationality of ends. Reality sets the standard of rationality. Facts about the world we inhabit—facts that are quite independent of human wishes or purposes—render certain ends unattainable, render certain ends incompatible with other ends, and render certain ends destructive of ends that are necessary for a person's ability to pursue any ends. In other words, when we dig to the deepest reaches of ends' rationality, the completely objective parameter on what is rational is reality. Facts that are not of anyone's choosing determine the rationality of various ends by establishing the means and the consequences of achieving those ends.

This is what I meant previously in claiming that we cannot remake reality according to our will or dictate the conditions of our ends' attainment. A person's ends do not liberate him from the limitations imposed by things' identity. No person can declare, "I want to live by a diet of cardboard, cement, and Tupperware" and proceed to do so; he would die. Thus, this would not be a rational end. No person can declare that he wants to live underwater, like a trout. By that route, again, he would die; it is not rational because it is not doable. While a person's ends help determine the rationality of his actions, they do not single-handedly determine what is rational. Because we live in reality—in a world where facts do not compliantly yield to any desire that a person might have—we must conform to reality in our adoption of ends as well as in the steps taken to achieve our ends. Just as a fish cannot live out of water, a person cannot live "out of reality" by defying his nature or the nature of his surroundings.

Consequently, the way to assess ends' rationality is by looking to reality, asking primarily two sorts of questions: Is this end attainable? and What would its attainment demand? Do its requirements impede any other ends, in particular, other ends that pass the first test and that are critical to one's ability to attain ends? A person must consider, in other words, whether he can achieve a proposed objective and how he could achieve it, what it would cost. If an end is incapable of being realized, it is irrational. If an end can be attained only by means that jeopardize more vital ends, it is irrational. ("More vital" literally and objectively: on the grounds that one's existence or one's ability to engage in this activity or to pursue any ends depends on these ends' realization.) In short, if an end is at odds with the requirements of reality, it is irrational.

No ends can be achieved by any means other than conforming to the relevant facts of reality. It is not only certain purposes that mandate rationality; it is not the case that if a person altered his purposes, rationality would no longer be required. *Any* purposes require rationality. A person ignores reality at his peril, for all his ends, including his very life, depend on actions realistically calculated to achieve them.[71]

We can evaluate ends as rational or irrational, then, by reminding ourselves of what grounds rationality's authority in the first place. The reason to be rational is reality; correspondingly, the standard of rationality is reality. None of this is to say that the determination of ends' rationality will typically be a simple affair. The complex networks of ends that individuals pursue and the cascade of effects that their actions carry for this variety of ends can demand intricate layers of analysis. But it is to say that we have an objective yardstick for measuring ends' rationality: reality.

Thus, the skeptics are mistaken in maintaining that pressing the roots of reason's authority exposes some inescapable subjectivity. On the contrary, examining reason's authority reveals reason's roots in the law of identity, in the fact that things will act according to their natures and that people pursuing any ends must heed the nature of the relevant existents.

Rationalism's Collapse

What has this excursion into the nature and authority of reason taught us about the tenability of Rationalism? Since Rationalism's basic contention is that we should be moral because rationality requires it, Rationalism must have a compelling answer to the natural follow-up question: Why be rational? It does not. And as long as it preaches allegiance to reason devoid of empirical elements or "unsullied" by ends, it will be incapable of providing one.

By considering the basic nature of a rational action, we saw that any action's rationality is dependent on its ends. The justification of an action cannot be detached from the issue of motivation. Without reference to purposes, assessments of rationality are impossible. Indeed, without identifying one's own purposes, the practice of rationality is impossible. Yet this is what the Rationalist refuses to recognize. He insists that reason is somehow compelling in its own right.

The actual source of reason's claim on us is the fact that reality requires rationality for success in attaining any of our ends. Rationality *is* essential for human beings. Since Rationalists employ an impoverished conception of reason, however, nothing that I have said in defense of reason bolsters the Rationalist account of morality.

In effect, Rationalists preach reason as a matter of faith. They do so, I suspect, because they essentially accept the skeptics' portrait. That is, Rationalists seem to fear that if we reach "outside" reason to provide reasons for reason, we will find what skeptics allege: subjective foundations that render all rational processes arbitrary. Rather than reject reason as inadequately grounded, however, Rationalists assert its inherent authority. Correspondingly, they conceive morality to be inherently obligatory. Rationality requires morality—for no reason. Yet for reason's authority to be self-contained would mean that it is based on . . . nothing.

Working through a Rationalist's defense of morality, people often have the sense that Rationalism misses the nerve of "Why be moral?" Answers in terms of self-contradiction or "pure" reason do not speak to the genuine concerns of someone raising the question. By now, we can appreciate the explanation of this: Rationalism's impoverished notion of reason. What initially seems a straightforward answer to "Why be moral?"—reason demands it—crumbles on inspection. Because Rationalism severs reason from its roots in reality, it provides no good reason to be moral. It misses the nerve of the issue of moral authority because it misses reality. In fact, we have seen, the rational justification of an action depends on rational ends. Thus, appeals to "rationality" detached from all ends could not provide a genuine reason for anything, let alone furnish the basis of morality's authority.

Our inquiry into the nature of reason thus reveals how feeble the Rationalist account of moral obligation is. Its thesis that reason demands morality is based on a grave misrepresentation of reason. This also undermines its four original elements of appeal, as we can now readily observe.

Rationalism's purported logic is cosmetic. Since nothing can be truly rational apart from its relationship to ends, no reason to be moral can be found without such ends. Rationalists refuse to provide them, however, protesting that ends would taint reason.[72]

It is important to realize that the weakness in Rationalism is not mere incompleteness. My conclusion is not that Rationalists have shown that the moral is the rational but that they simply need to supplement their account with some purpose. Rather, Rationalism has *not* shown that the moral is the rational, for we cannot determine whether anything is rational without reference to ends. The introduction of ends is not a later addition to an account of a rational procedure. It is essential to the determination of an action's rationality.

Correspondingly, Rationalism's alleged firmness and wide reach, obligating all rational agents without exception, are completely groundless. They are based on the assertion of a rationally dictated moral obligation that has not been demonstrated (and could not be, using the Rationalist's hollow conception of reason). We cannot determine an obligation's rigor until we have first secured that it is, indeed, an obligation. Similarly, the breadth of morality's authority is an extension of its authority over any individual; one can only claim that everyone is unequivocally bound by morality by the same grounds that bind any single person. Yet Rationalism has not demonstrated the grounds of *anyone's* obligation since it has not provided the ends that moral action serves and that would render moral action rational. While the aspiration to an account of unyielding, universal moral obligations may be admirable, Rationalism's reliance on an emaciated conception of rationality could never deliver it.

Finally, Rationalism's neutrality is illusory. If Rationalism instructs us to be moral for the sake of no purpose—for no good reason—it simply fails to show the grounds of moral obligation. The only way it can generate substantive prescriptions and a compelling justification is by abandoning its professed neutrality and smuggling in some values, as objectors to its formalism have long maintained.

Interestingly, the absence of neutrality is not necessarily a weakness in a moral theory. Neutrality's propriety depends on what a theory is neutral about. Here, it is the wish to be agnostic about the question of ends that actually renders Rationalism impotent. Since we cannot assess the rationality of an action apart from its ends, in refusing to embrace ends, Rationalists disavow the very thing that could allow them to identify a moral course as rational.

In the final analysis, Rationalism offers a pointless morality. Kant acknowledges as much, admittedly less explicitly, when he insists that morality is an end in itself and urges duty for its own sake. A pointless morality, however, could never furnish an adequate explanation of why we should be moral.[73]

CONCLUSION

While we have not conducted an exhaustive inventory of possible explanations of the grounds of morality, we have inspected the essence of the historically major positions. From doing so, the only lesson we can draw is that these have not provided satisfactory answers to "Why be moral?"

The question "Why be moral?" is undoubtedly a difficult one. Yet it is, logically, the first question of ethics. It makes no sense to propose how human beings should live until we know why the guidance of a moral code is wanted. How to live properly depends on what we seek to accomplish. As long as that remains unknown, whatever elaborate explanations of morality's demands one constructs—Kantian, Hobbesian, Butlerian, or any other—are as precarious as a house a cards.

In the face of these failures, one can take either of two courses: cling to certain moral tenets despite the lack of grounds for them, belittling the question of morality's authority, or press on in search of a sound basis for morality. To take the former route is to jettison reason from the realm of ethics. For those not ready to take that course, we will see in the next chapter a different approach to grounding morality.

NOTES

1. In this chapter, I will sometimes refer to "Why be moral?" as simply "the question."

2. A phrase made famous by Kurt Baier in *The Moral Point of View* (New York: Random House, 1958).

3. Brian Medlin has declared (approvingly) "that it is now pretty generally accepted by professional philosophers that ultimate ethical principles must be arbitrary" (Medlin, "Ultimate Principles and Ethical Egoism," *Australasian Journal of Philosophy* 35, no. 2 [August 1957]: 111). F. H. Bradley wrote that "there is but one fitting answer" to the question 'what is the use of goodness?': 'we do not know, and we do not care' (Bradley, "Why Should I Be Moral?," *Ethical Studies* [G. E. Stechert, 1911], 57). Among others who reject the question as illegitimate

are John McDowell, "Are Moral Requirements Hypothetical Imperatives?" *Proceedings of the Aristotelian Society* 52 (Suppl. 1978): 13–29; Dan W. Brock, "The Justification of Morality," *American Philosophical Quarterly* 14, no. 1 (January 1977): 71; and J. C. Thornton, "Can the Moral Point of View Be Justified?" in *Readings in Contemporary Ethical Theory,* ed. K. Pahel and M. Schiller (Englewood Cliffs, N.J.: Prentice Hall, 1970). Thomas Nagel allows that "strictly," "Why be moral?" is "senseless or in principle unanswerable" (Nagel, *The Possibility of Altruism* [Princeton, N.J.: Princeton University Press, 1970], 5).

4. Bradley, "Why Should I Be Moral?," 53.

5. John Hospers, "Why Be Moral?" in *Readings in Ethical Theory,* 2nd ed., ed. Wilfred Sellars and John Hospers (Englewood Cliffs, N.J.: Prentice Hall, 1970), 744–45 (emphasis in the original).

6. Hospers, "Why Be Moral?," 745.

7. Hospers, "Why Be Moral?," 746 (emphasis in the original).

8. Stephen Toulmin, *Reason in Ethics* (Cambridge: Cambridge University Press, 1964), 146; see also 148–49, 153–56.

9. Toulmin, *Reason in Ethics,* 162.

10. Hospers, "Why Be Moral?," 746; Toulmin, *Reason in Ethics,* 162–63, 165, n. 2. Another philosopher dismissive of the need to explain why we should be moral, Brian Medlin, in the course of an argument against ethical egoism, writes, "I'm a philosopher, not a rat-catcher, and I don't see it as my job to dig vermin out of such burrows as individual egoism" (Medlin, "Ultimate Principles and Ethical Egoism," 114).

11. I have some uneasiness about the terms "moral reasons" and "nonmoral reasons," for we do not find two types of reasons in nature, preordained moral or nonmoral. On the view that I will defend in chapter four, all reasons are potentially moral reasons, insofar as all facts potentially bear on the telos that morality steers us toward. Since I cannot assume the truth of that here, for immediate purposes, I take "moral reasons" to refer to types of reasons whose designation as moral depends on acceptance of a particular moral code's prescriptions. That is, once one accepts a certain account of what a person's moral obligations are, a "moral reason" would be one carrying implications for the morality of proposed actions. For example, if Tom accepts the Ten Commandments and a certain action would constitute stealing, Tom has "moral reason" not to steal because doing so would violate that moral code.

12. Kai Nielsen makes this point in "Why Should I Be Moral? Revisited," in *Why Be Moral?* (Buffalo, N.Y.: Prometheus, 1989), 288.

13. Toulmin, *Reason in Ethics,* 163.

14. Henry Sidgwick cites the possibility that either Egoism or Utilitarianism rests on the intuitively known first principle that happiness is the only rational ultimate end of human action. He later concludes that the method of Intuitionism yields the substantive doctrine of Utilitarianism (*The Methods of Ethics,* 7th ed. [1907; reprint, Indianapolis: Hackett, 1981], 201, 406–7).

15. See, for example, John Finnis's discussion of the seven fundamental forms of good as equally self-evident in the Natural Law theory that he embraces (Finnis, *Natural Law and Natural Rights* [Oxford: Clarendon Press, 1980], 85–97).

16. I leave aside ancient Greek moral theories because they did not conceive of the issue in the same way as later theorists. The Greeks viewed morality as woven within the larger fabric of living well, such that moral behavior was not carved as a special category in need of unique motivation. Also, I will not analyze the detailed arguments of advocates of the schools considered (which would require a book in itself) but will distill the essence of each.

17. Butler's book *The Analogy of Religion* was the standard text used to train Church of England clergy for generations (J. B. Schneewind, *Moral Philosophy from Montaigne to Kant,* vol. 2 [New York: Cambridge University Press, 1990], 525). J. O. Urmson reports that Moore, because of his utilitarianism, was not immediately recognized as an Intuitionist (Urmson, "A Defense of Intuitionism," *Proceedings of the Aristotelian Society* 75 [1974–75]: 111).

18. Stephen Darwall, Allan Gibbard, and Peter Railton, "Toward *Fin de Siecle* Ethics: Some Trends," in *Moral Discourse and Practice,* ed. Stephen Darwall, Allan Gibbard, and Peter Railton (New York: Oxford University Press, 1997), 6–7. The basic account of reflective equilibrium is given in John Rawls, *A Theory of Justice* (Cambridge, Mass.: Belknap Press, 1971), 20, 51.

19. T. K. Seung, *Intuition and Construction* (New Haven, Conn.: Yale University Press, 1993), ix. Bernard Williams, *Making Sense of Humanity and Other Philosophical Papers* (New York: Cambridge University Press, 1995), 183; Robert Audi, "Ethical Reflectionism," *The Monist* 76, no. 3 (1993): 295–315, and *Moral Knowledge and Ethical Character* (New York: Oxford University Press, 1997); Lawrence Blum, *Moral Perception and Particularity* (New York: Cambridge University Press, 1994); Jonathan Dancy, *Moral Reasons* (Cambridge, Mass.: Blackwell, 1992).

Intuitionism's influence extends beyond academic philosophy. The historian Daniel Walker Howe cites the influence of the British Intuitionists on early American culture, reflected in such things as the preaching of William Ellery Channing, a prominent spokesman for the young Unitarian religious denomination, and of Jonathan Edwards, who held that "the soul [of the saint] distinguishes as a musical ear"; in Ralph Waldo Emerson's writing a prize-winning essay praising the Intuitionists; and in the views of much of the faculty at Harvard in the nineteenth century (Howe, *Making the American Self* [Cambridge, Mass.: Harvard University Press, 1997], 43, 204, 244). In his recent book for popular audiences, *Integrity* (New York: Basic Books, 1993), Yale law professor Stephen Carter repeatedly sounds Intuitionist themes. And while every use of the word "intuition" does not reveal a commitment to Intuitionism, one frequently encounters appeals to intuitions that suggest it, as in the late Supreme Court Justice William Brennan's explanation that his jurisprudence preferred "a range of emotional and intuitive responses" to the "lumbering syllogisms of reason" (*New York Times Book Review,* July 6, 1997, 19).

20. H. A. Prichard, "Does Moral Philosophy Rest on a Mistake?" *Mind* 21 (1912): 154, 155, 156, and "Duty and Interest," *Moral Obligation and Duty and Interest* (New York: Oxford University Press, 1968), 236.

21. Joseph Butler, "Upon Human Nature" (sermon 2), in *Five Sermons,* ed. Stephen L. Darwall (Indianapolis: Hackett, 1983), 37, 38; "Dissertation," in *Five Sermons,* 69; *Five Sermons,* 34–35.

22. Prichard, "Does Moral Philosophy Rest on a Mistake?," 162. Rawls writes that according to Intuitionism, agreement in our moral judgments is based on "recognition of self-evident truths about good reasons. And what these reasons are is fixed by a moral order that is . . . given by the nature of things and is known, not by sense, but by rational intuition" (Rawls, "The Dewey Lectures," *Journal of Philosophy* 77, no. 9 [September 1980]: 557).

23. Samuel Clarke, "A Discourse of Natural Religion," in *British Moralists 1650–1800*, vol. 1, ed. D. D. Raphael (Oxford: Oxford University Press, 1969), 192, 193, 194.

24. Rawls, *A Theory of Justice*, 34. Urmson emphasizes this pluralism in his account of Intuitionism.

25. W. D. Ross, "What Makes Right Actions Right?" in *Readings in Ethical Theory*, ed. Wilfred Sellars and John Hospers (New York: Appleton-Century-Croft, 1952), 184.

26. Butler, "Upon Human Nature" (sermon 3), 43. One can detect a hint of Aquinas's famous doctrine in Natural Law theory that an erring conscience binds. Finnis discusses this in *Natural Law and Natural Rights*, 125–26.

27. Ross, "What Makes Right Actions Right?," 192.

28. The weakness of many alternative theories may explain why Intuitionism has become the fallback position of so many.

29. Sidgwick, while no opponent of intuitions, acknowledged that intuitions are easily confused with other phenomena, such as "blind impulses to certain kinds of action or vague sentiments of preference for them, or conclusions from rapid and half-unconscious processes of reasoning, or current opinions to which familiarity has given an illusory air of self-evidence" (*The Methods of Ethics*, 211–12).

30. David Schmidtz makes similar points in *Rational Choice and Moral Agency* (Princeton, N.J.: Princeton University Press, 1995), 135.

31. Nor does the experience of feelings of guilt necessitate positing a "conscience" that is guilty. Feelings depend, in part, on beliefs (e.g., anger, on the belief that an injustice has been done; fear, on the belief that something that one values is in danger). A feeling of guilt usually reflects the belief that one has failed to act as one should have.

32. Correspondingly, the self-evident does not need proof. Facts that are self-evident constitute the building blocks of proof; we start with what is self-evident and construct proofs of further claims from there. (This is why, when police have credible eyewitnesses to a crime, they do not need to devise ingenious inferences or elaborate proofs to show the identity of the criminal.)

33. I say half the population because opinion is probably roughly split on some of these issues. If we take into account shifting ranks of supporters of the allegedly erroneous positions on these and other controversial moral questions, it may well turn out that most people suffer from impaired moral faculties, by the Intuitionist's reckoning.

34. Ross, "What Makes Right Actions Right?," 176. In Ross's lexicon, a prima facie duty is a conditional duty or something that tends to be a duty but is not always one's actual duty. For his explanation, see 175, n. 2, and 176–77.

35. Prichard, "Does Moral Philosophy Rest on a Mistake?," 156, n. 7; Ross, "What Makes Right Actions Right?," 192.

36. W. D. Hudson, *Modern Moral Philosophy* (New York: Macmillan, 1970), 104. Alasdair MacIntyre has observed that Intuitionists are "on their own view, telling us only about what we know already. That they sometimes disagree about what it is that we all know already only makes them less boring at the cost of making them even less convincing" (*A Short History of Ethics* ([New York: Macmillan, 1966], 254).

37. Peter Vallentyne, "Gauthier's Three Projects," *Contractarianism and Rational Choice,* ed. Peter Vallentyne (New York: Cambridge University Press, 1991), 3.

38. The roster of Contractarians includes Thomas Hobbes, David Gauthier, John Rawls, G. R. Grice, Jan Narveson, Christopher Morris, Thomas Scanlon, Gilbert Harman, and Jeffrey Reiman. For a brief discussion of some differences between Gauthier and Rawls, see Vallentyne, ed., *Contractarianism and Rational Choice,* 2–3; for differences between Gauthier and Hobbes, see Jean Hampton, "Two Faces of Contractarian Thought," in Vallentyne, ed., *Contractarianism and Rational Choice,* 31–55.

39. Thomas Hobbes, *Leviathan,* ed. C. B. MacPherson (New York: Penguin, 1968), 186.

40. Hobbes, *Leviathan,* 191–92, 188. For an interpretation of Hobbes as a Natural Law thinker, see Aloysius Martinich, *The Two Gods of Leviathan* (New York: Cambridge University Press, 1992). Note that Hobbes qualifies the obligation to adhere to Natural Law with the proviso that one is bound to obey them when one can do so safely (Hobbes, *Leviathan,* 215).

41. David Gauthier, *Morals by Agreement* (New York: Oxford University Press, 1986), 9.

42. Gauthier, *Morals by Agreement,* 2, 5, 269, 339.

43. Psychological egoism is the descriptive thesis that human beings always do act to promote their own self-interest. One encounters weaker and stronger forms of psychological egoism, varying in the degree to which a person is thought to control his actions. Strong versions maintain that human beings necessarily act in self-interested ways; weaker versions maintain that while self-interest is not the inescapable motivation of human action, people do, as a matter of fact, act to advance their own self-interest.

44. Ronald Dworkin, *Taking Rights Seriously* (Cambridge, Mass.: Harvard University Press, 1978), 151. Some of the other points in this paragraph were also suggested by Dworkin, who was addressing Rawls's theory of justice.

45. This image of morality as a hindrance is at least as old as Plato. The discussion of Gyges's ring (with the power to make its wearer invisible) in Plato's *Republic* is a classic instance. Glaucon insists that any man who had such a ring would use it to flout morality's strictures; if people thought they could get away with immoral deeds, they would perform them with abandon.

46. Hobbes, *Leviathan,* 204–5.

47. In Hobbes's view, this would mean being free from concern for others' threats as well as for others' reactions to one's own behavior, such as one's violations of the contract.

48. Hobbes wrote that "whatsoever is the object of any man's appetite or desire;

that is it, which he for his part calleth good: and the object of his hate and aversion, evil; and of his contempt, vile and inconsiderable. For these words of good, evil, and contemptible, are ever used with relation to the person that useth them: there being nothing simply and absolutely so; nor any common rule of good and evil, to be taken from the nature of the objects themselves" (Hobbes, *Leviathan,* 120). Also, recall the "democratic pluralism" that forms a significant part of Contractarianism's appeal.

49. Nor can the Contractarian casually embrace egoism. For the belief that a policy of promoting one's self-interest is morally good requires proof. I say this not from hostility toward egoism but from hostility toward hedonism and the prevalent idea that egoism is adopted merely on the basis of its agreeable feeling. Egoism can be considered proper only if we have established the basis for assigning *value* to self-interest. "I like it" is insufficient. Chapters four and six will clarify this.

50. I speak of Contractarianism in this way on the grounds that restrictions reining in the contract by specific standards of rationality or of individuals' self-interest would render the theory a version of Rationalism or Egoism.

51. Hobbes, *Leviathan,* 186–87.

52. Contemporary Rationalists besides Gewirth include Alan Donagan and J. David Velleman. Classifications are complicated by many authors' tendency to borrow from an assortment of moral theories and to forge new variations. Bernard Gert, for example, sometimes thought of as a Rationalist, explicitly resists the assimilation of his view to any classical ethical theory (Gert, *Morality—a New Justification of the Moral Rules* [New York: Oxford University Press, 1988], xviii). Similarly, it is not clear that all avowed Kantians embrace the elements of Kant's theory that would qualify them as Rationalists.

53. Immanuel Kant, *Foundations of the Metaphysics of Morals,* trans. Lewis White Beck (New York: Macmillan, 1990), Academy Edition, 411, 412; see also 387–89.

54. Kant, *Foundations,* Academy Edition, 403, 431–32; see also 416–17 on morality's disavowal of concern with actions' results. By a maxim, Kant means "the subjective principle of volition," the underlying policy that an agent relies on when he acts. It is not what the agent thinks he should do, but simply the broader principle beneath what he actually does (400, 421).

55. Kant, *The Doctrine of Virtue* (pt. 2 of *The Metaphysics of Morals*), trans. Mary Gregor (Philadelphia: University of Pennsylvania Press, 1964), 57.

56. Kant, *Lectures on Ethics,* trans. Louis Infield (Indianapolis: Hackett, 1963), 149, 152.

57. Kant, *Foundations,* 429.

58. Alan Gewirth, *Reason and Morality* (Chicago: University of Chicago Press, 1978), 21ff., 26, 135, 139, 515. Gewirth's subsequent work has not departed from this basic position.

59. As Gewirth notes in *Reason and Morality* (194).

60. Note that if one conceives of morality as inhibiting a person's interests, "catch" is an apt term, reflecting the view of morality as a trap.

61. Gewirth boasts of the neutrality of the PGC in *Reason and Morality* (140).

62. Several authors link reasons for action with interests rather than desires. See G. R. Grice, "Motive and Reason," in *Practical Reasoning*, ed. Joseph Raz (Oxford: Oxford University Press, 1978), 168–76; Philippa Foot, "Reasons for Action and Desire," *Virtues and Vices*, ed. Philippa Foot (Berkeley and Los Angeles: University of California Press, 1978), 148–56; John McDowell, "Are Moral Requirements Hypothetical Imperatives?," *Journal of the Aristotelian Society* 52 (Suppl. 1978): 13–29; Thomas Nagel, "Desires, Prudential Motives, and the Present," in Raz, ed., *Practical Reasoning*, 155ff.

63. Prichard, "Does Moral Philosophy Rest on a Mistake?," 151, and Stephen Darwall, "Reasons, Motives, and the Demands of Morality," in Darwall et al., eds., *Moral Discourse and Practice*, 307.

64. Note that if a moral theory cannot be rationally defended in the proper sense of "rational", a natural strategy for hiding this would be to insist that it does not need to be, maintaining that motivation is irrelevant to the justification of morality.

65. On the issue of morality's overriding authority, see Schmidtz, *Rational Choice and Moral Agency*, 128ff., and Brock, "The Justification of Morality," 71ff.

66. Terence Irwin, *Aristotle's First Principles* (Oxford: Clarendon Press, 1988), 336–38, and Scott MacDonald, "Ultimate Ends in Practical Reasoning: Aquinas' Aristotelian Moral Psychology and Anscombe's Fallacy," *Philosophical Review* 100, no. 1 (January 1991): 42.

67. It is also unrealistic. Engaging in *nothing but* activities directly promoting one's highest value is not the best means of promoting that value. Rest, breaks, and distractions are sometimes necessary. When a person is so tired that he cannot think clearly, for example, he should take a nap or a day off. This does not mean that he values sleep more than the goal that he postpones while sleeping but rather that he appreciates that sleep is sometimes necessary to allow the effective pursuit of his more valued ends.

68. For some discussion of fundamental justification, see Peter Danielson, *Artificial Morality* (New York: Routledge, 1992), 19ff., and Christopher W. Morris, "The Relation between Self-Interest and Justice in Contractarian Ethics," *Social Philosophy and Policy* 5 (1988): 119–53.

69. Medlin raises this sort of reasoning ("Ultimate Principles and Ethical Egoism," 111). I do not mean to suggest that reason is exclusively concerned with means and ends, nor that "reason skeptics" are skeptics in the usual, more thoroughgoing philosophical sense. This is merely a convenient label for those who advance this argument; they may think of themselves not as skeptics but as simply being reasonable about the limits of reason.

70. Obviously, I am not claiming that all facts are static or impervious to human action. Human beings are capable of effecting change in the world; we can manipulate, adapt, and combine certain materials to suit our purposes. It is important to distinguish metaphysical facts from manmade facts, however, for example, facts such as the chemical composition of water, the existence of Mount Ranier, and humans' inability to walk on water, versus facts such as the ingredients of Pepperidge Farm cookies, the existence of Grand Central Station, and humans' ability to fly across the Atlantic on the Concorde. The latter are the result of human will and

action. My immediate point is that wishes cannot alter metaphysical facts; we can successfully navigate reality only by accepting and adhering to things' nature. We might be able to use natural gas as an energy source, for example, but we do so by respecting its nature and devising ways of manipulating it to serve that purpose. See Ayn Rand, "The Metaphysical versus the Man-Made," in *Philosophy: Who Needs It* (New York: Bobbs-Merrill, 1982), 28–41.

71. Note that if a person embraced the end of being irrational, seeking to enjoy the "release" that he finds in that, he still must heed reality's requirements in order to be able to pursue that end. Complete irrationality would, in due course, lead to his demise. (More on this in chapter four.) And we have already observed that even the person intent on suicide must conform to reality in order to successfully bring it off. Note the difference between the person who actively seeks to kill himself and the person who does not care whether he lives or dies, who is utterly indifferent to his fate. Only the latter person, if he is truly devoid of all purposes, lacks reason to be rational.

72. Kant, of course, was concerned that the inclusion of such empirical elements would prevent the universality of moral prescriptions. He took the necessity of such universality as a given (Kant, *Foundations,* 388–90).

73. Rationalism's failure reverberates beyond the field of ethics, contributing to the wider decline in the prestige of reason. Because Rationalism purports to explain morality via reason, its failure encourages the inference that reason has had its chance and could not deliver and thus that reason, as a method, must be deficient.

3

Intrinsic Value:
A False Foundation

G iven the failures of systematic attempts to justify moral authority, we might expect people to cast off morality's demands. Yet this is hardly what we find. People debate the morality of numerous issues (treatment of minorities, government policies, business practices, personal deceptions) with a fervor suggesting well-founded certainty. Many continue to treat moral appraisals as a uniquely grave class, pronouncing right and wrong as incontrovertible, all-important matters of fact.

Some people, of course, do conclude that morality is a charade. They regard both its basic categories and its finer distinctions as a colossal, useless rigmarole, an anachronistic echo of a more mystical era. Fueled by theorists' failure to justify popular moral beliefs, such people deny that moral claims carry any valid authority.

Others retreat to subjectivism. Subjectivists do not renounce morality altogether, but they insist that one person's moral standards cannot be applied to others. "Truth" depends on the subject. Denying any transcendent moral facts, subjectivists contend that what is true for one individual (e.g., the propriety of fidelity) is not necessarily true for another.[1]

Many people (perhaps most), however, adopt a third position. Repulsed by the implications of relativism and unable to shake the belief in *some* universal moral truths, they are undeterred by theorists' failings and hold tightly to their moral judgments. The chief basis for their doing so is belief in intrinsic value. Whether people are familiar with that term or not, the belief that certain things are good in themselves is widespread. Explicitly or implicitly, for many, intrinsic value is the anchor for derivative beliefs about what is good and bad, right and wrong, virtuous and vicious.

Given its wide and understandable appeal, we should investigate the validity of this belief. Does intrinsic value truly exist? If it does, it will offer another possible foundation for moral authority.

The list of ethicists who have embraced intrinsic value is a roll call of respected figures, including Henry Sidgwick, John Laird, G. E. Moore, Richard Brandt, W. D. Ross, Roderick Chisholm, and the "value realists" Franz Brentano, Max Scheler, and Nicolai Hartmann. Contemporary advocates include Ronald Dworkin, Elizabeth Anderson, Robert Nozick, Thomas Hurka, Hugh La Follette, Shelley Kagan, Robin Attfield, David Brink, and Laurence Bon Jour.[2] Consequentialists often allege the intrinsic worth of the ends they urge us to promote.[3]

Intrinsic value has been attributed to concrete objects as well as to states of affairs, activities, conditions, qualities, experiences, relationships (e.g., the Mona Lisa, aesthetic appreciation, rational thought, developing one's talents, enjoying good health, being a parent). Among the things most frequently said to possess intrinsic value are life, happiness, pleasure, art, education, love, friendship, freedom, justice, self-expression, self-realization, and communion with God. These days, disputes over assisted suicide, humans' treatment of animals, developing the wilderness, and federal arts subsidies routinely prompt declarations of the intrinsic value of life, or nature, or art.[4]

The basic impulse animating the idea of intrinsic value is a simple question: Don't certain inherently worthwhile goods serve as the foundation for all other values? And thus for morality? Indeed, are not such goods necessary to make sense of other goods? Aren't all other goods good in virtue of their relationship to these things of intrinsic value?

To investigate whether this is so, I will organize my analysis around three issues: exactly what intrinsic value is, the evidence supporting it, and the most prevalent reasoning given on its behalf.

WHAT IS INTRINSIC VALUE?

The first question to tackle is exactly what intrinsic value refers to. Modern discussions usually begin with G. E. Moore, who held that intrinsic value "depends solely on the intrinsic nature of the thing in question." "Saying that a thing is intrinsically good . . . means that it would be a good thing that the thing in question should exist, even if it existed *quite alone,* without any further accompaniments or effects whatever." W. D. Ross held that the intrinsically good is "that which is good apart from any of the results it produces." Fred Feldman observes that philosophers have used "intrinsically good" to mean that a thing is "good in itself—that it has its value in virtue of what it is, rather than in virtue of how it is connected to other things."[5]

Today, authors frequently characterize intrinsic value somewhat differently. According to L. W. Sumner, intrinsic value is something "worth having or pursuing for its own sake, not merely by virtue of some further good with which it is somehow connected." Elizabeth Anderson contends that intrinsic goods are things that it makes sense for a person to care immediately about, independent of its making sense for him to care about any other particular thing. Ronald Dworkin calls something intrinsically valuable "if its value is *independent* of what people happen to enjoy or want or need or what is good for them." Robin Attfield explains that something is of intrinsic value if there are "non-derivative reasons for seeking it."[6]

These accounts cloak significant differences. Christine Korsgaard has pointed out that claims that something is good in itself concern the *source* of the thing's goodness, while claims that something is valued for its own sake concern people's attitudes toward it. We often conflate two separate distinctions: that between something's being sought as a means or as an end and that between something's value being intrinsic or extrinsic, that is, derived from some external source.[7]

We can thus distinguish two main strains of intrinsic value: the "good-in-itself" conception and the "sought-for-its-own-sake" conception. The good-in-itself model construes intrinsic value as packed within the allegedly valuable thing, independent of and thus unaffected by the existence or condition of all other things, persons, and interests. On the alternative sought-for-its-own-sake model, intrinsic value consists of the fact that a thing is sought *not* as a means to or constituent of any other end. As a recent text puts it, such value is seen as "good without being good *for* anything."[8] What is important here is that, on this model, the alleged intrinsic value turns on a person's reasons for seeking something rather than on the nature of the thing itself.

The fact that these two senses are rarely distinguished is probably not accidental. Appeals to people's reasons for seeking things provide a smooth entree for the idea of intrinsic value. Since we are all familiar with the difference between seeking things as means and as ends, appeals to this difference find a receptive audience. Yet the price of the greater plausibility of sought-for-its-own-sake intrinsic value is its very intrinsic-ness. The discovery that something is sought for its own sake tells us only about people's motivations in pursuing that thing. That says nothing about the propriety of their quest or the actual value of the thing sought. No definitive conclusions about a thing's good-in-itself intrinsic value could emerge strictly from observations about individuals' reasons for seeking that thing. Indeed, such deference to individual's desires would allow the very subjectivism that the embrace of intrinsic value is typically intended to reject. That is, if we treated the fact that a given object is sought for its own sake as proof that it is intrinsically valuable in the more robust, good-in-itself sense, we would be embracing the subjectivist view that people's attitudes are sufficient to create value.

The two conceptions of intrinsic value are no doubt related. The belief that some things are good in themselves will often be the reason that those things are sought for their own sake (or the reason that people believe that those things ought to be sought for their own sake). But this does not erase the distinction between the two conceptions. The sought-for-its-own-sake strain—representing people's attitudes toward their ends—cannot deliver objective value. When intrinsic value is characterized solely in terms of the reasons for which something is sought, the embrace of intrinsic value collapses into subjectivism. Thus, our inquiry will focus on the good-in-itself conception. That notion, unabashedly embraced by Moore, Ross, and others, represents more truly *intrinsic* value. In this sense, to say that something is intrinsically good is to say that its goodness is completely self-contained. (This conception also matches the ordinary meaning of the term "intrinsic," whose principal definitions are "situated within; interior, inner; inward, internal . . . belonging to the thing in itself, or by its very nature; inherent.")[9]

Alas, the good-in-itself conception is a much more difficult one to defend. To see this, begin by reposing the question, What is it? What does this alleged value refer to?

It is striking how often intrinsic value is characterized in terms of what it is not. Advocates are evasive when pressed to define intrinsic value in positive or existential terms. They emphasize that it is *non*relational (recall Moore and Feldman), that it is value *apart* from a thing's consequences (Ross), *independent* of other aims (Dworkin). Robert Nozick contends that an intrinsically valuable thing need not be "linked with anything else"; intrinsic value stands "apart from further consequences and connections."[10]

Such negative depictions are not sufficient to illuminate a genuine property, however. (They are especially inadequate when the alleged property is employed to generate moral prescriptions.) Claiming that intrinsic value is different from other types, at best, provides only part of the story. We also need an explanation of what the *value* consists of, an explanation of how "intrinsic value" qualifies under the genus of value. Without that, we have no grounds for accepting its existence.

Moore, of course, would insist that goodness is a simple, nonnatural property and thus does not "consist" of more primitive elements. But this hardly resolves the difficulty. It leaves unexplained the basis for identifying particular things as possessing this property. Consider Moore's classic brief for intrinsic value:

> Let us imagine one world exceedingly beautiful. Imagine it as beautiful as you can; put into it whatever on this earth you most admire—mountains, rivers, the sea; trees, and sunsets, stars and moon. Imagine these all combined in the most exquisite proportions, so that no one thing jars against another, but each contributes to increase the beauty of the whole. And then imagine the ugliest world you can possibly conceive. Imagine it simply one heap of filth, containing everything that is most disgusting to us, for whatever reason, and the whole, as far as may be, without one redeeming feature. Such a pair of worlds we are entitled to compare. . . . The only thing we are not entitled to imagine is that any human being ever has or ever, by any possibility, can, live in either, can ever see and enjoy the beauty of the one or hate the foulness of the other. Well, even so, supposing them quite apart from any possible contemplation by human beings; still, is it irrational to hold that it is better that the beautiful world should exist, than the one which is ugly? Would it not be well, in any case, to do what we could to produce it rather than the other? Certainly I cannot help thinking that it would.[11]

A bit later, Moore continues: "If it be once admitted that the beautiful world *in itself* is better than the ugly, then it follows, that however many beings may enjoy it, and however much better their enjoyment may be than it is itself, yet its mere existence adds *something* to the goodness of the whole."[12]

Moore is defending hard-core, good-in-itself intrinsic value. Yet his thought experiment leaves the crucial question completely unanswered: In what sense is the beautiful world valuable? Apart from the idea that people contemplating the alternatives supposedly would prefer it? What does its value consist in?

Moore does not say. His explanation is strikingly similar to an elaboration of sought-for-its-own-sake value. Rather than pointing to the fact that a number of people seek some end for its own sake, Moore is relying on the fact that he would seek that end and tacking on the supposition that most readers would join him in this. But the essence of this account is as subjectivist as more overt defenses of sought-for-its-own-sake value. Moore's claim that certain things possess the simple property of goodness attaches a label to this preference without illuminating it as anything other than a preference.

Moore was careful to distinguish the reason that something is true from the reason that a person accepts it. The intuition that gives a person a reason to believe in intrinsic value is not proof of such value's external, independent existence.[13] This distinction is rarely respected by advocates of intrinsic value, however. (It is not clear that Moore himself is faithful to this distinction.) Many people accept intrinsic value on the basis of prefer-ence, subsequently treat intrinsic value as a fact about the world, and build moral instructions on it. This is how those who view intrinsic value as a bulwark against subjectivism typically proceed. To legitimately play this role, however, we must be shown intrinsic value's existence as something more than the object of people's preferences. We must be shown its value.

The difficulty in defining intrinsic value marks an ominous beginning for those who would defend it. Indeed, it is a crippling failure, for intrinsic value's proponents are asking us to believe in "a something, I know not what." If the alleged value is genuine, natural questions concerning how intrinsic value is valuable must be answered. Advocates of intrinsic value offer the positive claim; thus, the burden is theirs to substantiate it. They will be hard-pressed to do so as long as they fail to clarify exactly what intrinsic value is. To the extent that they do supply a definition, they face a daunting challenge, for whatever properties they identify as constitutive of intrinsic value (or as the base on which it supervenes or as identical with this unique, simple property), they must demonstrate that these amount to value. If the concept of value does something more than replicate the con-cept of "what people prefer," as advocates of intrinsic value are them-selves inclined to hold, we must be shown the grounds that warrant use of that label.

THE EVIDENCE FOR INTRINSIC VALUE

The case for intrinsic value is further strained when we consider how we can detect it. What are we to look for to determine which things possess intrinsic value? Obviously, what counts as evidence depends on what in-trinsic value is. The fuzzier the basic conception, the more difficult it will be to isolate evidence on its behalf. Casting intrinsic value in negative terms, as most of its defenders do, aggravates the problem by limiting the prospects of locating positive markers of its presence.[14]

Advocates have suggested various means of determining whether some-thing possesses intrinsic value. Moore employed what is sometimes called the method of isolation, maintaining that we must consider whether a thing is such that, if it existed absolutely by itself, we would judge its existence good. The two-worlds passage cited previously exemplifies this method. Moore supports assertions of intrinsic value with confident appeals to the "sober judgment of reflective persons." Like many others, he holds that the question of whether dispositions or actions are good in themselves "must be settled by intuition alone."[15]

This Intuitionist perspective does not always surface bearing that name, but the belief that intrinsic value is self-evident is commonplace. In his recent book *Intrinsic Value,* Noah Lemos contends that we can attain "modest a priori knowledge" of things' intrinsic value. Acquaintance with intrinsic value is analogous to knowledge of axioms. "There are a great many things that one can be justified in believing," Lemos writes, "even if one cannot show them to be true or deduce them from premises that are more evident." While Lemos disavows a distinct faculty of intuition, he holds that "what justifies me in believing that someone's being happy is intrinsically good is that I believe it on the basis of my comprehending consideration of it, and nothing defeats this reason for me." He supports his advocacy of intrinsic value by appeals to widely shared preferences; for example, "few of us would choose everlasting life as a cricket over a finite human life," and few of us would "trade the finite remainder of our normal lives for the indefinitely extended life of a contented imbecile."[16]

In a similar vein, Panayot Butchvarov maintains that "it is a difficult task to elucidate the way we are conscious of the goodness of, say, affection and pleasure. But what matters is the brute fact that we find it unthinkable that we should be mistaken in judging that they (in themselves) are good."[17]

Other advocates link intrinsic value to organic unity. Nozick holds that "[s]omething has intrinsic value . . . to the degree that it is organically unified." Organic unity depends on a thing's degree of diversity and the degree of unity to which that diversity is brought. While Nozick is attempting to identify the basis of intrinsic value—that in virtue of which things possess it—the possession of the requisite unity is itself allegedly self-evident.[18]

Yet another contingent maintains that the evidence for intrinsic value rests in observers' experience. Rather than attaining a purely intellectual grasp of a thing's intrinsic value, feelings or dispositions alert us to its presence. C. I. Lewis held that experiences of certain emotions amount to "felt goodness," direct findings of value. Philip Blair Rice contends that the presence of intrinsic value is "determined by direct introspection." Charles A. Baylis writes that "the best initial evidence" for ascribing intrinsic value to something "is that we find ourselves prizing things of that kind, i.e., liking, approving, desiring, preferring, and commending them, for their own qualities."[19]

Some recent authors have modified this experiential account of the evidence for intrinsic value, supplementing it with a reflective element. Peter Railton holds that what is intrinsically valuable for a person will carry "internal resonance"; it must have a connection with what that person *would* find compelling or attractive if he were rational and aware. An individual's intrinsic good consists in attainment of what he would, in idealized circumstances, want to want for its own sake were he to assume the place of his actual self.[20] Elizabeth Anderson maintains that what is intrinsically valuable is the object of a rational favorable attitude. We experience certain things as worthy of our appreciation; we "sensibly" care about them. (One of her examples is natural beauty.) It is reasonable for us to have these attitudes "independent of our caring about any other particular things or people."[21]

On even modest reflection, it becomes obvious that none of these accounts of the evidence for intrinsic value can substantiate its existence. Crucial questions are again left unanswered. Why does the presence of organic unity constitute value? How does a person know that his "favorable" disposition is stimulated by *value*? Moore's isolation method instructs us simply to swap intuitions (which, notoriously, do not always converge). If we fail to elicit others' endorsement of the same things as intrinsically valuable, our only recourse is to look longer. But what are we to look *for*? Without answers to these questions, such "evidence" can hardly confirm the independent existence of things that are good in themselves.

By now, we can appreciate why intrinsic value is frequently linked with Intuitionism. For the last resort in defense of intrinsic value is the claim, reminiscent of the quintessential Intuitionists Clarke, Prichard, and Ross, that we simply perceive it.

A belief in intrinsic value does not necessarily commit a person to full-fledged Intuitionism. Whether it does depends on the nature of our alleged awareness of intrinsic value and on the role that intrinsic value plays in relation to other moral conclusions. Many people believe that some things contain intrinsic value, although they proceed to reason about numerous moral matters, regarding argument as necessary to justify most moral claims about what people should and should not do. Intuitionism, on the other hand, purports that such moral judgments are knowable without argument. Yet however limited the role one accords intrinsic value in answering moral questions, if the way to detect intrinsic value is, essentially, to intuit it, then to the extent that one accepts any intrinsic value, one is an Intuitionist. The only way to avoid this implication is to demonstrate some alternative means of awareness of intrinsic value.

Notice, however, that not every Intuitionist must accept intrinsic value. Recall that the core Intuitionist thesis is that knowledge of moral truths is immediate and nonderivative. That, alone, says nothing about the nature of value. Intuitionism is an epistemological doctrine concerned with the way in which we acquire certain knowledge. It is not a doctrine about *what* it is that we come to know. Thus Intuitionists can, consistently, regard intuition as a means of learning moral facts that do not include the existence of intrinsic value—learning, instead, of other types of value, or our obligations, or the virtue or vice of certain sorts of actions. A given Intuitionist might think that intuition is a means of uncovering intrinsic values, then, and another might not. In short, Intuitionism does not entail belief in intrinsic value, although acceptance of intrinsic value typically involves at least a quotient of Intuitionism.

With that relationship clarified, let us return to our main track. The "evidence" for intrinsic value invariably boils down to claims that intrinsic value is self-evident. Even those who do not openly acknowledge this take for granted that the evidence they offer is evidence of value. Appeals to "worthy desires," "comprehending consideration," and "organic unity" are as far as they probe; no further steps demonstrate how these amount to value. The value is treated as obvious, in need of no further certification.[22]

Conspicuous by its absence from all accounts of the evidence for intrinsic value is reference to the governing standards. Lemos admits as much when he writes that we can know of intrinsic value's existence before ascertaining what justifies this "knowledge." Lemos asserts, "Even if there is no general criterion or method by which we can pick out those propositions . . . that are intrinsically acceptable, it hardly follows that we cannot be justified in believing that certain particular propositions have that status."[23]

Obviously, something could exist without our current awareness of any evidence for it. But what advocates of intrinsic value claim is not that intrinsic value *might* exist; they claim that it does. The absence of objective evidence for intrinsic value, alongside the utterly subjective basis on which people assert it (their feelings or intuitions), leaves us without grounds to credit its existence.

Because its exponents provide no tenable criteria by which to assess claims of intrinsic value, appeals to intrinsic value are reminiscent of the "look-say" method of teaching reading. Look-say attaches sounds to particular letter strings and trains students to recognize those strings and pronounce the corresponding sounds. Because look-say does not teach the underlying architecture of words, however, a child acquires no techniques for navigating new words. He is trained to know what to say when confronted with words he has already seen but develops no understanding of why strings are pronounced as they are and thus is helpless when faced with previously unseen terms. In phonics, by contrast, students learn the sounds of individual letters and clusters. Instruction to "sound it out" reminds students that they have the resources necessary to conquer the foreign sequence of symbols that a new word presents.

The intrinsic value thesis resembles look-say teaching insofar as it offers no conceptual understanding of value. In renouncing objective criteria, advocates assume the same position as the instructor who points to a word, pronounces it, and prods students to mimic him. The identification of intrinsic value is made on an ad hoc basis, completely uninformed by the broader patterns or principles that obtain across all instances of intrinsic

value. Supporters may claim that intrinsic value consists of particular qualities (organic unity, felt goodness, and so on), but until they show that
these add up to value, insistence on intrinsic value is merely an assertion
of faith. The advocate of intrinsic value insists that he can spot it but provides no satisfactory account of how—and thus no means of verifying his
claims.[24]

Rice reveals the essence of the doctrine when he maintains that we can
recognize intrinsic value when it occurs, although we cannot state its conditions. This confession conjures former Supreme Court Justice Potter
Stewart's infamous declaration that he might never be able to define hard-
core pornography, "but I know it when I see it."[25] Such a stance should
be an embarrassment to systematic ethics. It is hardly the route to a stable,
objective basis for moral instruction.

The failure to provide an adequate account of evidence for intrinsic
value, then, exposes the doctrine's latent subjectivism. The only common
denominator among allegedly intrinsically valuable things lies in the reactions of observers. "Intrinsic values" are united solely by the fact that they
elicit similar responses in many people. (Prevalent declarations of the in-
commensurability and pluralism of values testify to the absence of disci-
plining standards.)[26]

The subjectivism is at times astonishingly explicit. Thomas Nagel
claims that "sensory experiences which we strongly like or dislike simply
in themselves have agent-neutral value because of those desires." According to Butchvarov, Moore held that consciousness is diaphanous, such that
whatever it is conscious of, whatever contents occupy its attention, must
be real, existing things. Correspondingly, if people are conscious of moral
properties such as goodness, those properties must be real.[27]

Few people will claim that all the objects of their desire have intrinsic
value, of course, but how will they distinguish those that do? By introspection. By appealing to qualities of their experience rather than facts concerning the external objects. Even the insistence that people seek a particular thing *for itself* is an appeal to the nature of their desires. It offers
nothing about the nature of the object or the bases of anyone's desires but
simply points to the existence of those desires. It thus represents a variation on the subjectivist theme, supplementing one's personal taste with the
addition of others' tastes.

Railton, seemingly, struggles to escape subjectivism. Yet his elucidation
of intrinsic value as what a person *would* want, after fully informed, rational deliberation, does not introduce the elements necessary to transform
this into an objective value. Desires remain decisive. More reflective subjectivism remains subjectivism.[28]

It is important to realize that subjectivism infects the very idea of intrinsic value and not only those theories that explain it by naked appeal to

observers' desires. Because advocates furnish no external evidence warranting ascriptions of good-in-itself value, the case for intrinsic value must turn inward. The source of value must be located in the consciousness of the person asserting it. Yet this surrenders the very thing that those drawn to intrinsic value seek: value independent of personal taste.

The failure of intrinsic value to deliver what its advocates seek may explain the considerable fiddling one finds with the meaning of intrinsic value. Baird Callicott, a prominent environmentalist theorist, has recently formulated a theory of relational intrinsic value. Thomas Hurka characterizes intrinsic value as a function of a good's "explanatory power," its ability to organize and encompass other goods, and its connection "to deeper perfectionist values." Hugh La Follette contends that a value is intrinsic depending on how strongly "interwoven" it is with others. Health and knowledge, for example, are intrinsically valuable because of the large number of purposes that they assist. And many intrinsic value advocates eventually gravitate toward the view that only experiences can have intrinsic value. Ross held that beauty does not contain intrinsic value, but aesthetic enjoyment does. Moore traveled a similar path between *Principia Ethica* (1903) and *Ethics* (1912).[29]

All these revisions, however, surrender intrinsic value's intrinsic-ness—its independence of relations to other things. The motivation is understandable: Since it is impossible to provide evidence for intrinsic value, the only way to maintain the existence of intrinsic value is to change the meaning of one of the salient terms. Advocates must either broaden the meaning of "intrinsic" or broaden the object to which intrinsic value is attributed. An experience is a more plausible candidate for intrinsic value since a relationship to a person is now incorporated into the object allegedly bearing intrinsic value.

That intrinsic value has become a moving target complicates attempts to track it. These maneuvers do nothing to fortify the case for intrinsic value, however, for they unearth no evidence for the existence of anything that is, in the rigorous, good-in-itself sense, intrinsically valuable. To defend intrinsic value by changing its description is to admit failure in finding evidence that can justify belief in it.

THE REGRESS ARGUMENT

Despite these rather devastating difficulties concerning intrinsic value's identity and the evidence of its existence, many persist in accepting intrinsic value on the belief that it is necessary to prevent an otherwise infinite regress. Knowledge of intrinsic value is not based on an accumulation of positive evidence. Rather, the contention is, we know of intrinsic value by default. Some things must have intrinsic value in order for anything else to have value.

As Monroe Beardsley explains this argument, the existence of any instrumental value implies the existence of some intrinsic value. "To justify ascribing a value to X requires not only that we show it is a means to Y, but also that we justify ascribing a value to Y."[30] To complete the justification, therefore, some things must be regarded as valuable in themselves.

Many have embraced intrinsic value on just this reasoning. Attfield asserts that any theory of value must recognize intrinsic value somewhere, or there is nothing to give value its point. Nozick contends that "something must be valuable in itself; otherwise value could not get started." Henry David Aiken sees intrinsic value as providing a criterion for determining whether instrumentalities are instrumentalities having value. Ross put the point more poetically. If all value were dependent on relation to an interest, nothing would "possess value in itself. But in that case value would seem always to be borrowed, and never owned; value would shine by a reflected glory having no original source."[31]

This argument is seductive because it seeks what a rational theory of value should seek: the bedrock foundations beneath claims of instrumental value. It exudes the aura of logic. Yet its logic is fatally flawed. We can see this through four observations.

1. The regress argument seems a natural fit for the sought-for-its-own-sake conception of intrinsic value since it only makes sense to seek things as means given other things that we seek as ends. The argument accurately observes that certain things are sought as ends. Use of the sought-for-its-own-sake conception, however, would prevent the argument from demonstrating the existence of good-in-itself value. As we have previously noticed, the fact that something is sought for its own sake informs us only about people's attitudes, beliefs, or aims in seeking that thing. Nothing follows from these concerning the independent existence of good-in-itself value. Seeking a thing does not confer such value on that thing.

Since the argument quickly sinks, when given a sought-for-its-own-sake reading of intrinsic value, let us proceed with the stronger interpretation of the argument.

2. The regress argument posits that something must have good-in-itself intrinsic value in order for any instrumental value to get off the ground. The transition to good-in-itself value is not so smooth, however. A comparison with the First Cause argument for the existence of God is instructive.[32]

First Cause arguments are notoriously riddled with critical questions: How did God get started? Why does the genesis of things begin with God—no later and no earlier? By virtue of what does God have self-generating power? In parallel fashion, it is reasonable to ask, Where does intrinsic value get its value? What reason do we have to stop the chain of explanation with these "intrinsically" valuable things? Why suppose that value resides in these objects rather than in some others? By virtue of what does any alleged intrinsically valuable thing possess this unusual value?

The comparison with First Cause arguments reveals that the regress argument moves the question of the ground of value without answering it. The regress argument does not illuminate the distinctive character of intrinsic value; it does not identify its roots or name those features that confer this special status. Rather than explaining *how* intrinsic value arises, the argument simply points and attaches the label "intrinsic" when it has exhausted other observations.

The problem is, a label is not an explanation. Calling something intrinsically valuable simply cordons it off from other values. Bestowing a name does not enhance our understanding of what renders an object intrinsically valuable. (Nor, of course, does it impart much guidance for detecting or pursuing intrinsic value in the future.) The fact that a moral theory must start somewhere does not warrant an arbitrary starting place. To insist that some things "must" have intrinsic value does not show that any things do.[33]

3. A natural reply to this objection feeds directly into the next difficulty. One might respond that the regress argument holds that some things must have intrinsic value *if* some things have extrinsic value. Since some things clearly do have extrinsic value, intrinsic value is assured.

Yet a simple obstacle thwarts this reasoning: its impoverished conception of how to escape the threatened regress. An argument by default, purporting to offer the only possible explanation of some otherwise inexplicable phenomenon, must truly exhaust all alternatives. The regress argument, however, overlooks the fact that acceptance of intrinsic value is not the only conceivable way to make sense of instrumental value.

Certainly, arguments defending value must stop somewhere. Yet that observation alone does not settle where they should stop, or, more important, the value-status of the starting points. It does not show that they are intrinsically valuable.

The regress argument observes that some things are not sought as means. Thus, if such things are valuable, their value must be noninstrumental. But, in fact, that does not mean that their value must be intrinsic, for that is not the only alternative.

Value admits of more species than this traditional dichotomy supposes.[34] Instrumentality—being a means to an end—is only one of several types of relationships capable of being valuable. A thing might be valuable because it is a component of a multifaceted good, for example, or a necessary condition for the achievement of an end or because it intensifies a person's enjoyment of some experience or is a token of cherished associations (sentimental value). The point is, for a thing's value to be noninstrumental does not entail that its value is nonrelational. Other sorts of relationships might explain a thing's value. Since intrinsic means nonrelational, noninstrumental status does not entail intrinsic status.

Consequently, a thing may be valuable in a way that is neither instrumental nor intrinsic. Job security may not be a direct cause of a person's overall happiness, but it may be a necessary condition. (Whether it actually is involves an argument we need not enter.) Similarly, close friends or a vibrant romance might be neither means to happiness nor prerequisites but desirable elements that enhance it. More generally, it is quite possible that nothing is valuable to a person unless it contributes to his most fundamental objectives. Even life may not be valuable for the person whose experience is so infused with pain and despair that he cannot enjoy his life. But if this is so, then it is not intrinsic value that is the wellspring of instrumental or other relational values. It is a person's embrace of certain overarching objectives.

Advocates of intrinsic value might reply that these nonintrinsic values I have cited are various forms of instrumental value, while the end that they serve—whether as necessary conditions, as enhancers, or whatever—is an intrinsic value. But this would beg the question. My point is that a careful inspection of values reveals that we are not restricted to two crude categories of value, intrinsic and instrumental. It is a mistake simply to fold the further types of value that we observe into a broadened conception of instrumental value. Intrinsic value is not the only type of value besides means–end value.

While advocates of intrinsic value might claim that the values I have identified reduce to intrinsic or instrumental, in other words, such a claim is refuted by the reality of these distinctive relationships. When an apparent value does not fit the means–end mold, what intrinsic value advocates rush to call intrinsic value actually reflects a different kind of valuable relationship. The stone that holds sentimental value for me is not intrinsically valuable; it may have absolutely no value to most people, and it may have had no value to me apart from the circumstances under which I acquired it. But nor is its value akin to that of a scissors or ladder or other things that serve as means to attain particular ends. Similarly, the wine that enhances my enjoyment of dinner may be of no value to people who do not enjoy wine or who suffer allergic reactions to wine; its value is not universal and not intrinsic, even to me. But nor is it comparable to the ladder, without which I would not be able to reach the roof, or the scissors, without which I would not be able to cut the tape.

The point is not simply to expand our knowledge of species of relational value, however, for that might nurture the belief that intrinsic value is the foundation on which they all depend. Further, we must appreciate that whatever is served by any of these types of relational value need not be intrinsically valuable. Something might be instrumentally valuable because it is a means of my obtaining an object of great sentimental value. Something might be instrumentally valuable because it is a means of my obtaining something that enhances my enjoyment of a certain activity (without that activity or my enjoyment of it being intrinsically valuable). Something might be valuable in virtue of its being necessary for, or a component of, some larger aim of mine without that aim being intrinsically valuable. In short, things can be valuable in relation to other things that are not themselves intrinsically valuable.

The upshot of all this is straightforward: Instrumental value is perfectly intelligible independently of intrinsic value. The regress argument, in attempting to explain instrumental value, has not exhausted all available options. Instrumental value may presuppose noninstrumental value, but that is not synonymous with presupposing intrinsic value. The fact that some things are valuable *not* as instruments does not imply the hidden presence of "intrinsic" value—natural endowment with this unique, inherent property.

4. Finally, we should notice yet a further flaw in the regress argument. It is a simple but significant failing.

The argument plays on an ambiguity in the notion of "instrumental value." A thing's instrumental value could consist wholly in the fact that it is effective as a means. This carries no judgment of the value of the end that it advances. The value refers only to the thing's practical efficacy. Alternatively, to call something instrumentally valuable might mean that the ends that it serves are themselves worthwhile. This wider construal of instrumental value would require antecedent value in the purpose served in order to legitimize ascriptions of instrumental value.

Which sense of instrumental value does the regress argument employ? The first, narrow sense tells us nothing about the value of the target, so it could not deliver the conclusion that is sought. We would make no progress toward the demonstration of intrinsic value in certain ends if we merely established that certain things were effective means to those ends.

The second sense of instrumental value does imply value in the end, but only by assuming that value from the outset. That is, if the value of the end is necessary to understand the instrumental value of any means—if that is allegedly part of what "instrumental value" signifies—then the value that the regress argument intends to demonstrate is presupposed from the start. Thus, the argument is not a proof of the existence of intrinsic value but an elaboration of the relationship between two kinds of value that are already taken for granted. As a defense of intrinsic value, this reasoning is circular. The identification of certain things as instrumentally valuable would show the existence of things that are intrinsically valuable only by smuggling such existence into the thicker notion of instrumental value.

The only conclusion we can reach from all this is that the regress argument's initial aura of logic cannot withstand scrutiny—and cannot sustain intrinsic value.

ARTIFICIAL ALTERNATIVES

Consider one last defense of intrinsic value—this one, really, a reply to certain critics. When opponents of intrinsic value sometimes insist that it is the *pleasure* of a beautiful sunset or the *enjoyment* of life that is valuable, intrinsic value advocates contend, they are suggesting that the only things that are valuable are states of consciousness. But this is untenable, such advocates maintain.[35] Such states are reactions to events. Our definite preferences about those events—preferring our children's actual success to our deluded misimpression of it or preferring genuine accomplishments to the sense of accomplishment that a virtual-reality machine might provide—reveal that value lies beyond one's consciousness. Since the "feel" of both the genuine and the simulated experiences is the same, the value does not lie within the conscious experience but must emanate from those external objects or events that trigger those experiences. The value, intrinsic value advocates insist, is *out there.*

This argument is right, I think, to extricate value from the pleasant experience that often accompanies it. But its conclusion is hasty, and its error is instructive.

Consider the argument's reason for placing the value external to the experience. How do intrinsic value advocates know that one experience is valuable and another is not? On the basis of people's preferences. They appeal, for example, to the fact that we would rather have actually achieved a worthy end than falsely believe that we had. If preferences are decisive, however, this is hardly a case for the mind independence of good-in-itself value. Preferences are simply another reflection of individuals' states of consciousness. This account of value is not, then, as mind-free as it pretends to be.[36]

I am not disputing the distinction between what is necessary for pleasure (consciousness) and the object of pleasure. Nor am I disputing the distinction between pleasure and goodness. Both distinctions are important. What I am challenging is the presumption that if value is not fully in the feel of a person's experience, if it is not "all in your head," it must be wholly "out there," vacuum packed within external objects.[37]

What this argument helps us appreciate is that a false dichotomy distorts much discussion of intrinsic value. The debate is typically premised on the assumption that value is either given or made; it rests either within external objects or within a person's consciousness. Yet the fact that attempts to posit independent intrinsic value so often collapse into subjective assertions (which we observed when we considered the evidence for intrinsic value) signals confusion in the assumed structure of the alternatives.[38]

The lesson to draw is that debate over the location of value—is it created in our minds or discovered in our surroundings?—is misguided. In the coming chapters, I will pursue the proposal that value designates a relationship. Value is neither wholly internal nor wholly external but a function of a particular connection between external objects and a person's ends.

CONCLUSION

The denial of intrinsic value may seem cold, particularly if one agrees that some of the perennial candidates for intrinsic value (beauty, freedom, life, and so on) are pretty wonderful. Denying that these things are intrinsically valuable does not deny that they are valuable, however. Nor does it preclude their being especially valuable, carrying significant ramifications for other values or for the propriety of various actions. Our examination of the meaning of intrinsic value, the evidence for intrinsic value, and the strongest argument given on its behalf, however, has demonstrated that the existence of intrinsic value cannot be substantiated.

The basic impulse driving many people to posit intrinsic value is the wish to plant morality on a firm and objective footing. This is a goal that I share. The irony, however, is that assertion of intrinsic value represents a variant of subjectivism. Because no external evidence warrants claims of intrinsic value, such claims ultimately rest on the advocate's taste. In the place of objective evidence, the intrinsic value cognoscenti are armed with confidence that they know it when they see it. The assignment of intrinsic value rests, fundamentally, on the fact that a person or persons firmly believe that something has it. This leaves its advocates helpless against anyone who detects intrinsic value elsewhere, exposing belief in intrinsic value as something that is as fickle as subjectivism and as arbitrary as Intuitionism. Since intrinsic value's apparent objectivity is deceptive, the effect of indulging this thesis is the further entrenchment of subjectivism.

In sum, intrinsic value does not provide the sure, sturdy foundations that a rational justification of morality requires.

NOTES

1. I will use "subjectivism" to encompass relativism as well. Ultimately, subjectivism may collapse into moral skepticism since relative truth is not truth, but that is not an issue we need pursue here.

Notice that subjectivism does not attempt to explain why people should be moral. In maintaining that moral truth is subject customized, subjectivism defaults on the rationale for morality as well as on the provision of moral guidance. Whatever a given individual believes he should do *is* what he should do; his opinion is true, *for him.*

2. The classification of historical figures is more delicate, as the term's deliberate, self-conscious use seems to have been a fairly recent development. Certainly, the distinction between things sought as ends and things sought as means was employed by Aristotle, yet it is not clear that he conceived of intrinsic value in the rugged sense of many modern advocates. And while many ethicists through the years have sought ultimate starting points for their accounts of morality, they did not necessarily assign intrinsic value to those starting points. For discussions of the history of the concept of value, see John Laird, *The Idea of Value* (1929; reprint, New York: August M. Kelley, 1969), and William Frankena, "Value and Valuation," *Encyclopedia of Philosophy,* vols. 7–8, ed. Paul Edwards (New York: Macmillan, 1967), 229–32.

3. The trend among certain Consequentialists to urge satisfaction of preferences is clearly more subjectivist, as the idea that the paramount end to promote is people's getting whatever they want replaces the idea that we should promote some intrinsically valuable ends. Some have advocated satisfaction of "informed" or "rational" preferences (e.g., James Griffin, Stephen Darwall, Richard Brandt, and Peter Railton), as if to resist this subjectivist slide.

4. Kant seemed to think that morality was itself intrinsically valuable. He distinguished the price of a thing from its dignity, contending that price denotes relative worth and dignity denotes "intrinsic worth." A thing of dignity is "above all price." Kant wrote that "Morality, and humanity so far as it is capable of morality, alone have dignity" (Immanuel Kant, *Foundations of the Metaphysics of Morals,* trans. Lewis White Beck [New York: Macmillan, 1990], Academy Edition, 435).

5. G. E. Moore, "The Conception of Intrinsic Value," *Philosophical Studies* (London: Routledge and Kegan Paul, 1922), 260, and *Ethics* (New York: Henry Holt, 1912), 65 (emphasis in the original); W. D. Ross, *The Right and the Good* (Indianapolis: Hackett, 1988), 68; Fred Feldman, "On the Intrinsic Value of Pleasures," *Ethics* 107 (April 1997): 457.

I will sometimes use "the concept of intrinsic value" to refer not only to the concept itself but also to assertions of intrinsic value's existence. The context should make my meaning clear. Throughout, I am concerned exclusively with values for humans.

6. L. W. Sumner, "Two Theories of the Good," *Social Philosophy and Policy* 9, no. 2 (Summer 1992): 3; Elizabeth Anderson, *Value in Ethics and Economics* (Cambridge, Mass.: Harvard University Press, 1993), 19 (see also 2–3); Ronald Dworkin, *Life's Dominion* (New York: Knopf, 1993), 71 (emphasis in the original); Robin Attfield, *The Ethics of Environmental Concern* (Oxford: Basil Blackwell, 1983), 175.

A few further accounts: Thomas Nagel claims that intrinsic values are not reducible to their value *for* anyone (*The View from Nowhere* [New York: Oxford University Press, 1986], 153). C. L. Stevenson held that "intrinsically good is roughly synonymous with good for its own sake, as an end, as distinct from good as a means to something else" (quoted in John O'Neill, "The Varieties of Intrinsic Value," *The Monist* 75 [April 1992]: 121). Noah Lemos holds that some state of affairs is intrinsically good if and only if that state of affairs obtains and is intrinsically worthy of love (Lemos, *Intrinsic Value* [New York: Cambridge University Press, 1994], 15). A. Campbell Garnett refers to intrinsic values as having "value in themselves, apart from their consequences" (Garnett, "Intrinsic Good: Its Definition and Referent," in *Value: A Cooperative Inquiry,* ed. Ray Lepley [New York: Columbia University Press, 1949], 84). John Hospers holds that intrinsically valuable things are good "because of what they are in themselves; we consider them worth having or pursuing not merely as ways of getting other things but because of their own intrinsic nature" (quoted in Gilbert Harman, "Toward a Theory of Intrinsic Value," *Journal of Philosophy* 64 [December 1967]: 794).

7. Christine M. Korsgaard, "Two Distinctions in Goodness," *Philosophical Review* 92 (April 1983): 169–70. For further discussion of different possible meanings of intrinsic value, see Judith Jarvis Thomson, "On Some Ways in Which a Thing Can Be Good," *Social Philosophy and Policy* 9 (Summer 1992): 96–117; Shelley Kagan, "The Limits of Well-Being," *Social Philosophy and Policy* 9 (Summer 1992): 169–89; and O'Neill, "The Varieties of Intrinsic Value." Lemos points out that it is possible to love something for its own sake, such as the fact that one is a Texan or that the Red Sox beat the Yankees, without having any reason to think it is intrinsically good (*Intrinsic Value,* 194).

8. Robert N. Van Wyk, *Introduction to Ethics* (New York: St. Martin's Press, 1990), 100. Van Wyk meant to characterize intrinsic value itself, not simply one type of it. Joseph R. des Jardins also offers a stark instance of the sought-for-its-own-sake conception, writing that "an object has intrinsic value when it is valued for itself and not simply valued for its uses" (des Jardins, *Environmental Ethics* [Belmont, Calif.: Wadsworth, 1993], 144).

Among those employing the good-in-itself conception are William Frankena, *Ethics* (Englewood Cliffs, N.J.: Prentice Hall, 1963), 66; Charles A. Baylis, "Grading, Values, and Choice," *Mind* 67 (1958): 485–501, quoted in Monroe Beardsley, "Intrinsic Value," *Philosophy and Phenomenological Research* 26 (1965): 10; Richard Brandt, *Ethical Theory* (Englewood Cliffs, N.J.: Prentice Hall, 1959), 302; Brandt, *Value and Obligation* (New York: Harcourt, Brace and World, 1963), 18–19; Thomas Hurka, "Virtue as Loving the Good," *Social Philosophy and Policy* 9 (Summer 1992): 149; Nagel, *The View from Nowhere,* 129. These writers may not be aware of the potentially different interpretations of intrinsic value; thus, they may not intend to be defending one version of intrinsic value as opposed to another.

9. *Oxford English Dictionary* (New York: Oxford University Press, 1971). All subsequent references to intrinsic value will be to good-in-itself value unless otherwise specified.

Bob Kane has suggested to me (without embracing) another conception of intrinsic value in which one feature of the good-in-itself core is a magnetic appeal that disposes people to pursue the things containing it. This would be a fortified version of good-in-itself value. Yet it is not apparent that this constitutes an essentially distinct type of value. If people's pursuit of such objects were our sole means of knowing of those objects' alleged intrinsic value, this sounds like the sought-for-its-own-sake conception, with the basis for ascribing good-in-itself value still elusive. If, on the other hand, we had some different means of detecting the presence of this magnetic core of intrinsic value, this would simply be a type of good-in-itself value about which we would have further information (namely, its alluring effects on people).

10. Robert Nozick, *The Examined Life—Philosophical Meditations* (New York: Simon and Schuster, 1989), 167–68, and *Philosophical Explanations* (Cambridge, Mass.: Harvard University Press, 1981), 414. Lemos describes the traditional view as holding that intrinsic value is a "non-relational" property (*Intrinsic Value,* 3).

11. Moore, *Principia Ethica* (New York: Cambridge University Press, 1903), 83–84.

12. Moore, *Principia Ethica,* 85 (emphasis in the original).

13. Moore, *Principia Ethica,* 143–44. See also his disclaimers in the preface concerning how claims about what things ought to exist for their own sake are incapable of proof (viii, x).

14. Evidence for sought-for-its-own-sake intrinsic value is more readily available since it consists of information about individuals' desires, but this is useless as a basis for ascriptions of good-in-itself value.

15. Moore, *Principia Ethica,* 94, 173, 187. Moore believed that we can err in intuiting goodness, although he provides no standards by which to distinguish accurate from inaccurate intuitions.

16. Lemos, *Intrinsic Value,* xii, 52ff., 81, 188; see also x, 12, 138, 195. Lemos considers the a priori knowledge "modest" because it is neither certain nor indefeasible (150, 195). Brentano also considered intrinsic value self-evident (154), and Ross relied on self-evidence in regard to claims concerning which actions are prima facie right.

17. Panayot Butchvarov, "That Simple, Indefinable, Nonnatural Property *Good,*" *Review of Metaphysics* 36 (September 1982): 74.

18. Nozick, *The Examined Life,* 163; see also 167–68 and *Philosophical Explanations,* 446. In *Philosophical Explanations,* Nozick raises questions about why organic unity is valuable, although his answer is, frankly, difficult to make out (see 415ff. and 446ff.). In *The Examined Life,* he claims that "a thing's organic unity *is* its value" (164, emphasis in the original).

Moore advocated the "principle of organic unities," according to which "the intrinsic value of a whole is neither identical with nor proportional to the sum of the value of its parts" (*Principia Ethica,* 184; see also 27–28, 36). Lemos defends this principle in chapter 3. The view of some of the ancients that the best life is a unified whole, a harmony of varied qualities, activities, and ends, is an early instance of seeing value in unity, as Bob Kane has reminded me. The value that unity may offer in different contexts need not be intrinsic, however.

19. Lewis and Baylis, quoted in Beardsley, "Intrinsic Value," 8, 10. Philip Blair Rice, "Science, Humanism, and the Good," in Lepley, ed., *Value,* 282. Rice allows that intrinsic value is known "by indirect but equally empirical methods in the case of others." He contends that intrinsic value is marked by a certain "hedonic tone."

Franz Brentano, Max Scheler, Alexius Meinong, John Findlay, and Maurice Mandlebaum also held this feelings-are-evidence position (Lemos, *Intrinsic Value,* 180–83).

20. Peter Railton, "Facts and Values," *Philosophical Topics* 14 (Fall 1986): 9, 17. Railton's notion of intrinsic value is somewhat unusual in that he holds that the intrinsic good of individuals may differ. Something could be intrinsically valuable for a particular person without arousing similar responses in others (and thus without being intrinsically valuable for others).

21. Anderson, *Value in Ethics and Economics,* 5, 21, 205, 206. Anderson considers her account a development of Brentano's in certain respects.

22. Butchvarov contends that for Moore, goodness is a genus, and inclusion in a genus is something that we see rather than prove (Butchvarov, "That Simple, Indefinable, Nonnatural Property *Good*," 58, 60, 66–67).

23. Lemos, *Intrinsic Value,* 136–37, 159.

24. Conceivably, an advocate of intrinsic value might believe that such an account is possible but simply not necessary to identify things possessing intrinsic value. This view, however, would leave the process of locating intrinsic value mysterious and is thus subject to all the same objections concerning the alleged objectivity of value that is identified in the absence of specified, justified standards.

25. Rice, "Science, Humanism, and the Good," 281; Stewart's concurring opinion in *Jacobellis v. Ohio,* 378 U.S. 184 (1964), 197.

26. Not all such declarations refer to intrinsic value, of course, but many intrinsic value advocates have been pluralists. See, for example, Moore, *Principia Ethica,* 27; Lemos, xi; Nozick, *Philosophical Explanations,* 446; and the earlier work of Max Scheler, Nicolai Hartmann, and Franz Brentano.

27. Nagel, *The View from Nowhere,* 167; Butchvarov, "That Simple, Indefinable, Nonnatural Property *Good*," 54–55. The context of Nagel's claim implies that he means an intrinsic agent-neutral value. Earlier, with refreshing candor, Nagel acknowledged, "I don't know how to establish whether there are any [intrinsic] values, but the objectifying tendency produces a strong impulse to believe that there are" (153).

28. Garnett similarly invokes hypothetical preferences, contending that a life devoted wholly to pleasure is not the best life because few would agree that it is ("Intrinsic Good," 85). Obviously, this also relies on a subjective standard (people's agreement).

29. Callicott, reported in Jim Cheney, "Intrinsic Value in Environmental Ethics: beyond Subjectivism and Objectivism," *The Monist* 75 (April 1992): 227; Thomas Hurka, "Why Value Autonomy?" *Social Theory and Practice* 13, no. 3 (Fall 1987): 372, 373, 380; Hugh La Follette, *Personal Relationships—Love, Identity and Morality* (Cambridge, Mass.: Blackwell, 1996), 84; Ross, *The Right and the Good,* 130. See also Lemos on Moore's transformation (*Intrinsic Value,* 6, 88ff., 94), and Frankena, "Value and Valuation," 231. I will have more to say on the proposal that intrinsic value resides in experience later in the chapter.

30. Beardsley, "Intrinsic Value," 6–7. Beardsley refers to this as the "dialectical demonstration"; he himself is not endorsing this argument.

31. Attfield, *The Ethics of Environmental Concern,* 160; Nozick, *Philosophical*

Explanations, 414; Henry David Aiken, "Criticisms by Aiken," in Lepley, ed., *Value*, 296–97; Ross, *The Right and the Good*, 75.

Van Wyk maintains that unless at least one thing is intrinsically good, the instrumental goodness of anything would not give us reason to want it (*Introduction to Ethics*, 100). Hume wrote that "something must be desirable on its own account" (Hume, *Enquiry concerning the Principles of Morals* [New York: Liberal Arts Press, 1957], 111). Antony Flew circulates the same idea in his entry on "Value," *Dictionary of Philosophy*, ed. Antony Flew (New York: St. Martin's Press, 1979), 365.

32. Beardsley compares the two ("Intrinsic Value," 6ff.). See also George R. Geiger, "Values and Inquiry," in Lepley, ed., *Values*, 105, and Harman, "Toward a Theory of Intrinsic Value," 800.

33. Geiger makes a similar point more colorfully: "To arrest the logical or chronological process is to do no more than seize upon some apparently spectacular element and hypostatize it, or at least divorce it from a context. It is like jumping naked into the snow to quench a fever" ("Values and Inquiry," in Lepley, ed., *Values*, 105–6). Just as the jump does not address the source of the fever, the arbitrary assertion of intrinsic value does not explain the source of value.

34. Korsgaard considers "mixed values," such as mink coats and enameled frying pans, neither intrinsically valuable nor purely instrumentally valuable ("Two Distinctions in Goodness," 184–85).

35. Anderson addresses this sort of objection (*Value in Ethics and Economics*, 206ff.). She believes that such reasoning commits a "crude hedonistic error," taking the object of intrinsic value to be an observer's favorable response rather than the stimulant of that response. Note that those intrinsic value advocates who adopt the view that it is states of consciousness that have intrinsic value would be guilty of this very error.

36. In his much-cited discussion, Nozick reasons against settling for life hooked up to an experience machine: "Perhaps what we desire is to live (an active verb) ourselves, in contact with reality." This, of course, is what machines cannot deliver. Note, however, the pivotal role of desire (Nozick, *Anarchy, State, and Utopia* [New York: Basic Books, 1974], 45).

37. For a good discussion of some of the confusions swirling around these issues, see Stephen L. Darwall, "Pleasure as Ultimate Good in Sidgwick's Ethics," *The Monist* 58 (July 1974): 475–89.

38. We find an example of this external–internal dichotomy in Dworkin's contention that an art work is intrinsically valuable since "we say that we want to look at one of Rembrandt's self-portraits because it is wonderful, not that it is wonderful because we want to look at it" (Dworkin, *Life's Dominion*, 72).

4

Morality's Roots in Life

Having seen the failures of traditional attempts to provide the foundations of morality, we can now turn to the account that I believe is true. It was presented by Ayn Rand, primarily in her essays "The Objectivist Ethics" and "Causality versus Duty."[1] Here, I will elaborate and defend Rand's account.

Rand's thesis is that the foundation of morality resides in the nature of values. Values, in turn, depend on the fact that organisms face the alternative of life or death. We can understand what values are only against the background of this fundamental alternative. The requirements of human life furnish the standard of value for human beings and, derivatively, the basis for all moral prescriptions. Life is the yardstick by which we measure whether a thing is good or bad and whether an action is right or wrong. A person should pursue value and abide by a moral code in order to advance his own life.

To explicate Rand's theory, I will proceed in three stages. In the first section of this chapter, I will present the core of Rand's argument, explaining how values are unintelligible apart from their relationship to life and how life cannot be sustained without the organism's achievement of values. In shorthand, life makes the concept of value both possible and necessary. In this section, I will also explain the relationship between the goal of value and the standard of value as well as the basic relationship between values and specific moral prescriptions.

In the second section of the chapter, I will explain the major implication of Rand's account: Value and morality are objective. By understanding values' basis in facts—values' roots in their actual relationship to an organism's life—we can appreciate how morality overcomes the notorious fact–value "gap." This clears the way for the breakthrough offered by

Rand's theory. Rand's demonstration of morality's foundations establishes a firm basis for moral judgments that are objectively true.

Finally, in order to prevent possible misunderstandings, I will address several questions and objections that may naturally arise. Responding to these should clarify the exact contours of Rand's position and strengthen our grasp of its logic.

THE ARGUMENT FOR MORALITY'S BASIS IN LIFE

Let us begin by clarifying the central concepts involved. Rand describes morality as "a code of values to guide man's choices and actions—the choices and actions that determine the purpose and the course of his life."[2] This describes what myriad moral systems—ancient and modern, Eastern and Western, religious and secular, deontological and utilitarian—attempt to provide. Reference to the Ten Commandments, Kant's categorical imperative, the principle of utility, or the Golden Rule, for instance, is intended to steer an individual's decisions about concrete actions.

A value is "that which one acts to gain and/or keep."[3] People act to gain or keep material possessions as well as such things as relationships with others, professional positions, knowledge, opportunities, beliefs, and outlooks. Thus, a house, a friend, a job, or self-esteem could all be values. Insofar as morality is intended to guide a person, however, it seeks to identify those objects that human beings should pursue. Values in this positive sense—things that a person truly should act to acquire—are united by the fact that they are good for a person. They bring beneficial effects, minor or major, on a person's life.[4]

This raises a further distinction, one between values and benefits. Not all benefits result from the beneficiary's action. Certain salutary events can occur without the beneficiary's having done anything to bring them about. I might benefit from rainfall insofar as it spares me the time and expense of watering my garden, but I have not done anything to precipitate the precipitation. A baby benefits from being fed or clothed, just as a man may benefit from mouth-to-mouth resuscitation, but in neither case does the person's action trigger these benefits. Other benefits, by contrast, can be obtained only by the individual's own exertion of effort. Normally, a person must take some action to produce food or shelter, to find good friends or good books, or to achieve a rewarding career or a rewarding marriage. Thus, a value is that which one *acts* to attain. "Benefits" designate the broader class of advantageous events.[5]

This difference carries direct implications for morality. If some benefits are beyond a person's control, he can only hope for them. If the attainment of others depends on a person's conduct, however, he can act for them.

Thus, a rational morality attempts to guide a person's actions toward beneficial ends. It identifies proper values and provides direction for how to achieve them.[6]

The nature of value can be fully appreciated only by understanding what gives rise to value. Values are not self-evident. One cannot spot a value *as a value* in the same way that one can recognize a tree as a tree, a chair as a chair, or blades of grass as blades of grass. A beverage might look harmless but actually be toxic; a person might look menacing but be completely harmless. Something's being a value depends on facts about it that are not necessarily readily apparent. Thus, it is crucial to understand what renders something valuable.

Rand observes that life gives rise to the very concept of value. The alternative of life or death is what allows and what necessitates the pursuit of values. The quest for life makes the idea of value intelligible and imposes the need to identify values and to act to achieve them. Thus, it is life that mandates human beings' adherence to a moral code. Life is the end of value and establishes the standard of value. As such, it is the source of moral obligations, which are prescriptions for how to achieve that end.

Obviously, this is a vast claim. It will be best understood if I explain separately its major components.

Life Makes the Concept of Value Possible

The first part of the case for value's roots in life is the claim that life makes values possible.[7] Without the alternative of life or death, the very concept of value would be empty. To see this, consider when it makes sense to attribute value to something. What sorts of things can have values? *To what sorts of things* can certain objects, events, or states of affairs be valuable? To a rock or a coffee mug? To a hill or a pad? To a cave or a house? Things can happen to these objects and affect them in various ways. Some of them might be moved from the sunlight to the shade; they might be pulverized or painted, placed in a museum, auctioned, or featured as the subject of a PBS documentary. Could any of these events be good or bad for the object?

No.

Such events may be good or bad relative to some human ends.[8] If I was planning to use a particular mug for my morning coffee, it is bad for me if it is pulverized or painted an unappetizing shade of green. If a rock fetches four million dollars at auction, that is good for its owner. If a pad containing the only copy of the novel that I am writing is drenched in coffee, that is bad for me. Yet none of these developments is good or bad for the object. Why not?

Some of my examples are manmade objects, while others are found in nature; thus, that difference is not pivotal to value. Nor is the obstacle to the applicability of value the fact that these objects are not conscious. Plants are not conscious, yet they can flourish or struggle, as various things may be good or bad for them (e.g., rainfall, drought, pests, Miracle Gro). Whether a plant is placed in the sun or shade does make a significant difference to it. Animals (exhibiting varying levels of consciousness) are also affected by external events in ways that our original examples are not. Severe weather or a lake's infusion with algae, for instance, can be good or bad for certain animals insofar as it affects their mobility, which affects their ability to flee predators or to obtain food. Even human beings, while unconscious, can do well or badly (which is why we monitor their condition). What, then, is the salient difference between the sorts of things for which value is and is not applicable?

The common denominator among plants, animals, and humans is that all are alive—and can cease to be alive. We may die at any time. Crucially, our lives depend on our actions.

Any fate that befalls an inanimate object is neither good nor bad for it because nothing is at stake for it. Inanimate objects have no ends on the basis of which we can evaluate the effects of various occurrences on them. We can notice events' effects on inanimate objects; some, obviously, can destroy them altogether. The rock that is pulverized or the house that is consumed by fire no longer exists. Yet we have no grounds for regarding such effects as good or bad for the rock or for the house since those objects are not engaged in a quest to exist. They are not struggling to resist certain effects and to accomplish others. Indeed, inanimate objects lack agency through which they *could* struggle to attain any ends. Thus, the phenomenon of values—things which one *acts* to gain and/or keep—is inapplicable.

Live organisms, by contrast, do have something at stake: their lives. That provides the basis for evaluating some effects on them as good and others as bad. Life is conditional; any organism's life is always at risk of being extinguished. Inanimate objects stand equally exposed to the risk of destruction, of course. What restricts values to the realm of living organisms, however, is the fact that an organism's existence is dependent on its own actions. "Inanimate objects do not need to *do anything* to remain intact," as Harry Binswanger observes.[9] An organism, however, must act in ways that will sustain it. To remain alive, it must achieve certain subordinate ends or values. Some of the requisite activities are automatic (internal physiological processes), while others (for human beings) are deliberately chosen. If a person's heart or kidneys stop functioning, for example, he will die. If a person does not nourish himself or make a living for long enough periods, he will die. This is precisely why evaluating actions' effects is important: to lend guidance for what kinds of actions a person should take so as to maintain his life.[10]

Since life is pivotal in this account, we should be clear about what life is. Life is a series of actions. More specifically, it is a process of self-sustaining and self-generated actions.[11] All living organisms—from para-mecia and mushrooms through salmon and hawks to bears and humans—initiate certain actions to maintain their existence. This process of actions, once begun, does not continue indefinitely, however. Life is an ongoing either/or; it can continue or cease, and its continuation imposes require-ments. Life is contingent on certain needs being satisfied.[12]

It is only this conditional character of life, Rand argues, that enables us to distinguish some things as valuable on the grounds that they contribute to the sustenance of an organism's life. Without that goal and the possibil-ity of death, we would have no basis for evaluating the impact of various events.[13]

Much ordinary thinking about plants and animals reflects implicit recog-nition of life as the source of value judgments. When we assess certain events as beneficial or harmful for plants or animals, the barometer that we employ is the life of the organism. Some events further their lives—enhancing their hardiness and growth, minimizing their vulnerability to diseases, increasing their prospects for longevity—and others hinder it. What allows these evaluations is not the fact that one experiences varying feelings in reaction to such events. Rather, it is the fact that the organisms stand to gain from them; their lives can be strengthened or set back.

Thus, Rand's claim is not that any thing's existence (be it living or non-living) is intrinsically good and its destruction intrinsically bad. A living organism's existence establishes the measure of other things' goodness or badness only to the extent that that organism's existence is sought as an end. It is the pursuit of life that gives rise to values. Inanimate objects do not (and cannot) seek their continued existence.

Imagining Immortality

Thus far, to demonstrate how life makes value possible, I have contrasted living things with inanimate objects. Yet another contrast is instructive: immortality. To appreciate fully the salience of life to value, we should also consider the prospect of being *always* alive. (This is inspired by Rand's discussion of an immortal, indestructible robot that cannot be changed, damaged, or destroyed.)[14]

If a person were assured of going on forever, what sense could it make to regard some states of affairs as better than others? I am not merely imagining a person's life being extended by decades or centuries. Rather, imagine his life being literally endless. He is indestructible and will live for all eternity. Whatever the person did this afternoon, he would have an infinite amount of time to do other things. He would incur no loss by choosing one activity rather than some other. (I will address pain shortly.)

In actual, mortal life, of course, doing one thing now means forgoing other possible uses of one's time—which is a finite currency. Spent time cannot be retrieved; days are not equipped with a handy "undelete" key. A person must bear the consequences of how he spends his time. Engaging in one activity may neglect a serious need and set the person back in the larger struggle for life, such that he will have to compensate by taking other actions in the future. If a person postpones tending to an illness, for example, it may worsen and require more drastic action later. If he does not bother to take his medicine every morning, a few months down the road, he may need to stay in bed every morning. Since all of a person's actions can affect the progress of his life, what he does now may restrict what he can do in the future. If a person were immortal, however, he would have nothing to lose through his choices of activities.

The point is not that such a being would have all the time in the world to compensate for past actions. Rather, he would not have to "compensate." Because no activity could threaten his life, no action could have an effect that would require future repair. The effects of his activities simply would not matter. Under these circumstances, what basis would we have for thinking that certain things were good for him and others bad?

One might think that it would be bad for such a being to be sick since that means missing the opportunity to do certain things. Even if he had lots of later opportunities, illness could cause him to miss this one today. Yet the immortal being could not become sick. Illness is physiological malfunction, an unhealthy physical condition. If prolonged or uncorrected, it can kill a person. Yet in the case under consideration, the being is guaranteed life; nothing could truly threaten it. The concept of illness depends on the concept of health, but when immortality is taken for granted, we have no basis on which to distinguish such conditions. Immortality precludes the phenomenon of illness.[15]

Moreover, if the immortal being did not do something today, for whatever reason, he would retain infinite time to perform that action in the future. Thus, the sense in which not doing something *now* would be bad remains opaque. Whence the significance of one moment, in eternal time, versus another? For a mortal man, what lends significance to a particular segment of time is the fact that his life is finite. How a person spends any portion of his time is important because time is limited and because his action affects the future course of his life. In choosing to spend an hour doing one thing rather than others, a person affects his future options. If a teenager puts off doing his homework tonight, for example, he will have to do it tomorrow night and no longer will be able to go to the movies, as he had planned. He might be able to see the film next week, but that will naturally prevent his doing something else—seeing the baseball game, waxing his car, and so on. Nothing can recover spent hours, and a person is left to face the consequences of his use of them. In the immortal being scenario, however, given the prospect of endless time, it is difficult to see how any slice of time could assume significance.

This may prompt a related objection. One might think that some activities are likely to be more pleasurable, even if a person were immortal. Isn't it preferable to spend more time engaged in pleasurable activities? And isn't that the basis for attributing value to various things?

Here again, however, the possibility of pleasure depends on our mortality. We could not find certain things pleasurable if we did not face the alternative of life or death. Survival needs are the source of organisms' pleasure–pain mechanism. As most organisms normally function, we experience pain at things that are harmful and pleasure at things that are good for us. Babies enjoy milk, warmth, and play, all of which are good for them. Satisfying hunger (for adults as well as children) generally feels pleasurable. Eating too much or eating bad foods precipitates distinctly unpleasant indigestion. Toxic substances frequently carry noxious odors. Rancid food, which can cause serious illness, typically tastes bad. Exposure to extreme temperatures or fire is painful. Aches signal infections, inflammations, strains, and the like—abnormalities that threaten well-being. Indeed, an impaired capacity to feel pain is not a blessing but a hazard because it weakens the person's ability to recognize and react to dangers.

My point is not that every sensation of pleasure or pain unfailingly corresponds to life-or-death consequences. (In addition to automatic bodily sensations of pleasure and pain, human beings also experience emotional pleasures and pains that are sometimes based on mistaken beliefs.) My contention, rather, is that the evolution of the pleasure–pain mechanism is grounded in its service to an organism's life. We possess the capacity to feel pleasure and pain because these alert us to the life-enhancing or life-endangering effects of various phenomena. This does not entail that human beings enjoy a foolproof attraction to life-furthering things and a foolproof aversion to life-diminishing things. If it did, we would not require morality's guidance. Yet the general fact that life depends on certain conditions is what gives rise to pleasure and pain. Consequently, if we stripped away the possibility of death, we would be eliminating the very thing that makes pleasure and pain possible. Thus, we cannot suppose that an immortal being would continue to experience pleasure or pain.[16]

The larger point here is not about pleasure but about value: Immortal beings would lack the end that serves as the basis for distinguishing things as good or bad. It makes sense to speak of values only against the background of needs. Needs rest on the alternative of life or death, however. It is only because we face the threat of death that we have needs. Needs boil down to existence needs. The immortality scenario highlights this important intermediate step in the logical chain between life and values: Living provides us with needs, and needs make possible values (those ends that a person must act to gain in order to fulfill his needs). The existence of needs is a necessary condition for the existence of values. Needs furnish the foundation for viewing certain ends as good and certain activities as right on the grounds that they contribute to the satisfaction of some need.

The reason that the proposal that value presupposes the life-or-death alternative may encounter some initial resistance, I think, is our comfortable familiarity with the realm of preference. In the civilized world, people seem to face many more choices among preferences than among needs. Cheerios or a bagel? A documentary or a sitcom? The beach or the mountains? Life-and-death issues of genuine need seem extraordinary anomalies for most of my readers or are so easily satisfied as to hardly register on our minds. Thus, it is easy not to notice that preferences depend on needs. Preferences are so natural and prominent a part of ordinary life that it is difficult to imagine life without them.

Yet this very sentiment is telling. For it *is* difficult to imagine life without preferences. In truth, when we contemplate immortal beings, what we are contemplating is a radically different sort of entity. A being that will never die is not just like us, except in one small detail; the difference is not akin to a difference in hair color. An immortal being is not alive in any sense that we know. Once we remove the possibility of death, life's ever-present alternative, we have changed the subject entirely. We are no longer considering the relationship between values and *life*.

Recall that life is a series of self-generated, self-sustaining actions. Where no self-sustaining action is required, however, no self-sustaining action is possible. This follows from the nature of self-sustaining action. Whatever a destruction-proof robot or immortal being does is not sustaining its existence since that is already guaranteed. Where survival is inherently assured and death is impossible, then, we are no longer talking about life. Rand's robot is not a living being; that is why she calls it a robot.[17]

To summarize, where an object has no needs to be filled, we have no basis for judging effects on it in terms of value. An inanimate or ever-active entity might be changed drastically, beyond recognition. We can imagine a mountain reduced to a billion bits or a robot transformed to resemble Greta Garbo. Since nothing hinges on these alterations for the entity, however, we have no grounds for regarding them as good or bad for the entity, as better or worse than the previous condition or than any other conceivable developments. Impact on the fundamental alternative of life or death is indispensable for values.

Life Makes the Concept of Value Necessary

All of this has argued for the conclusion that we can understand value only in relation to life—that life makes value possible. We can now turn to the further crucial dimension of value's roots in life: Life makes value necessary.

Since life is conditional on the fulfillment of certain needs, it is imperative to know the nature of those needs and how they can be fulfilled. Many of the requisite activities are internal and automatic. A person need not, on waking every morning, order his heart to pump, his blood to circulate, or his lungs to inhale. Not all of life's requisite activities are automatic, however. We must deliberately wash and exercise, furnish nourishment, build shelter, combat disease, make money. We must take certain actions in order to survive. To know what to do, we must distinguish things' effects on us. Building on this, we must identify values, those things that we should pursue in order to fulfill our needs and further our lives.

If it were not for life's conditional character, we would have no need for values. If our lives were somehow assured, we would have no reason to discriminate good from bad ends or right from wrong actions because we would have no need to take one sort as opposed to the other. (This is one of the lessons from considering the robot.) It would not matter what a person did because nothing would hinge on his actions; he would have nothing to lose (and nothing to gain) by taking one course over another. Indeed, a person assured of life would have no need to take any action at all.

In fact, however, if a person wishes to keep his life, he must heed its requirements. While our lives can be affected by events beyond our control, they depend crucially on our own actions. Living requires action, but more, it requires right action—action that maintains one's life. Human beings who wish to remain alive must figure out which sorts of actions will foster life and which will hinder it. This is the basis for identifying which things are good and how one should act: contribution to survival.

Living demands that we pay attention to our surroundings and notice the effects of objects, people, and actions on our lives. If certain food consistently makes a person sick, for example, he should not continue to eat it. If a certain person is violent, unreliable, or rash, he would not make a good boyfriend, dissertation supervisor, or psychotherapist. If a person loses his job and has no savings, he should make efforts to earn income to pay next month's rent. If he loses his job because of his chronic carousing and subsequent bleary-eyed performance at the office, he should exert more self-discipline.

The simple point is that our actions carry consequences that shape our lives' extension, course, and character. It is for this reason that life makes values necessary. Distinctions between good and bad are a matter of self-preservation.

Some might deride such a strong claim as melodramatic. Philosophers are often uncomfortable with black-and-white images. Yet the relevant facts are unyielding. Little needs to be said on this point because it represents such a plain, undeniable empirical fact. The prerequisites of human survival are not negotiable. This is why we *race* to a fire, stop traffic for ambulances, and install alarms in intensive care units. Whatever a person's preferences, projects, or background, wherever and whenever he lives, the fact that certain substances are fatal if ingested is not open to debate. Drano is not mother's milk; a bloody butcher's knife is not a sterile scalpel. Human biology sets limits on what we can "get away with." This is as true for the identification of abstract moral values and virtues such as justice, honesty, and courage as it is for the identification of bodily needs. Different kinds of actions bring different kinds of effects. Treating others unjustly, for example, whether giving them more or less than they deserve, does not by itself change their character and does not change the effects of their actions. Injustice risks encouraging behavior that is harmful and discouraging behavior that is beneficial.

A given individual might temporarily engage in random actions, casually uninformed about what he is doing. When such a cavalier course is prolonged, however, it is only a matter of time before the gamble backfires. The AIDS virus is a tragic illustration. Those who do not practice safe sex often pay the ultimate price. Wishing that you will escape dangers does not exempt you from those dangers. Kidding oneself about the chances of contracting a disease is an all-too-real example of the self-destructive ramifications of dishonesty (in this case, in the form of self-deception).

In principle, human beings who wish to remain alive must identify what is good for them and what is bad for them and act accordingly, pursuing those things recognized as valuable. This is the manner in which life makes value necessary. Values are a matter of life-or-death necessity.[18]

It is the fact that living organisms confront the alternative of life or death, then, that makes value both possible and necessary. This alternative make values possible because things could be valuable only on account of their effect on an organism's life. Without impact on that alternative, we would have no basis for regarding some things as "to be pursued"; the phenomenon of values would not arise. At the same time, life makes values necessary because an organism's life depends on its achieving values that sustain its life. To live, a person must identify and take actions that will promote his life.

Both aspects are crucial to appreciate value's foundation in the alternative of life or death. It is not sufficient to show that life mandates values; the fact that life allows for the possibility of values is crucial to exclude other conceivable grounds for values. That is, the fact that the life-or-death alternative makes values possible secures that the only true values are life-promoting ones, that no other values could exist. This fact preempts acceptance of other, potentially conflicting "values." Detached from the goal of furthering life, any purported values could at best reflect preferences, which would lapse into hedonism.

It is important to appreciate that life is the source of value because life or death is the fundamental alternative that a person faces. By "fundamental," I mean that all of a person's other alternatives depend on this alternative and affect this alternative. The point is not simply that a person must be alive in order to choose among alternatives. Rather, all other choices carry consequences that affect whether a person lives or dies. Consequences need not be equally momentous or direct to be real. Even the most mundane, usually innocuous choices, such as of what to wear or what to drink, can have an impact on one's life by affecting intermediate ends—for example, by coloring the impression that one makes on prospective employers or voters or by affecting one's ability to think clearly and react rationally when taking an exam or performing surgery. Our actions' effects on our lives are inescapable.

Consequently, if a person seeks to live, all his purposes must be pursued in light of this end. Since any of a person's actions can affect his realization of this end, at the bottom of every alternative that he faces, he must consider its impact on his life.

At the same time, no other alternatives would involve needs or values if it were not for the fundamental alternative of life or death. Consider the most widely recognized human needs: needs for food, shelter, and clothing. These are needs only relative to an end: living. It is only if a person seeks to maintain his life that fulfillment of its requirements—satisfaction of these needs—is good. The life-or-death alternative thus stands at the foundation of all others, rendering them significant because of their impact on life. The alternative between healthy and unhealthy food, or between finding a job and not finding a job, or between a person you love and a person you loathe all *matter* only because of their impact on an individual's life—on his survival and on the subordinate goals that sustain his survival. Apart from effects on a person's life, alternatives would offer no values; events would simply be things that happen.

Life as the Goal and the Standard of Value

What emerges from values' roots in life is that life is the goal and sets the proper standard of value. The requirements of human life furnish the yardstick by which to make moral evaluations. In essence, the good is that which protects, furthers, or enhances one's life, and the bad is that which endangers, harms, or diminishes one's life.[19]

A "standard" is a criterion of measurement.[20] We employ standards to assist us in the achievement of goals. Instruments such as a scale, speedometer, blood pressure gauge, or Scholastic Aptitude Test, for example, all reflect certain standards (miles per hour, mathematical capacity) and measure qualities or relationships relevant to particular purposes. "Standardized" testing is designed to facilitate comparisons between students from widely differing educational backgrounds, for instance. When a person inquires about a good school, the response "By what standard?" invites him to elaborate on his purposes. Is he primarily seeking a certain level of cost, convenience, quality, prestige, or job-placement prospects? Decision making often seems impossible precisely when a person's purposes are muddled. If you are not sure what you want or, among several aims, what your top priority is, you cannot be sure what criteria to employ. In choosing a school, a person may well seek affordability, quality, *and* favorable job prospects. Determining which of these purposes is paramount often clears the way to identifying the appropriate standard and reaching a decision. The goal, in other words, establishes what can serve as an appropriate standard for evaluation.

The same holds in the moral realm; the goal sets the standard. A person's goal is his own life. In order to achieve that, he must abide by the requirements imposed by his nature as a human being. Thus, the standard of value refers to the requirements of human life. This standard allows a person to measure progress in advancing his goal. For anyone who seeks to maintain his life, the proper measure of value is a thing's impact on that end.[21]

Life's status as the standard of value is a "preethical" fact insofar as it holds for all living organisms, while ethics is applicable only for beings that can deliberately direct their actions. What is good and bad for organisms depends on things' bearing on their lives. The very concept of health presupposes life as the goal. Healthy functioning simply is life-sustaining functioning. In analyzing this biological concept, philosopher of science James Lennox has written, "The standard by which one judges the successful functioning of a biological system, then—the organism's life—is also the goal of that system. The concept of 'health' identifies, as a value, the state in which all of an organism's goal-directed systems are contributing to this goal."[22]

When it comes to human beings and moral value, however, it is important to understand that life is the standard of value *if* a person seeks life. Having rejected the idea of intrinsic value in chapter three, we cannot treat life as intrinsically valuable. Rather, the existence of value is conditional; value arises for those who seek to maintain their lives. It is only for people who wish to live that we can intelligibly distinguish things as good for them and bad for them relative to that purpose. If one wishes to maintain his life, various things acquire value depending on their relation to that end.[23]

At the same time, we must recognize that life is the only possible standard of value. Not any purpose that a person adopts can substitute as this standard. The fact that life makes value possible means that no alternative ends warrant the status of value, as we noted previously. Life assumes this central role because life or death is the fundamental alternative that a person faces, demanding that a person achieve ends that sustain his life. No alternative end could replace life as the source of value because no alternative end could be achieved by means that do not respect life's requirements. Life's demands are inescapable.

Given the unequivocal nature of human needs, then, it is the conjunction of the purpose of living and the requirements of reality that establishes life as the standard of value. If a person seeks life (embraces that purpose), then, given the facts of human nature and needs (reality), he must pursue certain values. Life is the standard by which we can identify those values.

Value as the Basis for Normative Ethics

While the goal of life sets the standard of ethics, the identification of this standard does not, by itself, tell us everything that we need to know in order to achieve that goal. Just as knowing one's purpose requires a standard of measuring whether that purpose is being advanced, so a standard must sometimes be supplemented by more specific information. In this case, the objective, life, is a long-range, widely encompassing project. Countless discrete actions can affect an individual's life, and recognizing the exact nature of their impact often requires sifting through layers of subordinate values and interlocking aspects of one's welfare. Actions' net effects are often not apparent. To say that life is the standard of value is, while important, extremely abstract. If the identification of this standard is to provide fruitful guidance, we need more specific instruction.

This is what normative ethics provides. Recall Rand's statement that morality is a code of values to guide a person's choices and actions. Such a code is imperative precisely because people are capable of acting in ways that do not sustain their lives. It is because we can err, in forming goals and in acting to attain our goals, that we require guidance. Because life comprises long-range and wide-ranging ends, we must conceptualize its requirements, identifying the kinds of effects that different types of actions carry for a person's life.[24] A proper moral code sets forth the fundamental values and virtues essential to human life. It identifies values that must be achieved in order to realize one's highest end, and it identifies the kinds of actions that are most productive of those values. On that basis, it prescribes principles to follow and virtues to cultivate. Thus, normative ethics will address issues such as the importance of honesty in dealing with facts, forming beliefs, and representing one's beliefs to others; the importance of justice in judging other people; and the importance of productiveness to satisfy one's needs and advance one's life. In effect, metaethics establishes that life requires guidance toward life-promoting actions; normative theory elaborates the more specific contents of that guidance.

To illustrate the basic relationship between normative ethics and the goal of life, consider a few examples. I offer these not as proof of particular virtues (which would require much more in-depth treatment) but merely to indicate the general character of a life-based code of guidance.[25]

Since action in the face of danger is often necessary to protect those things that nourish a person's life, courage would be a virtue in a life-directed ethical code. If a person is cowardly when his values are at stake—not speaking up against a threatening policy for fear of unpopularity, for example, or failing to apply for a career-enhancing position for fear of looking foolish in the attempt, or failing to rescue the child he adores from drowning—he will suffer. He relinquishes the value that he treasures. Yet life depends on gaining values rather than abandoning them. Cowardice does not sustain a person's life.[26]

Honesty would also be a virtue on this theory. If a person is dishonest, his misrepresentations do not change the facts that he must heed in order to act effectively to achieve his ends. Pretending that things are other than they are, whether to others or to oneself, does nothing to make them other than they are and does nothing to strengthen his ability to navigate the facts that he distorts. If a man lies to his wife about the affair that he is having, it leaves his dissatisfaction with the marriage uncorrected. If a man lies to himself about the affair that he correctly believes that his wife is having, he postpones discovering its sources and repairing the marriage's rifts. Even if a marriage would be better dissolved than restored, a person is better off the sooner he confronts this fact. Evasion only perpetuates a draining relationship. Dishonesty is not an effective policy for achieving the values that advance a person's life.

Justice would be a virtue for the same sorts of life-promoting reasons. If a person fails to judge others objectively and treat them accordingly, giving them what they deserve, he faces destructive repercussions. If a man hires a nanny, for example, not on the basis of careful evaluation of the applicant's recommendations or past employment but by irrelevant criteria such as her stylish wardrobe or British accent, he is risking his children's well-being. If a person forgives another who does not deserve it, he sets himself up to be victimized again. If a person condemns a friend and severs a relationship by leaping to conclusions and ignoring evidence, he deprives himself of all the value that he might have gained from that person. If, on the other hand, a person rewards a worthy employee or praises the merits of a political activist's efforts, he encourages more good work from which he stands to benefit. In short, injustice does not advance a person's life; justice does.[27]

These examples, again, are meant only to indicate the general pattern of the relationship between virtues and life. The important point here is that as a normative theory is fleshed out, all moral prescriptions are united in their service to human life. That ultimate value provides the single basis and barometer for an integrated, efficacious code of values and virtues. To say that a person should do something means that it is, all things considered, a rational means to a life-promoting purpose. Correspondingly, all vices are united by being detrimental to a person's life.

In this way, value serves as the anchor of ethics. Our explanation of the roots of the concept of value revealed humans' need to identify and pursue values—those things that advance our lives. Ethics is our guide to doing that. Thus, ethics has a definite function to fulfill: the furtherance of life.[28]

VALUE'S OBJECTIVITY

The basic argument for life as the root of value and morality is now completed. The recognition that life is the source, goal, and standard of value carries a significant implication that warrants special attention, however: Values are objective.

Life provides the standard of value, we have seen, because human beings have definite, inescapable needs. To maintain our lives, only certain sorts of actions will satisfy those needs. Consequently, beliefs that particular things are valuable are either true or false. The requirements of survival are determined by reality, independently of a person's beliefs or feelings. By saying that values are objective, then, I mean that "[o]bjects and actions are good *to* man and *for* the sake of reaching a specific goal."[29] Both aspects are crucial to objectivity: values reflect facts, but they reflect facts *as evaluated* by human beings, relative to the goal of living. The moral prescriptions derived from values—the beliefs that particular actions are right or wrong—are correspondingly objective.[30]

Human needs determine what is good for us and what is bad for us; they provide the measure of things' impact on the sustenance of our lives. Thus, at the most fundamental level, the nonnegotiable conditions of life dictate the objectivity of values. The same needs that mandate the identification of values in the first place also serve as the test of whether a given thing truly is good, that is, life advancing.

Value Is Relational

Value's objectivity is a function of value's relational character. Whether a given thing is valuable depends on its relationship to the end of an individual's life. As Rand explains, the attribution of value to anything "presupposes an answer to the question: of value to *whom* and for *what*?"[31]

Value does not depend simply on a person's attitude toward an object. Nor does it consist in an object's inherent qualities. Rather, to determine whether something is valuable, we must pose a more sophisticated question: What bearing does this thing have on this person's life? On his survival and on subordinate values that serve his survival? (Subordinate values could include such varied ends as his career, marriage, lifelong devotion to political justice or quest to master the works of Liszt.)[32]

Food is good, for example, because it is necessary to sustain a person. (It may also be good for the enjoyment it provides if enjoyment itself has life-enhancing effects, as I will argue in the next chapter.) Yet certain types and quantities of food can be bad, as when cholesterol clogs one's arteries or excess weight overtaxes one's heart. The test is food's effects on an individual's life. Similarly, another person might be good for a person, depending on his characteristics and their impact on the person. Reliability and perceptiveness are beneficial and thus good; unreliability and insensitivity are harmful and thus bad.

In the more obviously moral sphere, honesty is good because truthfulness in portraying facts is the most effective path to navigating facts successfully, to achieve life-enhancing purposes. Justice is good because objective evaluation of others is the best means for reaching accurate appraisals and treating others accordingly, which is the clearest path for advancing one's life. Courage is good because perseverance in the face of danger is sometimes necessary to secure one's values.

The point is, value is a function of the interaction between the thing called valuable and the person to whom it is valuable. Value is neither a static, preexisting quality awaiting human discovery nor an arbitrary invention erected by the mere fact of one's desire or unsubstantiated belief that a given object is valuable. A thing's value depends on what the thing is and on how it affects a person. Value denotes a thing's standing in a life-promoting relation to a given individual.

Notice how different this view is from the traditional alternatives. Those endorsing intrinsic value, Intuitionism, Rationalism, or various religious moralities tend to view value as simply given, free-floating "out there," to be read off the universe in some never-explained way. Contractarians, hedonists, and other subjectivists, on the other hand, treat value as a construct; essentially, our attitudes or desires are sufficient to confer value.

On the account that I have defended, in contrast, value is neither a ready-made given nor created by will. "The good is an aspect of reality in relation to man," Rand writes, meaning that both ends of this relationship are crucial to value.[33] The object in question must possess certain characteristics in order to advance a person's life, and the person must seek his life, for that thing to be valuable. Elements of the external world as well as of his consciousness (his desire to live) combine to render certain things valuable. Insofar as value marks a pro-life relationship, value depends on a variable and a constant: an individual's desire to live and human biology and psychology (i.e., his literal needs).[34]

To reinforce how such relational value is objective, remember that life makes values necessary. The fact that life *requires* values means that values have a job to do. Not just any ends or actions will do that job, however. Which things will fulfill that function is an objective matter of fact. This further exposes why subjective and intrinsic conceptions of value fail. What those theories offer as values—objects of preference or mysterious discoveries—do not fulfill values' function. What a person would like or what seems good are not reliable tests of whether such things actually advance a person's life.

To say that value is objective is not to say that it is easy to identify what is valuable. If it were easy, we would not need the guidance of ethics. Given the myriad effects that different things may carry on the gamut of a person's other genuine values, determining whether something is good and should be pursued is sometimes difficult.

That value is objective does mean, however, that values are not open to conflicting, equally valid interpretations. Values reflect facts about survival needs, and these are not a matter of convention or culture. One cannot alter the effects of honesty or justice in achieving life-furthering ends any more than one can substitute arsenic for orange juice without catastrophic results. Only the time scale of the effects differs. The most basic conditions of human survival are the same in the East and West, under atheism or Islam, under capitalism or communism, in the twenty-first century or 200 B.C. People's beliefs and practices are simply not the fundamental source of what promotes or diminishes our lives.

Choice does play an important role in ethics. As we have already observed, a person must choose to maintain his life in order for things to become valuable to him. Yet this choice does not single-handedly create value, for it cannot dictate the course for achieving one's life, making things valuable by fiat. We choose whether to seek life, but we do not choose the requisite means; those are given. Choice is necessary for value to exist but not sufficient.

Optional Values

While value is objective, we should also realize that a range of different things can be objectively valuable to different individuals. For a thing to be valuable means that it promotes a person's life. Many different things may bear this relation to a given individual, in various spheres of his activities and in varying magnitude. Some things will be values for everyone, while others will legitimately vary. (By "legitimately," I mean that their pursuit is consistent with the pursuit of life. Career choice can legitimately vary, for example.)

Moral values are the most fundamental values that apply for all human beings. They so apply because they are necessitated by our common human nature. No one can live by defying his own nature or circumstances. Thus, honesty, justice, and courage, I would argue, are virtues for everyone. Certain ends and certain types of actions are required for anyone to achieve his life.[35]

People can pursue numerous further, optional values, however, that may vary considerably from person to person. Individuals' needs, abilities, and taste in such areas as recreation, literature, music, work, clothes, vacations, humor, and personality may lead them to pursue things that serve a definite life-enhancing role for them but that would not play a comparable role in others' lives. Just as insulin injections may be good for diabetics but dangerous for hypoglycemics, what things are valuable depends on an individual's context. A $100 dinner might be bad for one person but good for another, depending on the extent of their resources, other demands on those resources, the occasion, and so on. The book that might be a good gift for a twelve-year-old may have no value for a Nobel physicist, just as the treatise that the physicist finds stimulating might be useless for the twelve-year-old. Peter Railton suggests that we "think of goodness as akin to nutritiveness. All organisms require nutrition, but not the same nutrients."[36]

My point here is that even among human beings, the objectivity of value permits for some variation in particulars. There is not one complete set of values that is identical for everyone. Nor is it the case that a given person in given circumstances will always find himself with only one right choice or proper course of action. Sometimes, morality sanctions each of several options because they would all equally advance his life. The requirements of human life remain the ultimate standard of value, however. Since any actions that a person takes are capable of affecting his survival, he must ensure that his optional values promote that end.

Fundamental values constitute the foundational common values that everyone must pursue. A person may have special needs or develop particular interests that generate many more values, however. Variations in people's circumstances allow for additional specific values and for the pursuit of common values to assume more colorful form. Indeed, optional values are simply preferred means of filling basic, shared needs. The fundamental values are identified rather abstractly and need to be pursued through more concrete activities. We all need to eat, for example, but while some people regard food as no more than the means of satisfying this need, nourishing themselves with whatever is cheapest or quickest to prepare, others become gourmet chefs and take great delight in cultivating culinary versatility. Their means of fulfilling their need for food may come to include a range of values—gourmet books, magazines, television programs, kitchen equipment, specific cooking skills—that you or I do not share. Or again, people need to make a living (even those who inherit wealth must maintain it). Thus, work is valuable to us. Yet here again, while some people regard their work as regrettable drudgery, others relish the particular kind of work that they do, such that it becomes valuable for far more than paying the bills.

What is important to realize, then, is that optional values are not alternatives to the basic moral values; they do not compete with them for our allegiance. In order to determine the legitimacy of any seemingly optional value, the question to ask is whether its pursuit will advance one's life. Whenever the answer is negative, the would-be value must be rejected. Values are legitimately optional and variable within limits, in other words; those limits are established by the requirements of survival.

Let us not allow our recognition of the possibility of optional values to obscure the bigger picture. My main contention here has been that values' objectivity is a function of values' relational character. Something's being a value depends on its serving a life-enhancing function for a being engaged in the struggle to survive. Our previous rejection of the doctrine of intrinsic value should make clear that values are not preexisting packages simply awaiting our discovery. Nothing is good in itself. Nor, however, are values arbitrary projections of a person's mind; we are not capable of creating values by whim. The requirements of survival are set by reality; what is valuable is valuable by virtue of its capacity to contribute *to* a specific person, *for* his life. This is the core of value's objectivity.

Value Is Based in Facts

By demonstrating the objectivity of value, Rand has illuminated the relationship between facts and values. She has shown how values are inextricably grounded in facts. Factual judgments and value judgments are not radically different in kind, as if pertaining to different universes; the notorious gap between facts and values is artificial.

Rand's theory is naturalistic in that values are an outgrowth of certain facts about the nature of life. If one seeks life, then things become valuable (good or bad) on the basis of their impact on that goal. The fact of that relationship is the ultimate source of goods and "shoulds."[37]

I am not asserting that normative conclusions can be deduced from non-normative premises. The absence of normative material in a deductive argument's premises affords no grounds for normativity to appear in the conclusion. But normative conclusions can be induced.

Twentieth-century reverence for deduction has led us to neglect the sources of the generalizations from which we deduce. How are such generalizations justified? Are they revealed in dreams, through special visions or voices? Are they produced by pollsters' calculations of popular opinion? Concocted out of thin air? If such general claims are to furnish the basis for deductions that yield knowledge, they must themselves be true.

Consider the classic example. You are no doubt convinced of the mortality of any person that you meet. It is a clear deductive inference from the general premise that all men are mortal. What is the basis for accepting that, however? Few of us reach it by pure deduction from the wider premise that all mammals are mortal. Rather, it is an inductive generalization based on numerous observations. The same holds for all sorts of simple deductions that we properly employ every day. Their grounds are generalizations built from observations of fact. All dogs are mammals—we realize, from observations; basil needs sunlight—we realize, from observations; rest is good for fever—we realize, from observations; material objects are subject to gravitational pull—we realize, from observations.

The point is, induction provides the basis for deduction. It supplies the premises from which we deduce further conclusions. Sound generalizations are products of inductive inferences.[38]

The larger lesson concerning the relationship between facts and values is that we *can* use reason to generate moral judgments. Indeed, we must use reason to figure out how to live. This was Rand's point in arguing that life makes values necessary. Human beings must pay attention to facts about ourselves and our surroundings to determine how to achieve our lives and all subordinate goals. We must identify values and act to secure them. Rand has shown that reality does not permit human beings to *not* reason about morality. If we do not reason to identify life's requirements and if we do not act as reason dictates, we will die. What stronger connection between facts and values could one demonstrate?[39]

Observations about human needs take us far in explaining the factual grounds of value, but these observations are not sufficient. To appreciate the further vital element, notice that in everyday life, people often engage in reasoning from facts to values without anyone's offering a squeak of protest. We observe effects of various objects, events, and actions on our ends and generate guidelines from there. We reason, for example, that if you want your new car to perform well and regular oil changes enhance performance, then you ought to change its oil regularly. Or, if you want your students to learn as much as possible and students learn more when they are motivated, then you ought to try to motivate them. Or, if you want to be admitted to medical school, you ought to study hard in biology and chemistry.

In all such cases, the "oughts" or value judgments are built on facts. Further, and most salient here, these prescriptions carry authority only if the person has a certain goal (he wants the car to run well, the students to learn, or admission to medical school). Rand proposes that ethics works in the same manner. You should abide by a moral code *if* you want to live. She writes,

> If [man] chooses to live, a rational ethics will tell him what principles of action are required to implement his choice. If he does not choose to live, nature will take its course. Reality confronts a man with a great many "musts," but all of them are conditional: the formula of realistic necessity is: "you must, if—" and the "if" stands for man's choice: "if you want to achieve a certain goal."[40]

In other words, all the true inductions in the world will not generate "shoulds" unless a person seeks the ends to which they prescribe the means. To determine proper moral guidance, identifying the purpose of morality—one's life—tells us what sorts of inductions are relevant and what information to pay attention to.

Induction alone, then, does not plant values in the soil of fact. It is induction coupled with the purpose of living that provides a factual base for normative judgments. Both elements are vital to understanding the objective basis of claims about what things are valuable and how people ought to live.[41]

OBJECTIONS AND CLARIFICATIONS

By analyzing the presuppositions of the concept of value, Rand has revealed value's inextricable roots in the quest for life. Things can attain the status of value only in relation to living organisms engaged in the effort to maintain their existence. When it comes to the guidance of human action, then, the necessity of achieving values establishes the framework for a rational morality. The maintenance and promotion of life is the reason for having a moral code. Living mandates morality. Correlatively, life provides the standard of moral evaluation, and one's own life is the reward of living morally.

In the next chapter, I will explore "life" in more depth. Before turning to that, however, it will be helpful to consider several questions or objections that this theory is likely to provoke. Addressing these should help to refine our understanding of Rand's view. I will begin with the simpler issues.

Is Life a Value, or Is Life the Source of Value?

The exact status of life in this account of value's foundations may seem ambiguous. At times, it sounds as if life is itself a value, an end on which a person should place great importance. If a person seeks anything else, he should secure his life in order to enable the achievement of his other goals. Yet at other times, particularly in the arguments that life makes value possible and necessary, life seems to be that which gives rise to value—a precondition for value rather than a value itself. Which is it? Is life a value, or is life the source of value?

The answer is, both. Life is the source of value for the reasons already explained. The idea of value is unintelligible apart from the aim of maintaining life. Only the aim of living gives us reason and grounds for distinguishing what is good and bad for an organism.

Further, however, life itself is also a value because it is something that we act to gain and keep. In Rand's account, values are pro-life ends, ends that a person should pursue because they advance his life. All sorts of specific ends—income, romantic love, golf clubs, *Garden Design* magazine, a high-speed Web browser—can be values. Life itself is also a value, however, because life *is* self-sustaining action. Life encompasses all other life-promoting ends and activities; it encompasses all the particular goals by which we keep ourselves living. Life is the goal of life in that it is what we are maintaining through all the more specific values that we pursue.

It is important to be precise about the relationships here. Life is not a value simply because someone seeks it or seeks something else whose enjoyment depends on his being alive. People seek myriad ends, but they are not thereby valuable because they are not necessarily life-promoting. To regard any end that a person embraces as a value would revert to subjectivism, deflating values into mere objects of desire. Since life is not compatible with any conceivable ends that a person might adopt, ends per se cannot be equated with values. The end of life, however, is not merely "compatible" with life; its achievement *is* life.

Life is the ultimate value insofar as all other genuine values depend on it and are the means to it. Other values are values because of their relationship to life; they presuppose the embrace of life. This embrace entails its actual pursuit. Thus, life, for a person who holds any true values (verified by the standard of life), must be that person's overarching aim.[42]

We should recognize the artificiality of speaking of life and subordinate ends as wholly separate concerns. Other ends (career, romance, piano playing, and so on) that are *bona fide* values are aspects or means of living rather than distinct, independent enterprises. A person does not face a choice between tending his life *or* his career, his life *or* his love of music, for example. In pursuing his career or music, he is tending his life. A person lives by pursuing scores of more specific ends; this is what pursuing his life consists of.[43]

The point, then, is that life occupies a dual role. Life stands as both the source of values and the ultimate value.

How Does a Person Choose Life?

The thesis that values' roots rest in life has been accompanied by the proviso "if a person seeks his life." Value's contingency on a person's choice raises a series of questions concerning the nature and role of this choice.

The first question is straightforward. What exactly is this choice? When and how is it made?

Admittedly, the embrace of life is not usually crystallized in an unmistakable, do-or-die moment when well-defined options are laid out and a decision is imperative. Most of us never face such an all-or-nothing, high-stakes decision, the stuff of soap opera cliffhangers. We do not receive anything akin to draft cards on reaching a certain age, ballots to be cast for life or against it. Occasionally, life presents stark choices, as when a serious accident demands momentous medical decisions, but this is the exception.

Rather, we choose life by choosing all sorts of specific things that constitute and further our lives. In embracing countless people, projects, objects, and destinations—in loving Megan, saving money, buying coffee, studying French, playing jazz, having a child, building a career, planning a vacation, or planting a garden—a person may be choosing life. By getting out of bed in the morning and having at the day, a person may be choosing life. In setting any life-enhancing aims for himself, be they modest or ambitious, trivial or profound, short or long range, a person may be choosing life. Remember that life consists of a person's activities, all that he does in pursuing his various ends. Thus, life is not a distinct aim that one can adopt in *addition* to learning French, saving money, building a career, and so on. To embrace life is to embrace the condition of *having* specific ends (and more, of having consistent and life-furthering ends).

I say that the person pursuing various ends "may" be choosing life to reflect the fact that not everyone does choose life. Not every choice that a person makes actually serves his life or reflects a desire to live. Many such choices do, however. And it is through all of a person's life-advancing choices—to eat dinner, treat an illness, enter a contest, ask someone for a date, apply to college, start a business, go into therapy—that he chooses life.[44]

The fact that we do not all embrace our lives in fully focused terms, with the alternative of life or death consciously identified as such, does not mean that our choice is less genuine. Not all choices are equally reflective.

Consider the varying degrees of forethought that stand beneath different individuals' choice of a school, an apartment, a husband, a doctor, a Christmas card, or a hairstyle. A person can grocery shop by strictly obeying a carefully constructed list, by making a random series of impulse buys, or by barely noticing what he is tossing into the basket, conducting the entire outing while mentally rehashing a just-finished argument with a friend. A person might invest his retirement savings by meticulously studying business reports, by unquestioningly agreeing to his broker's first suggestions, or by flipping a coin. All these more or less rational decisions remain choices.

In most cases, it seems, people answer the question of whether to live without consciously posing it. We do not often ask because the answer is so overwhelmingly positive as to make the question seem superfluous. We carry on with our lives, planning specific projects and activities, more concerned with living our answer than with contemplating it. (A great deal of attention to the fact of choosing life can also distract a person from the pleasures of immersion in life.) At moments, again, a person might confront the alternative more self-consciously. Sparked by tragedy or beauty, a philosophy course or a moment of intense happiness, a person is sometimes transported to a broader perspective on his life as a whole and to ponder his regard for it. Yet many people who never swore a loyalty oath to life would fiercely battle a threat to it. Many people struggle against fires, storms, diseases, and wartime sieges with the utmost tenacity. In short, a focused statement of devotion to life is not a necessary condition for choosing one's life in the most vivid, active terms.

While "the choice to live," then, may carry the misleading connotation of a single, momentous decision, what is essential is that this *is* a choice insofar as a person has alternatives. It is a constant choice. People can and do sometimes choose not to carry on. Suicide is a genuine option, as are all sorts of less definitive self-destructive actions. While the "embrace" of life might better suggest the wide-ranging activities that a person is affirming, in maintaining his life, "choice" conveys the presence of alternatives. The important point is, the choice is real. We are not fated, irrevocably, to live.

Is the Choice of Life Justified?

Even if we can now better appreciate that the choice to live is genuine, a further question arises. Given its pivotal role in the generation of value, one might wonder whether this choice is justified. Is the decision to live one that a person ought, rationally, to make? If the embrace of life is not justified, it seems that no objective ethical code could stand on it.

As we saw in chapter two, reasons and justification depend on purposes.[45] A given decision's rationality is mysterious until we know what it is meant to accomplish. (Recall the baseball manager's decision to change pitchers, for example.) A person cannot have a reason, let alone a justification, for an action unless the action is expected to carry some impact on one or more of his ends. Since ends themselves are not necessarily rational, they must be evaluated in light of further ends.

When we ask whether the choice to live is justified, we are asking about the most fundamental end that a person could have. We are essentially asking, Why should a person pursue his life? What makes life worth living?

On the account I have presented, to say that a person should do something means that the action in some way promotes his ultimate value. This presupposes that he has an ultimate value. Yet the choice to live is what gives rise to values. All "shoulds" depend on purposes; whether to pursue one's life is the question of whether to adopt any purposes at all.

What this means is that the choice to live is not subject to rational appraisal. It arises in a context devoid of the values that provide the standard for determining what a person should do. In this sense, the choice to live is primary. It is not justified by any prior ends. As Leonard Peikoff puts it, there is no "more basic value the pursuit of which validates the decision to remain in reality."[46] We cannot say that a person ought, rationally, to choose to live because we have no preexisting standards to underwrite the "ought."

"What makes life worth living?" is thus a question without a rational answer. My point is not to deny that life is worthwhile; the point is that one cannot reason another person into the choice to live. No roster of wonderful things constitutes *the* correct explanation of why all human beings should live. The choice depends on what kind of experience a given individual finds satisfactory.[47]

Reason can play an important subsidiary role in deliberations over whether to live. A person might be mistaken about the prevalence of unhappiness or pain in the world, for example, or about the ratio of failure to success, or about the prospects for his recovery from some affliction or for his country's political climate to improve. If a person is seriously contemplating suicide, others can remind him of all the things that he has enjoyed in the past; they can point out the flaws in his excessively dark forecasts. After all the miscalculations have been corrected, however, and a person sees clearly what is likely in his future, he either does or does not want it. Nothing logically necessitates the wish to live. At the deepest point, the embrace of life is beyond argument.[48]

The lesson is that the choice to live is prerational. It is a presupposition of the standards of rationality. We have already seen that the adoption of ends is essential for reason to exert any claim on us. Having the purpose of living gives a person reason to be rational. Without the fundamental end of living, I concluded in chapter two, one could have no reason to be rational.[49] At bottom, we found, the authority of rationality stands on two things: the nature of reality and a person's desire to remain within reality—that is, his desire to live.

Thus, the best answer to "What makes life worth living?" is: life. Inspiring an answer as this may be to many, it is not an answer that anyone is logically compelled to accept. A given person can take life or leave it, without committing any lapse of reason. Reason's requirements arise once a person embraces life.[50]

The fact that the choice to live is prerational does not mean that it is arbitrary in the derogatory sense so familiar in philosophy. A decision is arbitrary when it is "derived from mere opinion or preference; not based on the nature of things."[51] This is a defect, however, only where rationality is appropriate. The fundamental choice to live precedes the possibility of being culpably arbitrary by virtue of preceding the possibility of being rational. Since we have no higher value or standards by which to rationally evaluate the choice to live, we have no basis on which to criticize the choice as insufficiently rational.

The decision of whether to live, then, is itself neither justified nor unjustified. This reveals no infirmity in the ethics that I have defended because it is not the sort of decision that *could* be justified. To criticize this absence of justification is to apply standards that *depend* on the choice to live. The embrace of life is, however, necessary for the phenomenon of value to arise, as was explained in the first part of the chapter.

Does the Choice to Live Undermine the Objectivity of Value?

The fact that the choice to live is not rational may appear to be the undoing of this account, for it seems to leave control over one's moral obligations to personal discretion. The premise that value (and, derivatively, morality) is contingent on a choice that people may take or leave seems to entail that individuals can opt out of morality at will, freeing themselves of its demands. Moral obligations thus lose their grip since they are unlikely to command universal devotion. If the initial choice to embrace one's life is not rationally required, this seems to preclude the objectivity of value. Contrary to my claims that morality rooted in life is objective, the pivotal role of choice in values' foundations may seem the seed of subjectivism.

In fact, this objection rests on serious misconceptions concerning the nature of morality's objectivity.

First of all, it is important not to confuse objectivity with universality. The universality of an obligation concerns the number of people governed by it. If everyone is bound by a certain obligation, it is universal; if not everyone is, it is not. Objectivity, by contrast, concerns the basis of people's obligations, the reasons for which specific moral judgments are valid. Objectivity carries implications for the scope of an obligation's authority, but it is not the same thing as an obligation's scope (and thus its possible universality). If an alleged obligation is based on the fact that the prescribed action promotes a person's life, it is objective. If an alleged obligation is premised on the fact that a large number of people sincerely believe that it is an obligation, it is not objective.[52]

My contention is that moral values are compelling for all those who seek life. That some people may not seek life does not refute the objectivity of value, for it does not alter the facts concerning various actions' effects on life. If a person wishes to live, only certain actions will suffice. If a person does not take those actions, his life will suffer. Life's basic requirements do hold universally. It is the causal relationship between certain actions and certain effects that grounds morality's objectivity. The fact that some individuals do not seek life is immaterial because it does not alter the relevant relationships.

Second, it is important not to confuse objective value with intrinsic value. To insist that choice can play no role in the foundation of an objective moral code seems to treat moral "shoulds" as unshakable commandments to which we are born and bound, regardless of our ends. It treats obligations as inherent in the nature of things. But this is to assert some form of Intuitionism, or Rationalism, or the doctrine of intrinsic value—all of whose fatal defects I have already exposed.

Objective value is not intrinsic. I am not positing value as given and derivative obligations to promote values as binding on everyone, like it or not. The objectivity of value stems from the fact that certain types of action tend to promote human life and certain types of action tend to hinder human life. These facts are independent of particular individuals' tastes or desires. Actions' effects on human life are not a matter of our choosing. But remember that value is relational. Life-promoting effects are good only for those who wish to live. The fact that not everyone seeks to maintain his life does not compromise morality's objectivity, however, because it does not alter the fact that for those who do wish to live, only certain sorts of actions will succeed.

If a given individual chooses not to pursue his life, nothing is valuable for him. Various things will continue to carry their natural effects on his life, of course (food will nourish, poison will harm; courage will increase his chances of achieving ends, cowardice will decrease his chances). Yet none of these will be values since value depends on a thing's relationship to the end of one's life—an end that he has rejected. Correspondingly, moral prescriptions are inapplicable. Having renounced his life, this person has killed the source that warrants such prescriptions and establishes their authority.

This does not mean that he can pursue some alternate amoral life, however. The choice that we face is not between two ways of living: with or without morality. Rather, Rand has shown that there is a way to live—by adhering to a life-promoting morality—and a way to die. Those are our options.

Further, the fact that a given person rejects his life does not alter the moral position of others. Here, we meet a third confusion that may fuel this objection. The role of the choice of life in Rand's theory should not lead one to mistake her theory for some variant of Contractarianism. If one believes that social agreement is the basis for moral obligation, then any individual who does not agree poses a threat since he seems to enjoy an exemption that he may exercise in ways that injure others, leaving them without grounds for moral complaint. The view that I have presented rejects such contractarian requirements of consensus, however.

Social agreement is not the basis of moral obligation. It is not the case that if some people reject life, they thereby acquire "permission" to treat others however they like. Nor is it the case that those who do embrace life, if injured by those who reject it, may do nothing to defend themselves. Measures against those who threaten one's well-being would be justified on the same grounds that warrant any life-promoting actions. The effects of the life rejecter's actions might be indifferent to *him;* this does not mean that they are indifferent to others (nor that they should be treated as if they were).[53]

How it is appropriate for one person to pursue his life is not contingent on others' choices of whether to pursue theirs. The most fundamental source of moral "shoulds" rests in the requirements of human life; it does not depend on other people's attitudes toward their lives. What is salient for determining how people should treat an individual is not that individual's attitude toward his own life; it is his actions' impact on their lives. (One has reason to care about another person's attitude toward his life only insofar as one thinks that it may affect his own life.)

Notice that the worry about the choice of life precluding objectivity suggests that a person is better off outside the bounds of morality. Why else would one worry about those who decide not to comply with morality? This challenge to morality's objectivity will arise only if one believes that it is sensible for people to eschew morality. And that would be true only if noncompliance were more advantageous. (The resemblance to Contractarianism's debates about free riders is obvious.)

Blithe talk of opting in or out of morality as if it were a hand of poker ignores the stakes, however. "Opting out" means moving toward death. A person can forgo the pursuit of values only at his own peril. One could not be better off "cheating" because a life-based morality provides guidance to further one's own life. Every betrayal of such a code works against one's interest.

I suspect that much resistance to the claim that the choice to live is prerational stems from the firm grip of the belief that morality is a given, that its presence is a trans-temporal constant, such that one could never stand outside of it. Many seem to view morality as a "birth burden" that can never be laid down. A refusal to entertain seriously the possibility that morality is not part of the permanent furniture of the universe is simply engraved in many people's automatized thinking about morality. The worry about the prospect of individuals "opting out" of morality suggests that we are already "in," before having chosen anything. But this is precisely the conception of morality that Rand is challenging. Moral authority is not a freestanding, preexisting set of restrictions into which we are born. It is only the purpose of one's own life—keeping it, leading it, enjoying it—that establishes reason to identify values and to abide by a moral code. A person must wish to live in order for value and morality to apply.

Reluctance to admit the role of choice may also stem from inflating its role. On the account that I have defended, only the choice to live, coupled with facts of how that end can be achieved, generate value. Other objects of choice are not capable of playing the same role. Choice is not the sole, all-powerful author of value, in other words, since it does not establish what will further a person's life. The conditions that must be navigated in order to sustain one's life are unimpressed by personal preferences.

Yet these facts are what this objection overlooks. It suggests that one could cast off moral concerns without consequences. That is exactly what Rand has shown that we cannot do. The basic requirements of human existence cannot be circumvented. And this, again, is the heart of values' objectivity.

In sum, as long as we recognize that objectivity is distinct from universality and that moral prescriptions are neither intrinsically given nor socially constructed, we can see that the prerational status of the choice to live does not destroy morality's objectivity. On the contrary, that choice is vital to morality's authority. It is the only reason a person has to abide by the facts of what will foster his life.

Living without a Life-Based Code

The final objection to consider is a fairly obvious question: What about all the people who have not embraced life as the standard of value and basis for ethics? Humankind has made it through centuries without allegiance to such a code, evidently surviving by other means. Doesn't the existence of "live bad guys" (bad by the criteria of Rand's theory) refute the thesis that only a life-based code of values can sustain life?

The answer to this question depends on the relationship between adherence to the life-based code and achievement of its goal, life, as well as on the nature of that goal. Since the entirety of chapter five is devoted to clarifying the latter, my response here can be only partial. Nonetheless, several points concerning the relationship between morality and its end should defuse the concern.

I have argued that the achievement of values is necessary to fill human needs. What is particularly salient in regard to this question is the fact that our needs are long range. They are extended across time. Many of our needs require forethought and action well in advance of the time when they will be most pressing. "Reactive" living—simply responding to needs as they become urgent, tending needs as intermittent crises—is not a policy that can sustain human survival. We must anticipate future needs (next month's, next year's), identify the probable effects of certain means of fulfilling them on other needs, and devise suitable strategies for satisfying our needs. We must take precautions to avoid certain dangers and prepare ourselves, in case they do arise, to extricate ourselves or to limit their damage. We must recognize the cumulative effects of various seemingly trivial actions on our ongoing ability to meet our needs and on our overall well-being. Consider the need for retirement income, for example, which typically requires steps toward securing that income taken decades in advance. Or consider health and fitness, which may require countless disciplined decisions to maintain a certain diet or exercise regimen over a prolonged period. The fact that we cannot always easily discern what it is best to do for our overall well-being is precisely what necessitates a moral code. If human beings could effortlessly recognize how best to promote their lives in each situation as it arose, we would have no need for systematic guidance.

The point is, the long-range character of human needs heightens the probability of any single action's carrying effects on a person's survival. The longer the period between an action and its full impact and the less direct the path by which an action affects one's life, the more difficult it is to appreciate this. Yet the long-term character of human needs widens the compass of morality, imbuing a greater array of actions with significance vis-à-vis a person's life. Viewed in isolation, a given decision might appear inconsequential, although it actually carries significant repercussions for the agent's life. Discrete actions can affect an interwoven assortment of a person's ends, short and long range, stretched across decades. A single deception could ruin a career; a single fling could wreck a marriage—or have one impeached. Thus, a person must be attuned to any possible action's likely ramifications on the full network of his ends. Since the means of advancing one end often affects others, a person must integrate his understanding of any single action with all his other actions and ends. No action is sealed off from the progress of a person's life. Actions that appear to be life sustaining may not be, and actions that do not appear to be life impeding may be. Thus, one should not be misled by the fact that actions' effects are not always apparent into supposing that actions' effects are not real.[54]

The fact that human needs are long range carries a second significant implication for understanding how life depends on following a life-based code: Life allows room for error. That is, limited neglect of certain needs can be survived. In this sense, life is forgiving—to some extent. Its demands are not infinitely malleable; life does not allow room for gross error or for a steady stream of nothing but errors. But the same feature of our needs that requires attending to many incremental steps over a long period also permits an occasional failure to satisfy a need.

This is why people can be inconsistent, taking some life-advancing actions and some life-injuring actions. I do not mean that it is morally permissible to cheat on moral principles. I mean simply that it is, to a limited extent, causally permitted. A person can sometimes neglect a need and later compensate for that neglect. A person who has been remiss in caring for his health, for example, can reform, and may thereby help his future prospects. He cannot costlessly undo whatever damage he has done, and he cannot now gain what he might have while he was damaging his health, but he may be able henceforth to do better, to good effect. The same applies to moral reform. Turning from self-indulgence to self-discipline, for example, or from dishonesty to honesty strengthens one's ability to meet life's demands. (Obviously, not all neglect of one's needs is "correctable later.")

Not every action carries equally momentous consequences on a person's life. A glass of wine rarely carries the same risks as a bottle of valium (although for a surgeon or a pilot in certain circumstances, a single drink could obviously be quite devastating). Dishonesty about your reason for declining a party invitation is rarely as destructive as dishonesty about your credentials for a job. The stakes of a person's actions at every moment, with every decision, are not "do or die *now*."

Not all needs carry the same urgency. A person can go without food for several days; he can go without oxygen for a few minutes. This does not mean that a person does not need food. Some needs are simply more pressing in terms of the speed with which they must be satisfied and the gravity of their repercussions. Similarly, the costs of moral breaches vary. The effects of a moral lapse may be immediate or delayed, localized or far-reaching, easily reversed or corrected only by considerable effort. Consider lapses of honesty or recklessly indulging appetites for sex or drugs. Depending on the circumstances, such lapses could waste a day or blow a career, kill a marriage or kill oneself.

Life is not a high-wire act in which any false move seals instant doom. A person will not drop dead at his first failure to choose the life-promoting path. Consequently, the pulse of a person who has not practiced the life-based moral code does not refute Rand's theory. Believing that it does is like believing that a person who shows up for a doctor's appointment needs no examination since he has made it to the office. "He's alive, so he must be fine." This is ludicrous. Because such a snapshot does not capture everything relevant to the person's condition, further examination is needed. An illness need not kill a person to be bad for him. A cold or hepatitis does not spell instant death, but it nonetheless works against one's life—by sapping energy, dulling mental alertness, or weakening resistance to worse forms of illness, for instance.

Not every morally errant action is punished by death. This is not to retreat from the claim that life requires certain action. It is simply to acknowledge that the proximity between cause and effect varies in different cases. Death can be a protracted process.

The crucial fact is that the effects of a person's actions need not be conspicuous in order to be genuine. That an ulcer or a tumor is not visible to the naked eye does not render it benign. Similarly, the long-term, often multilayered route between a person's actions and their impact on his life should not lull us into supposing that morality is irrelevant or that the stakes are less definite than Rand has observed.

Finally, a different perspective may also be helpful for appreciating life's dependence on morality. Simply focussing on the nature of life is instructive.

Recall that life is a process of actions. This process can be flowing in one of two basic directions: life furthering or life diminishing, making the person more fit and likely to live or less so. A person can be described as dying when his actions proceed in a life-diminishing direction. In the usual sense, of course, anything this side of the morgue counts as living. If your vital organs are operating, you qualify. Yet among all those who are alive in this technical sense, we can make finer distinctions, as we find a wide spectrum of degrees to which a person might be promoting his life or impeding it. Just as some people's physical health is better than others', so some people's lives overall are in better condition than others'.

Bear in mind that our actions bring psychological as well as material repercussions. Both influence the direction of a person's life. Any action not only changes one's position vis-à-vis some external object (as when one catches a fish or builds a boat). It also reinforces a person's inclinations to act in particular ways—for example, to be productive or lazy, to exert willpower or to indulge the urge of the moment, to act on one's own best judgment or to follow the popular course. Our actions naturally train our cognitive and motivational muscles and condition us along particular tracks. These effects remain open to later revision, of course, but the more deeply entrenched a person's patterns of action, the more difficult change will be. The more ingrained a person's life-diminishing habits, the further from life he drifts. By living properly, as a life-based moral code directs, a person is thus advancing his life both externally and internally, strengthening inclinations to act in life-enhancing ways.

To illustrate, contrast two college students, Larry and Dan. Larry reaches an informed decision that he wants a career in medicine. He purposefully sets out after his objective, reading up on the best schools' faculties and programs, following research developments and trends in the various specialties, studying diligently, and actively participating in his college's pre-med society.

Dan, on the other hand, drifts, finding himself in school for no particular reason, not sure what he wants to do, not troubled about trying to figure it out. He sort of thinks that he wants to study literature, but he postpones doing anything about it and then rationalizes that if he had really wanted to, he would have done something about it by now. Dan dabbles in this and that, nothing sustaining his interest for more than a few days. His spare time is spent aimlessly, surrendered to whatever the guys in the dorm are doing—cruising, drinking, playing video games, watching television. Dan backs into things, accepting whatever job happens to open up, spending the night with whatever person happens to be around; he is prodded by chance rather than by deliberately chosen goals.

On the continuum of living or dying, I submit, Larry is living; Dan is dying. Larry is strengthening himself to achieve his goals and to live ever more happily. He is "toning up" to get the most out of life and, already, enjoying life and achieving some of his ends. Dan, on the other hand, is not advancing his life and is allowing his living skills to deteriorate. His abilities to achieve purposes atrophy from his failure to exercise them. His desires themselves are likely to dwindle (in both number and potency), as he subconsciously learns to regard desires as futile or as occasions for frustration since he does not act to achieve his desires and thus rarely does. He suffers a steady decline in his sense of efficacy and enjoyment of living.[55]

My broader contention is that immoral action impedes the process of living by halting the course of acting as life requires. In that sense, immorality represents an abandonment of one's life as one's highest end. Since the moral path is the life-promoting path, immoral actions are self-destructive; they are diametrically opposed to the end of one's life. Given that a person's life is a unity of tightly integrated elements, any deviations from the moral path risk significant damage.

Moral guidance seeks to identify those types of actions that, in principle, tend to sustain life. A rational moral code does not claim to ensure particular results any more than the best heart doctor would promise that the patient who adheres to a prescribed regimen will live for twenty years. Living healthily does not guarantee long life any more than living unhealthily guarantees early death. Some people smoke for decades and celebrate a ninetieth birthday. But living healthily increases the likelihood of long life. A similar relationship obtains in the moral realm (with the added dimension of moral actions' increasing one's prospects for enjoyment of life).

Because degrees of vice vary, because not all actions carry equally grave effects, and because some things that affect our lives are completely beyond our control, virtue does not ensure life, and vice does not ensure immediate death. The belief that smoking is unhealthy does not license the expectation that if a person takes one puff of a cigarette, he will drop dead on the spot. The belief that sun exposure is dangerous does not mean that one hour in the sun will trigger melanoma that proves fatal by nightfall. It would be no more reasonable, in regard to Rand's moral theory, to expect that any deviation from a life-based code will result in instant death. Such a reading would overlook the long-term, variegated nature of our actions and their effects.[56]

Allegiance to a life-promoting code is not needed in order to be a live human specimen with a functioning complement of vital organs. Mom, Dad, and hardwired physiology can sustain that for limited periods. A given day of physical existence is not what necessitates the achievement of values. Momentary morgue avoidance is not the test of Rand's thesis.[57]

My opponent might protest that he is not pointing to isolated individuals who have survived single days without practicing a life-based moral code. For centuries, millions have lived without it.

Yet in fact, those who profess allegiance to alternate principles survive to the extent that they cheat on such principles. For no principles that counsel actions antithetical to life or that neglect life's requirements can, if *consistently* practiced, sustain life. To live, we must engage in the kinds of action that our nature demands, or we must rely on others who do so. This is an empirically verified fact, unrelentingly demonstrated every day, too sure to tempt any of my audience to substitute Drano in their children's milk bottle. The same holds at the moral level, where we identify, more abstractly, the types of actions necessary to sustain life. If only certain virtues can achieve what is needed to live, then to the extent that a person does not act virtuously to fulfill his own needs, he relies on the virtue of others. It is others' honesty, productiveness, justice, integrity, and so on that sustain him. Notice that if the grocer or pharmacist or engineer on whom one depends is dishonest, all bets are off; under those circumstances, a person cannot confidently drink the milk that he buys or ride the plane that he boards.

Certain actions sustain life; certain actions hinder it. It is for normative ethics to identify principles of action that promote life. But the immediate point is unequivocal: We cannot live on anti-life actions. An individual might survive occasional dabbling in some destructive principles, just as many of us have survived bouts of pneumonia or food poisoning. A person cannot survive *because of* such actions, however; life-hindering actions are not a charter for living.

The alleged counterexample of "live bad guys," then, disintegrates on inspection. Such people fall on the "dying" end of the living–dying continuum. Insofar as they remain alive, their lives are propelled by virtuous (i.e., life-sustaining) behavior, whether their own or others', however erratically practiced. A fuller portrait of morality's goal in the next chapter should only underscore the tensions between life and immorality. Already, however, we can see that this objection misfires.

CONCLUSION

Breaking with the unwarranted assumptions and false alternatives that have stifled previous attempts to explain morality, Rand has grounded moral authority in inescapable facts and demonstrated the practical stakes of identifying and abiding by a code of values. She has presented the most convincing account of morality that I have seen and the most compelling account that I can imagine. Why be moral? Because our lives depend on it.

The key to understanding morality is understanding value. Since morality is designed to steer human beings toward good and away from bad, we must have a standard for identifying what things are good and bad. Rand has shown how the concept of value is intelligible only in relation to living organisms. It is only because organisms face the alternative of living or dying that we can distinguish ends that are good for them to pursue if they are to maintain their lives. This alternative, further, *necessitates* the achievement of value. Any person seeking to maintain his life must learn what types of actions his life requires and conduct himself accordingly.

The nature and requirements of life thus provide the foundation of morality. All prescriptions of what people should and should not do, of what sorts of actions are right and wrong, are grounded in actions' impact on this end. Life is the purpose of morality and determines the standard of morality.

A major implication is that value is objective. Contrary to traditional conceptions of value as either intrinsic or subjective, any particular thing's value is a function of the relationship in which it stands to a given individual's life. Whether the relevant relationship obtains is an independent matter of fact.

This constitutes the heart of Rand's theory. Given the central role of life in generating morality, it is important to understand life as fully as possible. In the next chapter, I will elaborate further on what this end encompasses.

NOTES

1. Ayn Rand, "The Objectivist Ethics," *The Virtue of Selfishness* (New York: New American Library, 1964), 13–35, and "Causality versus Duty," *Philosophy: Who Needs It* (New York: Bobbs-Merrill, 1982), 114–22.

2. Rand, "The Objectivist Ethics," 13.

3. Rand, "The Objectivist Ethics," 15. Humans are not alone in seeking values. To the extent that plants and animals act to acquire certain objects—for example, growing toward the sunlight or scurrying to find nuts—they are also pursuing values.

4. Henceforth, I will often use terms such as "acquire," "promote," "advance," or "gain" to refer either to gaining or to preserving a value. Thus, defensive action taken to protect values is also included.

5. Many benefits, of course, are products of a person's own action as well as factors out of his hands. Years of diligent effort might have prepared a person for a certain position, for example, but the external fact of another person's retirement may also be necessary to create his opportunity to assume the position.

6. Since our concern is with morality, in much of what follows I will use "value" in the positive sense to denote objects that a person should pursue. Also, while much of the ensuing portrait of value applies to all genuine values, we are most concerned with moral values, a subset. Moral values are distinguished by their being pursued by choice (as opposed to being automatically pursued, determined by certain physiological processes) and their being fundamental (as opposed to values reflecting a person's end in some narrow field, such as music or attire). For more on this, see Leonard Peikoff, *Objectivism: The Philosophy of Ayn Rand* (New York: Dutton, 1991), 214. I will discuss "optional" values later in the chapter.

7. Given Rand's theory of concepts, elaborated in *Introduction to Objectivist Epistemology* (New York: New American Library, 1966), I take her to mean both that the concept of value would not exist, and that no genuine values would exist, apart from life.

8. Or relative to the ends of animals or plants. My claims will be confined to the nature of value for human beings, however, unless the context clearly indicates otherwise (as occurs mostly in the early portions of the chapter).

9. Harry Binswanger, "Life-Based Teleology and the Foundations of Ethics," *The Monist* 75 (January 1992): 93 (emphasis in the original).

10. Peter Railton sounds a broadly similar theme when he writes, "It seems to me that notions like good and bad have a place in the scheme of things only in virtue of facts about what matters, or could matter, to beings for whom it is possible that something matter. Good and bad would have no place within a universe

consisting only of stones, for nothing matters to stones. Introduce some people, and you will have introduced the possibility of value as well. It *will* matter to people how things go in their rock-strewn world" (Railton, "Facts and Values," *Philosophical Topics* 14 [Fall 1986]: 9).

11. Rand, "The Objectivist Ethics," 15. This description concurs with one of the *Oxford English Dictionary*'s definitions of life: "the series of actions and occurrences constituting the history of an individual (especially a human being) from birth to death" (Oxford: Oxford University Press, 1971). Both Plato and Aristotle observed the self-generated dimension of life but did not clearly identify that a living organism's existence depends on this activity. See Plato, *Laws,* trans. A. E. Taylor, in *The Collected Dialogues of Plato,* ed. Edith Hamilton and Huntington Cairns (Princeton, N.J.: Princeton University Press, 1963), 895c, and Aristotle, *De Anima,* trans. J. A. Smith, 412b16–19, and *Physics,* trans. R. P. Hardie and R. K. Gaye, 255a, both in *Basic Works of Aristotle,* ed. Richard McKeon (New York: Random House, 1941).

12. For the sort of definition of life typically taught in introductory biology courses, see Helena Curtis, *Biology,* 4th ed. (New York: Worth Publishers, 1983), 19–20. For a more essentialized account, see Harry Binswanger, *The Biological Basis of Teleological Concepts* (Marina del Rey, Calif.: Ayn Rand Institute Press, 1990), 6–7, 63–64.

Note that some of our metaphorical uses of "life" reflect this realization that life is an active process, as when we refer to the life of a company, theater, or club to designate the duration over which it functioned.

13. Sometimes, metaphorically, we attribute "needs" to inanimate objects—for example, "the coffee mug needs to be placed on a shelf where it won't fall and break." Note that even here what enables the sense of the metaphor is an understanding of the conditions required for the thing's continued existence. Existence or nonexistence is the crucial alternative.

14. Rand, "The Objectivist Ethics," 16.

15. For an excellent discussion of this and similar questions pertaining to the robot hypothesis, see Peikoff, 209–13.

16. For a very good discussion of pleasure's basis in survival needs as well as some further references on it, see Binswanger, *The Biological Basis of Teleological Concepts,* 66–67, 129–37. Note that by speaking of a robot, which is not conscious, Rand's example averts the question of the possibility of pleasure or pain.

Also notice that the proposal that pleasure could represent value amounts to hedonism, collapsing the distinction between what is pleasurable and what is good. If value and pleasure were interchangeable, however, hedonists should obey Occam's razor and shave off the notion of value, ridding the vocabulary of redundant clutter. Hedonists are typically reluctant to do this because they welcome the more respectable connotations of "value" and benefit from maintaining the pretense (which it is, in their view) that value is something more than an object of desire.

17. I will discuss the difference between needs and preferences further in chapter five.

18. I will address the prudential character of this ethics in chapter six.

19. Rand, "The Objectivist Ethics," 17, 23.

20. This reflects some of the *Oxford English Dictionary*'s definitions of "standard": "an authoritative or recognized exemplar of correctness, perfection, or some definite degree of any quality;" "a rule, principle or means of judgment or estimation; a criterion, measure."

21. For further explanation, see Rand, "The Objectivist Ethics," 17, 23–25.

22. James G. Lennox, "Health as an Objective Value," *Journal of Medicine and Philosophy* 20 (1995): 507.

23. See Rand, "Causality versus Duty," 118–19, and further discussion in the second section of this chapter. A thing's conduciveness or destructiveness to a person's life is independent of the person's wishes, of course, but no such effects would register in the dimension of value unless the person sought to maintain his life.

24. See Peikoff, *Objectivism,* 217.

25. I mean this quite literally. A natural sequel to this book would be another, consisting entirely of an elaboration of the normative prescriptions that derive from this account of morality's foundations.

Note that the cardinal virtue, according to Rand, is rationality, and other virtues are applications of rationality to specific types of issues.

26. Obviously, cowardice should not be mistaken for well-founded fear. Under certain circumstances, it might reveal no lack of courage *not* to jump in the ocean, for example, if the would-be hero does not know how to swim or if the ocean is especially treacherous and trained lifeguards are already attempting a rescue. For a discussion of courage as a type of integrity, see Harry Binswanger, "Q & A from the Objectivist Graduate Center," *The Intellectual Activist* 10, no. 2 (March 1996): 15–17.

27. For a fuller account of why justice is a virtue and of the propriety of forgiveness, see my "Justice as a Personal Virtue," *Social Theory and Practice* 25, no. 3 (Fall 1999), and "Tolerance and Forgiveness: Virtues or Vices?," *Journal of Applied Philosophy* 14, no. 1 (1997): 31–41.

28. I will amplify the meaning of this end in the next chapter. Henceforth, I will sometimes use "life-driven code" or "life-based code" as a shorthand for the normative code that this theory of morality's foundations would dictate.

29. Peikoff, *Objectivism,* 241 (emphasis in the original).

30. There is a further layer of meaning to the claim that values are objective that I will not develop in the text but that I should briefly indicate. The meaning of the claim naturally depends on the nature of objectivity. Strictly, it is persons who are or are not objective in their judgments concerning value and moral prescriptions, not the values or prescriptions themselves. Objectivity pertains to a person's process of thinking, the manner by which one reaches conclusions. Correspondingly, the objectivity of values depends on the way in which a particular person came to regard a given thing as valuable. Part of what value's objectivity refers to is the factual relation between a given thing and a particular person's life that *requires* that he act in certain ways rather than others, if he is live. But value's objectivity also reflects the fact that values are conclusions of a volitional consciousness. Since objectivity pertains to the use of one's mind, values' objectivity also refers to a person's method of concluding that something is valuable.

The exact and full nature of objectivity is, obviously, an enormous subject of epistemology. It should not be necessary to pursue it in depth in order to convey the heart of the claim that values are objective. For our purposes, suffice it to say that an objective method of arriving at conclusions (about values or anything else) adheres to relevant facts, identified by the discipline of logic. While we can imagine a person regarding things as valuable via an array of possible mental processes (e.g., by being mentally lazy, persistent, evasive, honest, dishonest, honest but mistaken, honest and correct), the main thing for us to appreciate is that the identification of values must be guided by fidelity to reality in order to be objective. Harry Binswanger has helped me clarify this further layer of objectivity's meaning. For more on this, see Peikoff, *Objectivism,* chapter 4 on objectivity, especially 116–21; see also 241–49 on value as objective.

31. Rand, "The Objectivist Ethics," 15 (emphasis in the original). Among other philosophers who have highlighted the relational character of value are Samuel Pufendorf, Ralph Barton Perry, G. H. von Wright, Robert Kane, Peter Railton, and, in places, Robert Nozick. I also discuss the relational character of values in "Reconsidering Zero-Sum Value: It's How You Play the Game," *Journal of Social Philosophy* 28, no. 2 (Fall 1997): 128–39.

32. I will use "thing" or "object" as a shorthand for the range of things that could be valuable, be they objects, events, actions, persons, relationships, conditions, characteristics, states of affairs, or anything else that plays the relevant role in a person's life.

33. Rand, "What Is Capitalism?," *Capitalism: The Unknown Ideal* (New York: New American Library, 1967), 22.

34. Again, strictly, there is a little more to value's objectivity than this. Value is relational in the twin senses that a genuine value must stand in a life-advancing relation to a person, and it must stand in a proper relation *to his consciousness;* that is, he must come to regard it as valuable through a logical process.

Notice that this expands on our understanding of the difference between what is beneficial and what is valuable. For human beings, who are capable of consciously identifying values, the difference is not simply what we noted previously, namely, that one must *act* to secure values, while benefits might be experienced without a person's taking any action. Further, a person must understand that a given thing is good for his life in order for it to be objectively valuable to him. The belief that something is valuable is not sufficient for something to be a value, but it is necessary. For human beings, in other words, the proper designation of something as valuable means more than that it is beneficial (and more than that it is a benefit that one must act to attain). "Value" is a richer concept. I leave a full explanation, which would stray too far into epistemology and too far off our main track, for another occasion.

35. This is not an exhaustive list of such virtues.

36. Railton, "Facts and Values," 10.

37. We could trace these facts in more detail, of course. Fact: I want to live. Fact: Living is not automatic. Feeling a strong emotional desire for life is not enough to sustain it. Fact: Not everything that I might do is consonant with the preservation of my life; some actions are and some actions are not. Fact: It is not

always easy to tell the difference; actions do not telegraph whether they will promote or detract from my life. I might *feel* like the problem in my marriage is my
husband's fault, for example, when in fact the problem really lurks with me. I
might feel like this position with the prestigious law firm will be good for me when
in fact the work would be numbingly dull or antithetical to my moral principles. I
might feel that this growing attraction to drinking is harmless when in fact it is not.
Thus another fact: I had better figure out how to discriminate life-promoting from
life-damaging actions, if I am to live. (Doing so, obviously, will require me to heed
further, more specific facts.)

38. John Stuart Mill emphasized this in *A System of Logic,* reprinted in *Philosophy of Scientific Method,* ed. Ernest Nagel (New York: Hafner, 1950), 123–27,
134–35, 161ff., 170ff.

Obviously, many people learn some generalizations from others' reports, but the
original, firsthand grasp of these facts is gleaned from observation. Also, even if a
person did reach one of these conclusions via previous deductions, the general
premises of those arguments would depend on inductive inference from observation.

39. For some of Rand's direct comment on the alleged gap, see "The Objectivist
Ethics," 17, 22.

40. Rand, "Causality versus Duty," 118–19.

41. Harry Binswanger has offered a telling analogy to expose the absurdity of a
prohibition against deriving values from facts. The idea that we cannot derive values from facts because they are different sorts of things is akin to the idea that we
cannot derive statements containing references to toxicology from statements not
containing references to toxicology since such statements are different in kind.
This would mean holding that observations about an individual's physical condition (reporting symptoms of illness such as his temperature, color, aches, or energy
level) afford absolutely no logical grounds for conclusions about what medication
might alleviate his condition (statements that refer to toxicology). But this is ridic-
ulous. Such inferences are the means by which we integrate information to build
knowledge (and devise treatment to battle disease, among other things). Historically, we did not arrive at knowledge of toxins or medicine by deduction from
general principles mystically revealed but from systematic experimentation and
observation (Binswanger, "The Is-Ought Dichotomy—How Morality Can Be Derived from Facts," unpublished lecture).

42. I am not suggesting that a person must seek life under all circumstances. I
will address the propriety of suicide in chapter five.

43. Occasionally, an emergency might demand immediate attention and post-
poning pursuit of some other values. The fact that continuing to pursue lesser ends
would work against one's life in extraordinary circumstances does not mean that
life and other ends typically stand in that competitive relationship, however.

44. I also discuss this choice in *Moral Rights and Political Freedom* (Lanham,
Md.: Rowman & Littlefield, 1995), 43–48.

45. See chapter two's sections "Why Be Rational?" and "Justification of Action."

46. Peikoff, *Objectivism,* 211–12.

47. Since life is not imbued with intrinsic value, *that* cannot be a basis that rationally requires people to pursue life.

48. The political prisoner who chooses to die because he finds life under certain conditions intolerable is significantly different from the person who rejects life under any conditions. The prisoner's decision could stem from his love of life alongside the conviction that certain trials or injustices are too destructive or degrading to bear; they make a human existence impossible. The person who unconditionally rejects life suggests no such love of life.

49. Again, in the sections "Why Be Rational?" and "Justification of Action."

50. Since I am not offering life as *the* correct, rational answer to the question, this "answer" cannot be dismissed as question begging. If anything, it simply highlights the unusual, arational nature of the question. No answer outside of life can be given. One cannot appeal to anything that is not part of life to "prove" that life is worth living.

51. *Oxford English Dictionary.*

52. By "obligation," I mean simply that which a person morally ought to do. Obligations do not necessarily concern relations with other people.

53. The particulars of when and what forms of self-defense and punishment are legitimate are governed by the particular virtue of justice and are more intricate than we need to engage here. For our purposes, what is important is the principle that a person may act, rationally, to promote his life vis-à-vis other people as well as anything else.

54. For further discussion of this, see Peikoff, *Objectivism,* 213–20.

55. Most people are somewhere between the extremes of the continuum, engaging in some life-promoting and some life-diminishing actions. A person need not have consciously chosen death for his actions to follow a destructive path, however.

56. The expectation that a life-based morality should offer such airtight guarantees of immediate, fatal repercussions would make sense only if morality were a contrived game in which our fortunes were fixed by a god or a computer programmed to unfailingly punish vice. It is utterly unrealistic to experience.

57. Nor is it the aim of morality. See Rand's discussion of this in "The Objectivist Ethics," 23–25.

I recently encountered the same basic idea—that living consists of more than breathing—in an article cataloging the economic hardships in Cuba. The piece quoted a resident: "We may not be dying of hunger, but we're not living either" ("Living with Fidel," *The Economist* 350, no. 8109 [March 6, 1999]: 34).

5

Morality's Reward: Flourishing

If life is the ultimate source of value and moral authority, it is important to understand this source as fully as possible. Rand writes that the standard of value is "that which is required for man's survival *qua* man" and that man's survival *qua* man "means the terms, methods, conditions and goals required for the survival of a rational being through the whole of his lifespan."[1] In the last chapter, I argued that life means more than morgue avoidance, more than a breath or a pulse. If that is so, we need to explore further what this involves.

My thesis here is that the end of value and the reward of living morally is individual flourishing. Colloquially, people commonly distinguish flourishing from survival, with "survival" referring to subsistence with the barest necessities and "flourishing" referring to a much higher level of comfort and enjoyment. In fact, this distinction is misleading. Life, as the source and aim of ethics, *is* flourishing. These are not two alternative goals only one of which a person might adopt. Obviously, not everyone alive flourishes; to deny this would empty "flourishing" of meaning. But a flourishing life is the target and foundation of value.

Rand, I should point out, speaks of happiness rather than flourishing. I consider the two roughly interchangeable but will primarily use "flourishing" because "happiness" has more passive connotations. That is, people often think of happiness as something that does or does not happen to a person, with the person entirely on the receiving end of this fortuitous event. "Flourishing," in contrast, suggests action. It reflects not just a feeling of satisfaction with one's experience, as happiness does, but also a person's own activity as the chief source of that feeling. The fact that we speak of plants as flourishing, although they cannot be happy, testifies to this active dimension of flourishing. (I will say more later on the relationship between the feeling of flourishing and the activity of flourishing.)

The claim that flourishing is the goal of morality may naturally raise concerns that I am shifting the terms of the previous argument, equivocating about exactly what end it is that values and morality serve. Flourishing may, for instance, seem a more subjective matter than survival. Or it may seem to raise the bar of life's requirements. Or it may seem too much a function of a person's enjoyment to be a proper aim for morality.[2] Thus, I will explain this claim at length, proceeding in three stages.

The first task is simply to elaborate on the character of flourishing, to sharpen our image of what this condition is. Next, I will explain why flourishing is the proper end of value. To this end, I will argue that living as a human being's long-term survival requires *is* flourishing and that the "two ends" of life and flourishing are actually different perspectives on a single aim. I will also argue here that human beings need to flourish. Finally, I will explain why recognizing flourishing as the ultimate aim and foundation of value preserves morality's objectivity. The requirements of flourishing are every bit as factual as the requirements of surviving.

WHAT FLOURISHING IS

As I argued in the last chapter, the end of value pursuit is life. Morality is a do-or-die proposition; life hinges on our needs being satisfied. The biological examples were not metaphors or analogies but literal, factual reports of the necessary conditions of human existence. The fulfillment of needs is valuable to anyone wishing to live. Since fulfillment of our needs depends on our actions, morality guides us to the proper types of actions.

At the same time, values' telos is more than life in the minimal, technical terms of brain states or autonomous respiration that satisfy certain legal, insurance, or census purposes. The end of value is flourishing.

To see how this can be, we must understand exactly what flourishing refers to. Recall that life is a series of self-generated, self-sustaining actions. "Flourishing" refers to a life that is prospering or in good condition. Indeed, the nature of life itself clues us into the meaning of flourishing by revealing the features that render a life good.

Consider plants and animals. When are they well? An obvious sign of health for plants is growth—an increase in overall size or in the number of leaves, flowers, or fruits that a plant generates. Appearance also testifies to how well a plant is. Are its leaves straggly, frail, and limp or thick, hardy, and taut?[3] Animals' well-being is also gauged by growth and appearance as well as by their level of activity. Is the dog lethargic or energetic? Is it responsive or indifferent to food or play? We identify plants and animals doing well by observing whether the organism is functioning in a way that improves its survival prospects. Is it poised to withstand hardship or likely to be defeated by the first obstacles that it encounters? "Holding one's own" is decidedly inferior to flourishing because an organism merely holding on is drawing on its stored resources, thus leaving fewer in reserve to battle future challenges. It is weakening its long-term position. Growth, on the other hand, is a sign of energy to spare and thus of fitness to survive.

A similar account could be provided for human beings. We applaud an infant's development as healthy—his increasingly exercising his capacities to reach, grasp, crawl, stand, walk, talk, and reason—on the grounds that these contribute to his eventually becoming an independent being. Since his parents' round-the-clock support will not be available indefinitely, these developments are good because they propel the child toward self-sufficiency—that is, they strengthen his ability to live. The same applies to adults, although the effects of our actions on survival are often more subtle.[4] The twenty-something whom we commend for holding a steady job or completing a degree or managing a successful business is doing well insofar as his actions bespeak competence—if not excellence—at the task of living.

The lesson from these observations is this: "Flourishing" designates a good life. In the broadest terms, what makes a life good is its being led in a life-furthering fashion. A life is good and a person is flourishing when the series of actions that constitutes his life proceeds along a life-promoting course. Thus, flourishing refers to biological life that attains a particular character: It is marked by activity and growth of the sort that fuels survival. Flourishing represents meeting life's demands well, in other words, doing a good job of it. Flourishing is propelled by a person's strengthening his capacities to act as life requires. Flourishing, or a good life, is simply life-enhancing living.

Correspondingly, flourishing is something that a person does rather than something that he has. Well-being consists of *being* well. Flourishing cannot be reduced to a basket of possessions. Just as life is a series of actions, so living well is a matter of acting in a certain manner. A person flourishes by acting in ways that propel his life. Thus, flourishing is not captured by any batch of belongings (be they material objects or any other sort of goods, such as a particular job, status, or authority).

My intent in saying that the proper end of morality is flourishing is not to pronounce some bill of particulars as *the* combination of activities that constitutes flourishing (e.g., reading these books, pursuing these hobbies, earning this income). No fixed set of specific pursuits constitutes flourishing for all human beings. Across and within species, the particulars of individuals' needs vary. Having observed the legitimacy of optional values in the previous chapter, it should be apparent that people can flourish through different actions as a result largely of their own tastes, abilities, and circumstances. As with optional values, however, the requirements of flourishing are not determined by anyone's arbitrary declaration. Reality dictates flourishing's requirements. The demands of life determine when a person is living well by determining whether a person's activities further his existence.

It is important to realize that because flourishing is a function of how a person leads his life, flourishing results from a person's own actions. More exactly, it *is* those actions rather than a separate outcome of them. It is a mistake to think of flourishing as only the positive feeling that is the usual effect of such action. In fact, living well constitutes flourishing. Flourishing is not a distinct, after-the-fact result of proper living. The means of flourishing are themselves components of the end of flourishing. Flourishing is both end and means. By acting as life demands, a person attains the reward of flourishing—which consists simply of more living—of extending the very process of engaging in those activities. Just as a person does not putt *in order* to play golf but as part of playing golf, so a person acts morally as a part of flourishing. The activity of flourishing is what the end of value consists of. Proper action is constitutive of flourishing.[5]

Since flourishing is living well and since a person leads his own life, only he *can* live it well. This reveals a further significant feature of flourishing: Flourishing must be self-generated. Whether a person flourishes is essentially up to him.

Obviously, a person can be seriously affected by events beyond his control. A paralyzing car accident or the right card in Monte Carlo can bring lasting repercussions on the course of his life. Similarly, certain external goods—such as minimal wealth or health—are necessary for flourishing. They are not sufficient, however; the core of flourishing resides in how a person manages what lies within his control.[6] Welcome as good fortune may be, whether it ultimately enhances a person's life depends on what he does with it: on the propriety of his desires and the rationality of his avenues of pursuing them. People squander opportunities every day.[7]

While external events can be more or less conducive to a person's flourishing, insofar as flourishing is a function of one's activities, it is an end that a person must attain for himself. This is comparable to the way in which Aristotle conceived of *eudaimonia*. As John Cooper describes Aristotle's view, "*eudaimonia* is necessarily the result of a person's own efforts." As Julia Annas explains, on this view, "our final good cannot be something that other people could give us; it must be something we can achieve for ourselves . . . it is not a thing or state of affairs that others could bring about for me."[8]

My claim about flourishing reflects the same basic idea. A person can only flourish for himself. Because flourishing is not a collection of external goods, it cannot be transferred from one person to another. However well-meaning, loving, and generous a person might be, he cannot make another person flourish. While one person might aid another in significant material and spiritual respects, he cannot live for another person, and he cannot impart to another the sense of satisfaction that one's own efficacy can provide. Flourishing is inescapably a function of how an individual leads his life.

None of this account of flourishing entails that it is easy to determine whether a person is flourishing. We have previously observed that life is an extended, wide-ranging enterprise. Whether something serves a person's life can be a difficult judgment, given the layers of effects that a thing can carry on the complex network of ends that compose a person's life. What superficially looks good is not always actually beneficial. Because flourishing is not reducible to some set of possessions or positions, a snapshot of a person's condition at any moment is insufficient to justify conclusions about his flourishing. Among other things, we must know the sources of a person's present condition. Is it the result of his own activities, which he pursued because he recognized their benefit to his life?

Since flourishing means living in a pro-life way, it refers to the overall direction of a person's activities. A flourishing person takes positive strides that fulfill his needs and achieve his values—securing, expanding, and enriching his life. To know whether a person is doing this, it is helpful to know how his present ends and activities compare with his ends and activities of the past. Are these more or less worthwhile than those he pursued a few years ago? Is he seeking these ends through virtuous paths or by cutting moral corners? Is he exhibiting stronger or weaker discipline or integrity? Is he becoming more honest, productive, or just or less so? This relative assessment is not a sufficient gauge of flourishing, of course, since life's demands are independent of a person's particular history of meeting those demands. But since flourishing is an ongoing condition, a view of a person's overall trajectory is part of our means of measuring flourishing. (Knowledge that a person is not working as conscientiously as he did in the past, for example, absent any good reason for the change, would suggest that he is not acting as well as he can and is thus not flourishing.)

Flourishing refers to a person's complete physical and psychological health over a full life span—as opposed to in any isolated hour, day, or week. Anything less than this—flourishing in just one sphere of life or for one temporary period—would not suffice to sustain one's life. A person's life stands to be affected by anything that he does. Thus, a concern for flourishing cannot be a part-time occupation or an insulated compartment of a person's life. Flourishing is full time insofar as no moment fails to carry potential impact on one's life; flourishing is all-encompassing insofar as no spheres of activity are incapable of affecting one's life. Certain kinds of activities may typically carry weightier or more conspicuous effects than others. Drug addiction tends to be more dangerous than a Doritos addiction; deceit or cowardice tends to be more destructive than a sick sense of humor. Yet a person's flourishing is not immune to any type of activity that he might engage in. Thus, the person striving to flourish must be concerned with acting well in every aspect of his experience. As will become clearer in the next section, flourishing cannot be regarded as a peripheral, optional luxury.[9]

To summarize, flourishing means living in a life-sustaining manner. It is an active process that can be achieved only by a person's own efforts. Flourishing is both means and ends in the sense that by acting as life demands, a person enables himself to enjoy life—which simply means to enjoy more of the activities that constitute life. Flourishing is thus the condition of a life that is going well—"going well" by the same standard of all value: life.

WHY FLOURISHING IS THE PROPER END OF VALUE

At first blush, my linking of life with flourishing might seem to introduce problems. Having argued in chapter four that life makes value possible and necessary by appealing to actions' effects on survival, flourishing may strike one as altering the stakes. Survival seems a function of satisfying needs, while flourishing seems a matter of fulfilling wants, attaining a desirable quality of life. If these represent distinct ends, their requirements are not interchangeable, and they cannot stand as the foundation for the same moral prescriptions. Given the foregoing account of the nature of flourishing, however, we should be able to see that such worries are unfounded.

To understand why flourishing is the proper end of value and morality, we must appreciate two principal facts. First, "life" and "flourishing" are two perspectives on the same phenomenon; flourishing is a certain character of life rather than a separate objective. Second, a person *needs* to flourish; flourishing is not an optional frill but a necessity. Let's develop each thought in turn.

Living Is Flourishing

To think that we must choose between life and flourishing as the highest end of value and morality is to accept an artificial alternative. Rand holds that

The maintenance of life and the pursuit of happiness are not two separate issues. To hold one's own life as one's ultimate value, and one's own happiness as one's highest purpose are two aspects of the same achievement. Existentially, the activity of pursuing rational goals is the activity of maintaining one's life; psychologically, its result, reward, and concomitant is an emotional state of happiness.[10]

By "happiness," Rand is referring to the feeling component of flourishing. My discussion thus far has emphasized the activity of flourishing, the fact that flourishing is something that a person does. The feeling that such life-promoting activity typically gives rise to, however, is happiness. "Happiness is that state of consciousness which proceeds from the achievement of one's values."[11] Since the way to achieve genuine values is through life-advancing action (or, more specifically, through action in accordance with a moral code grounded in its service to life), the path to happiness (or to the feeling of flourishing) and the path to living are one and the same. If the feeling of flourishing is the satisfaction that one experiences from realizing the values that promote one's life, then a person does not face a choice between alternative avenues: one leading to life and another leading to happiness. Rather, the pursuit of life *is* the pursuit of flourishing—and the life that one seeks and that sets the standard of value and morality is a flourishing life, life in this peak or ideal form.

To dislodge this dichotomy between life and flourishing completely, we should examine its sources more closely. The idea that flourishing is a different goal from life is typically built on the association of flourishing with quality of life and with wants rather than necessities. But this is premised on distorted distinctions between quality and quantity of life and between needs and wants.

The Quality–Quantity Distinction

The distinction between quality and quantity of life is not nearly as sharp as it is often portrayed. The quality–quantity distinction is fair enough in some domains; a pound of beef is a pound of beef, while taste and tenderness are obvious ways to distinguish qualitatively and decide which butcher to patronize or which cut to order. When the subject is life, however, the issue is not so clear-cut.

People usually speak as if quality of life is the murkier concept, subject to competing views concerning what constitutes adequate quality. That, allegedly, is merely a matter of taste. What is quality differentiated from, however? What does quantity of life refer to? The typical answer, the mere fact of being alive, will not do, for it leaves important questions dangling. Doctors, lawyers, ethicists, and public policymakers argue over whether being alive is best defined by heartbeat, or brain activity, or respiration, for example. What kinds of self-sufficiency are required? What degrees of self-sufficiency? Is machine-supported respiration adequate? What level of brain activity is required? Recent medical technology has lent urgency to such questions. The fact that the boundaries delimiting quantity of life are themselves arguable indicates that the distinction between quantity and quality is not as crisp or as value neutral—as devoid of qualitative assessments—as is usually presumed. Indeed, the very concept of biological health is normative. We must identify a certain manner of functioning as the goal for an organism and as good for an organism in order to identify successful functioning, that is, the condition of health.[12]

The distinction between quantity and quality is not entirely specious, of course. As I acknowledged earlier, not everyone who is alive is flourishing; not everyone who is breathing is acting in a life-promoting manner or enjoying the contentment that the activity of flourishing characteristically brings. The important point, however, is that quality cannot be stripped off quantity and treated as if it existed independently. What is at issue when we speak of quality or quantity of life is actually a difference in perspective on the same phenomenon: a person's life. Neither can exist without the other: A person can have no quality of life without some quantity, and a person can have no quantity of life without its having some quality (however desirable or undesirable that quality may be). What we often think of as "quality versus quantity" actually reflects a difference of degree (of quality) rather than an emphatic break in kind. Thus, when I invoke flourishing, I do not mean flourishing as *opposed* to life, something to be substituted for life. Nor do I mean flourishing as something added on top of life. Rather, "flourishing" designates the condition that a life ideally attains.[13]

Most people do seek a qualitatively satisfying life. Suicide is often based on the belief that without a certain quality, life is not worth living. Many people would prefer a shorter, more enjoyable life to a longer life of inferior quality.

This does not show that a person can seek quality instead of quantity, however. A particular quality of life is not a distinct objective, independent of life itself. It is simply the character of life that a person seeks. Suicide, when committed for the sake of quality of life, is a choice about the conditions under which a person considers his life—its quantity and its quality—worth maintaining.

The point, then, is that quantity and quality of life are irrevocably entwined. As was demonstrated in chapter four, biological life is the foundation of the concept of value. What fosters survival sets the terms of what constitutes a qualitatively good life.[14]

The Needs–Wants Distinction

The other distinction that can distort one's understanding of the relationship between life and flourishing is that between needs and wants. People normally think of needs as essential and of wants as optional, frills that are nice but not necessary, things that a person could do without. Bread on the table and a roof over one's head are the sorts of things that everyone must have; caviar and a summer cottage on the coast are not. Many comforts, conveniences, and pleasures to which we are accustomed seem to fall in the latter category (e.g., movies, music, sports, Christmas gifts, and birthday parties). For that matter, higher quality in things that we *do* need, such as a more spacious home, more stylish clothes, or more exotic food, also seem dispensable. Thus, one might contend, if life requires satisfaction of needs and flourishing depends on fulfillment of wants, life and flourishing impose very different requirements. They cannot generate the same moral prescriptions.

Here again, however, the salient distinction is not as rigid as it initially seems. To appreciate this, consider the nature of needs.

In order to fill the most basic needs for food, shelter, or clothing, a person will need other things, such as the time and skills to produce food, shelter, or clothing or the money to buy them. He may need a job to earn money, education or training to obtain a job, and effort and discipline to acquire the relevant abilities and then practice them sufficiently to keep his job. Thus, these are needs as well. Basic health is a precondition for satisfying many of these needs, so it is yet another need. Severe mental illness can prevent a person's satisfaction of other needs, so mental health seems still a further need.

With only a little reflection, we can begin to identify several different kinds of needs. Some needs are primary and others are derivative, as these examples indicate. The needs for a job or income are derivative from the more basic needs for food and shelter since the latter needs create the former.

We can also distinguish external from internal needs. A person requires fuel from his environment (food, oxygen) as well as proper functioning of his kidney, liver, and lungs, for example, to make the necessary use of that fuel.

While material needs are the most easily noticed, a person also has spiritual needs. By "spiritual" I mean psychological, or pertaining to a person's mind. (I do not mean mystical.)[15] Spiritual needs encompass such things as art, friends, hope, inspiration, a sense of purpose or direction, and a belief in one's own efficacy and worth. Such things are needs insofar as their absence weakens a person's fitness to survive. (I will say more on this when I discuss depression in the next section.)

Obviously, needs differ in their complexity. Some can be satisfied easily, while others depend on the coordination of several interdependent steps. Needs can be short range or long range, demanding immediate attention or demanding actions taken well in advance of their ultimate fulfillment (think again of investing for retirement income).

Needs differ in frequency. Some needs are rare, some arise occasionally, and some recur on a regular basis. A person might need to extricate himself from a burning automobile once in his life, if that; he might need to relocate or find employment a half dozen times; he might require certain medical treatments every few years and food every few hours.

Needs' stakes can vary a great deal. The impact of the failure to satisfy a need can be limited or far-reaching. A person can lose a parking spot, a job, a wallet, a wife, or his license to practice medicine. Some losses might permanently bar a person from certain activities (e.g., forcing him to spend forty years in a wheelchair), while others temporarily inconvenience him (four weeks on crutches).

Similarly, needs vary in urgency. Urgency is a function of stakes and time: the gravity of what hinges on fulfillment of a need combined with the speed with which it must be satisfied. The shorter the time and the higher the stakes, the more urgent the need. The need to meet a deadline, for example, will be more or less urgent depending on how near the deadline falls and what the deadline concerns: satisfying the IRS, inclusion on an election ballot, or saving money with a detergent coupon.[16]

For our purposes, two lessons are most important. First, a person has an array of needs, including needs for things required to satisfy the most obvious and momentous needs. Our needs are layered in such a way that some needs depend on others. We need to obtain food; we need to be able to obtain food. We need to be productive; we need to maintain the energy, initiative, and will to be productive. We need a sense of self-worth; we need to act in ways that nourish a sense of self-worth. Since our most direct needs can be satisfied only through intermediate means, those become additional needs whose satisfaction is valuable to us.

The second lesson is an outgrowth of the first. Recognition of various types and levels of needs obscures the distinction between needs and wants. Once we observe all these differences *within* the category of needs, it is harder to maintain a sharp difference in kind between needs and wants. Recognizing the range of people's physical and spiritual needs (e.g., for exercise, rest, nutrition, sex, material goods, and productivity; social, romantic, artistic, intellectual, and relaxation needs; the need for variety itself) as well as these needs' varying degrees of simplicity, urgency, frequency, and so on demonstrates that needs cover much more, and more varied, territory than we casually suppose.

The point is, the way in which some of these needs differ from one another is not so different from respects in which wants allegedly differ from needs. The need for a vacation is related to the need for income, for example, much like the need for friends is related to the need for oxygen. The needs for friends or vacation may not be as apparent or urgent or ongoing as the need for money or oxygen, but they are nonetheless genuine, insofar as friends and vacation are necessary for sustaining a person's ability and motivation to fill other needs.

Life must be understood recursively. "Survival" refers to the continuation of an organism's metabolic processes as well as to other activities that foster that continuation. Correspondingly, a person's needs have not been met simply because a day's food and shelter have been secured, any more than famine sufferers' needs are satisfied when the Red Cross ships them two weeks' food supply. Such measures heed only the most superficial layer of needs. As a person's needs naturally develop and proliferate, so do the meaning and the requirements of his survival. Needs encompass *all* that is necessary for life—the most glaringly urgent physical needs, more subtle psychological needs, and the ancillary activities and conditions required to fulfill a person's expanding network of needs over the course of his life.

Snatched from its full context, then, any given desire may look like a want (as opposed to a need). But appreciation of the variety and complexity of needs should alert us to the fact that many apparent wants are actually needs. Our quick inventory of kinds of needs indicates the several respects in which something could be a need and the many respects in which something could serve a need.

My claim is not that wants and needs are synonymous or interchangeable. People can want things that are bad for them. Even when concerned strictly with innocent, life-furthering wants, it can sometimes be useful to distinguish wants from needs so as to tend pressing objectives before lesser ones. If it is imperative that a hospital patient eat only certain kinds of food, for instance, that should take priority over his desire for other foods. Since the wants–needs distinction may seem to challenge my identification of flourishing as the end of morality, however, the main message to grasp is that the distinction between needs and life-furthering wants is, at root, a difference in degree. Instead of a radical rupture between completely disparate phenomena, we actually find considerable continuity between needs and wants.

Consider again some apparent wants or dispensable desires. Many people would dismiss fax machines, e-mail, cellular phones, and automobiles' climate control mechanisms as frills. These conveniences or comforts are luxuries that we can live without. Indeed, people did live without these things for centuries. For that matter, people have lived without computers, microwave ovens, telephones, and cars or, earlier, without electricity, railroads, transistor radios, and typewriters. There was a time before AZT, chemotherapy, pacemakers, penicillin, antibiotics, and anesthetics—and people lived. Given individuals died, of course, who might have been spared had such advances been available. But the species endured.

What this indicates is that needs are identified relative to the context of what is available. What we consider essential has escalated over the years. Yesterday's luxury frequently becomes today's necessity. The average contemporary American home buyer who expects indoor plumbing is not being fussy. The "need for the unnecessary," the historian Daniel Boorstin has written, is "another name for human progress."[17]

Needs are more elastic than we often assume. (A "want" in wartime may be indispensable in peacetime.) Correspondingly, the line between needs and wants is not fixed such that we can confidently assign subordinate status to wants. If needs are not fundamentally different from wants, however, then the contention that flourishing is a matter of wants and survival is a matter of needs collapses. The worry that flourishing is not a fair interpretation of life as the end of morality is thus undermined by its reliance on this exaggerated conception of the difference between needs and wants.

To sum up this first part of the explanation of why flourishing is the proper end of value, then: The idea that life and flourishing are two independent objectives, between which one *could* equivocate, depends on exaggerated distinctions between quantity and quality of life and between needs and wants. Survival and flourishing are not alternatives to choose between. If one understands the nature of flourishing, one will realize that it is not attained by pursuing some track other than that which promotes one's life. The only way to flourish is by acting in the manner that life itself demands. To say that living is flourishing is not to count every breathing human being as flourishing. What I mean is that living *as life requires* is flourishing. Anything less than flourishing will not sustain the process of living. Correspondingly, when Rand claims that the standard of life is "that which is required for man's survival *qua* man," she is not raising the threshold of morality's demands, introducing some unwarranted, alien standard. Had she said "*qua* martian," misgivings would be justified. But Rand is simply calling attention to the fact that only certain kinds of action will suffice to sustain a human life. Human beings cannot survive except by acting as human nature demands. The actions that sustain human life, however, simultaneously fuel a person's flourishing. Indeed, performing the appropriate actions constitutes flourishing.

Not by Bread Alone

The second fact to appreciate, in order to understand that flourishing is the proper end of value, is that flourishing itself promotes survival. Flourishing is not a dispensable luxury; human beings *need* to flourish.

I adverted earlier to the difference between the activity of flourishing and the feeling of flourishing. "Flourishing" can refer either to the subjective feel of a person's experience or to the objective character of a person's life—to whether a person feels as if his life is going well or to the actions that constitute its going well. The latter is comparable to the grounds on which we might say that a plant or animal is flourishing. (I will use "the feeling of flourishing" or "subjective flourishing" and "the fact of flourishing" or "objective flourishing" as shorthands, respectively, for these two meanings.)

Objective flourishing is a manner of living. A person flourishes in this sense to the extent that he acts in accordance with a life-promoting moral code. The subjective sense of flourishing is made possible by that. Feeling as if you are flourishing is typically a product of objectively flourishing.

Happiness is another term for the feeling of flourishing. Feelings of happiness or depression are indicators of the objective status of one's pursuit of life and its constituent values. Such feelings can suggest whether a person needs to adjust his course. The disposition to experience these feelings serves as an internal monitor of the progress of one's quest for life. Happiness is the psychological experience correlative to a life properly led; it is a reflection, in a person's consciousness, of successful living.[18]

Broadly, then, flourishing is living well, and ideally this encompasses both the activities of flourishing and the feeling of flourishing. A person flourishes to the extent that he enhances his fitness to live. The psychological offshoot of this is the person's enjoyment of living, satisfaction with his experience.

My claim that human beings need to flourish applies to both senses of flourishing. The activity of flourishing—of living in a life-promoting manner—is crucial to survival. The only way to meet survival's requirements is through the sorts of actions that constitute flourishing. That should be clear from chapter four and from the previous discussion of how living *is* flourishing. The additional element that it is important to digest is that the feeling of flourishing—contentment, happiness—itself fuels life. Let me explain.

Human needs are spiritual as well as material. A person is an integrated unity whose mental life matters to his survival. A person's beliefs, emotions, long-range plans, higher-order desires, and attitudes concerning the prospects of realizing his desires all affect his actions. Unlike lower animals, we are not steered by instinct to life-sustaining actions.

Because a person's survival depends on his actions and because human actions are volitional, a person's psychological condition becomes critical to his survival. It is the basis on which he selects his ends and actions. Because these must be chosen, a person must wish to act. Thus, the will to live is crucial to satisfying life's requirements.

Human life comprises an elaborate network of interlocking needs. As we have noticed already, many of our needs are complex and long range, such that a great many things can, to differing degrees, affect their fulfillment. Since the fulfillment of needs often requires the orchestration of multiple variables stretched across months or years, a single event's impact may be difficult to appreciate. Consider all the activities that go into composing an opera, pursuing a degree, winning a championship, or starting a company. None of the isolated hours devoted to completing a multiyear project may be obviously constructive to outside observers. But a contribution need not be monumental or obvious to be genuine.

Because a human life is such an extensive, multifaceted enterprise, it becomes singularly imperative to sustain motivation. When success in some endeavor is neither in sight nor certain, it is easy to lose the conviction of its possibility. This is why enjoyment becomes valuable. The feeling of flourishing enhances a person's life primarily by fueling his appetite for living. Many of life's "dispensable" embellishments—friends, music, movies, sports, stylish writing, good cooking—stoke a person's enthusiasm for life. Reaping satisfaction from incremental progress on some long-range goal (such as from finishing a course or reducing a debt) can also be valuable. The belief that one is "getting some place" can sustain a person's efforts through trying times. Further, taking pleasure in success at component projects can strengthen the belief in one's ability to accomplish the larger, principal objective.

The difficulty of certain of our projects is also reason to pursue some less demanding ends. Without a quotient of comparatively low-investment gratifications, the ratio between struggle and reward can come to seem oppressive and discouraging. It can deter a person from engaging wholeheartedly in enterprises that would richly advance his life. Success at more modest enterprises can keep afloat belief in one's ability or simply keep a person upbeat during the pursuit of more arduous, long-term goals that yield fewer immediate gratifications. It can help toward the completion of a dissertation, for example, for a person to cultivate some peripheral ends, such as learning a musical instrument or sport. While such lighter pursuits may appear more frivolous than survival serving, they are actually an important part of the overall campaign for life insofar as they enhance a person's enjoyment and engagement in life.

The point is, the quality of a person's experience—whether he feels as if he is flourishing or as if flourishing is within his reach—makes a tremendous difference to his motivation to act in a life-furthering fashion. It is as necessary for a person to fill his spiritual needs by achieving values as it is for a person to fill his physical needs by exercising or eating.

The feeling that one is flourishing can contribute to a person's objective flourishing, which means that it strengthens his life. Needs for education, freedom, friends, and art are somewhat different from needs for food and shelter. It will not kill a person to miss a concert. It will not kill a person to lose a close friend. Yet insofar as concerts and friends enrich a person's life, such things do support his survival.

This is the key point overlooked by the presumption that value can serve *either* life or flourishing. While "frills" enhancing the enjoyment of life may seem to carry more impact on flourishing than on sustenance, their contribution to survival is vital.

Man does not live on bread alone. Human beings have a need to flourish (to feel as if they are flourishing) as genuine as the need for bread. "Frills" feed life because the enjoyment of life is itself life promoting. Flourishing has survival value.

Another way to appreciate this fact is to contemplate the contrasting case: depression. Consider the descending spiral of a person losing his interest in life. The absence of pleasures in a person's life steadily drains his energy. If effort is required merely to maintain a ho-hum status quo, the debilitating attitude will fester: Why bother? When a person is not enjoying his experience, this diminishes the appetite for action, which translates into fewer and less decisive actions.

Depression exacts a toll on both a person's material and psychological well-being. Depression is marked not only by a lack of enjoyment in one's activities but also by inertia, listlessness, and lethargy. The clinically depressed person will struggle to get out of bed in the morning or to leave his home. A depressed person typically does not sleep or eat well; his mental alertness sags, and he is prone to make poor decisions. Such traits can clearly detract from the satisfaction of life's material needs.

Depression's psychological toll is the decay of the person's morale. This is particularly marked by the erosion of two essential qualities: hope and purpose.

When life seems to offer little enjoyment, a person will embrace fewer ends and lose things to hope for. And if a person believes that his ambitions are unlikely to succeed (e.g., he is convinced that the campaign is a losing cause, that he will never complete the degree, or that success at any endeavor would not prove very satisfying anyway), it will be much harder to motivate action. When a person regards his aims as unattainable, trying to attain them will seem pointless.

Thinking "I can't get what I want" is different, of course, from thinking "I don't want anything anyway." My point is that the former tends to encourage the latter. When depressed, a person believes that he cannot achieve the contentment he yearns for. Since it is painful to cling to desires viewed as beyond one's grasp, the person will gradually release the desires themselves.

The very lack of effort that depression engenders naturally increases the probability of failure since the less effort exerted to succeed, the less likely success will be. Thus, a lack of enjoyment can lead to pessimism, which saps initiative and makes failure more likely, reinforcing one's pessimism and the apparent logic of not bothering to attempt anything. Hope is a vital ingredient for breaking this paralyzing cycle.

The other essential quality that depression poisons is purpose. When not enjoying life, no destination holds much appeal. And hopelessness undermines the point of maintaining any firm purposes. Yet purpose is valuable as the organizing principle propelling a person's activities. (The expression "leading a life" may reflect the idea that a person's life should be driven in some direction.)

Purposes provide direction; they guide a person's actions toward definite destinations. This naturally raises the probability of one's actions advancing one's life since a vision of what ends one is after is indispensable to achieving the concrete values that propel one's life.

Without definite purposes, a person's days would amount to a series of disconnected dead ends, his activities trailing off around no particular terminus and bringing a person neither the advance of his life nor its correlative satisfaction. Life is a very abstract goal, encompassing all the self-generated, self-sustaining activities that a person engages in—everything from tying his shoelaces or sharpening a pencil to paying a bill or getting married. Purposes, modest or major—to play the guitar, to strengthen one's backhand, to practice medicine, to be a good mother—lend form and content to that overarching aim.

David Schmidtz's analysis of *maieutic* ends in *Rational Choice and Moral Agency* similarly testifies to the importance of purpose. *Maieutic* ends are ends that are achieved through a process of coming to have other ends. "A *maieutic* end is an end of bringing ends into existence, of giving oneself ends to pursue." The ends of settling on a career or spouse, for instance, are *maieutic* ends.[19]

Schmidtz affirms the value of purposes when he writes, "To have ends to pursue is to have something to live for." Moreover, Schmidtz recognizes *maieutic* ends as directly strengthening a person's existence. "Finding reasons to live improves our survival prospects. To whatever extent we care about survival, and to whatever extent finding things to live for strengthens our will to survive and thereby improves our survival prospects, we have a rationale for the overarching end. Finding things to live for is instrumental to the further end of survival."[20] Purposes are reasons to live.

The salient lesson from all this is simple but important: Enjoyment tends to buoy a person's appetite for life and sharpen a person's fitness for living. Often, the more a person enjoys something, the more he wants to do it. And the more he wants to do it, the more he cares about doing it well, as skillful performance can heighten his enjoyment. Playing tennis well is usually a lot more fun than playing poorly, for example, and that realization can stimulate efforts to improve one's game. Further, the sheer fact of engaging in an activity with some frequency (which enjoyment encourages) often improves one's skill. Practice usually helps a person become a better tennis player, piano player, teacher, lawyer, and so on. What holds for these activities that make up a person's life holds for life itself. Enjoyment of life—the feeling of flourishing—tends to enhance one's capacity to succeed at living.

The broader point is that a mutually reinforcing dynamic develops between the fact of flourishing and the feeling of flourishing: between living well and enjoying its effects, between achieving values that advance one's life and loving one's life. The better a person is at living (the more in accordance with a rational moral code), the more likely it is that he will love his life because his experience will be more loveable. The more a person loves his life, in turn, the greater his motivation to live well (as morality, and as life, demands).

By now, then, it should be clear that flourishing is not a good based on some grounds independent of those that I have presented as the foundation of value. Flourishing is not measured on a separate axis. Prolonged absence of "the good things in life" will diminish a person's appetite for living itself. Lack of friends, or music, or certain comforts, for example, can erode a person's will to live and eventually, as a consequence, his fitness to live. Flourishing is not a peripheral or arbitrarily adopted end of value; flourishing is valuable *on life-based grounds*. Enhancing our lives, as flourishing demands, is instrumental to sustaining our lives.[21]

Even if flourishing is measured on the same axis as survival, one might wonder why it must be so high on the axis. The textbook gloss of flourishing can make it seem dauntingly exalted: achieving excellence across the board, a nonstop spiral of striving, growth, setting ever stiffer challenges, and reaching new heights in achieving them.[22] On what grounds is flourishing so lofty? Does flourishing really require such elevated accomplishments?

The answer, here again, stems from the requirements of life. Essentially, flourishing demands a rising series of achievements because survival requires a rising series of achievements. People's needs change over time. As a person ages, his needs expand such that he must stretch in order to meet them. Needs become more numerous and more complex. A ten-year-old needs more food than a two-month-old. As a child ages, he needs more sophisticated language skills and more sophisticated amusements. An adult needs finer coordination and motor skills, greater physical strength, and a greater ability to concentrate than does a toddler.[23]

It is not enough for a person to fulfill only his most basic needs. Nor will it do to satisfy only the same needs that he has tended in the past or to fulfill such needs through the same expenditure of effort. Some energy must be directed to satisfy new needs. Survival demands that individuals grow and improve both physically and spiritually. The standard of value remains life. How that is satisfied, however, evolves as a person's life evolves. The end itself, we might say, is a moving target—a person's life imposes greater demands as it unfolds.

Because life requires action to fulfill our expanding needs, the failure to improve can be deadly. A glance at other organisms is again instructive. Plants' growth is good not simply for people's aesthetic enjoyment. Growth is good *for them* because it equips them to battle possible future adversity (e.g., a drought, a storm, or pests). The same is true of animals. Growth signifies hardiness, resilience, a fortified capacity for endurance. If an organism simply stagnated, it would have no reserves to call upon should immediate resources ever prove inadequate to meet some challenge.

The same holds for humans. We applaud children's progress from complete dependence on their parents to doing things on their own because by becoming increasingly self-sufficient, they are becoming better able to live. The person whose development is arrested at a certain point will be incapable of filling all his needs.

Individuals' psychological as well as physical needs broaden and mature. The people or books or music that engage a person at one time often give way to more refined tastes later. We frequently witness individuals' thresholds of satisfaction escalating; it typically takes more to satisfy a person in the present than it did in the past. The apartment or car that thrilled one as an undergraduate would probably not be satisfactory twenty years later. The activities or achievements that brought satisfaction or pride a few years ago often fail to stimulate the same response today. Because of further knowledge or abilities, it may be appropriate to attempt and demand more of oneself over time—as a therapist, cyclist, or friend, for example. The mode of survival acceptable at one stage of one's life is inadequate at a later stage.[24]

The point is, our needs expand in ways that demand an ascendant capacity to meet them. Psychological growth is necessary to fuel a person's sense of hope, purpose, and enjoyment, all of whose value we have already observed. When days seem nothing but filling the same old needs in the same old ways, the dank fog of drudgery rolls in. The charm of life is energized by the new—by the uncertainty, excitement, and purpose of fresh objectives and fresh challenges. Meeting these, however, calls on us to grow. The "lofty" character of flourishing, then, is necessary because survival requires it.

The larger point, again, is that flourishing is vital to survival. Earlier, I wrote that the only way to flourish is by acting in the manner that life itself demands. By the same token, the only way to live is by acting as flourishing demands. Life is a process of action, and the continuation of that process depends on a person's ongoing acquisition and exercise of the requisite resources and skills. Because life requires action and because life's demands grow, maintaining the status quo will not suffice. A person must keep moving forward in order to fill his changing and expanding needs.

Far from the identification of life with flourishing being a troublesome peculiarity of my account, note that recognizing life as flourishing actually reflects the way that we routinely think of life. A lame duck is alive, but that is not the model that a biologist would use to describe the requirements of a duck's survival. A child with spina bifida is alive, but that is not the model that a pediatrician would use to measure the health of another child. Similarly, in elaborating the demands of morality, the appropriate image of life to employ is of a healthy, thriving specimen.

Flourishing means "peak living," filling one's needs in optimal fashion. To say that life requires flourishing is another way of saying that we need to act as our nature requires and to act *well* in this respect. Our lives depend on it.

Suicide

Understanding that morality's end of life has a richer meaning than barren subsistence should help us understand why a moral code built on these foundations can allow suicide. This may seem surprising. A life-based code of values condemns actions that are detrimental to life. What could be more detrimental to life than extinguishing one's life? Yet suicide is not necessarily wrong. It is important to be clear about the precise grounds for suicide's status, however.

Some might suspect that if values' end were life itself, suicide would be prohibited; but if the end is flourishing, suicide can be allowed because a person might not like his particular quality of life. The "broader" aim of flourishing, in other words, affords room to reject some lives as insufficiently desirable. This is not my basis for recognizing the permissibility of suicide, however, since I have rejected the idea that life and flourishing pose distinct alternatives.

Rather, the reason that suicide can be morally allowed is that life is not intrinsically valuable. Life is not to be maintained at any cost, like it or not. A life-based code is not a sentence to live, saddling people with the obligation to endure, however painful the circumstances. Life is the standard of value and source of moral obligation *if* it is a person's goal, but it is up to the individual whether to embrace that goal. Nor is it the case that if life is a person's goal, it must interminably remain his goal nor that, once chosen, life may never be unchosen. The only alternative to abiding by a life-based code of values is death, but that is the real alternative that suicide offers.

Discussion of the character of flourishing brings into relief why a person might be likely to wish to live. Appreciating that the life that a person pursues is a good life makes more vivid why a person would be inclined to embrace life. Nonetheless, that choice remains pivotal; a person must choose life in order for morality's demands to carry any authority. Regardless of whether or why a person chooses to live, life holds no intrinsic value that commands a person's devotion. Thus, no such value could serve as the basis for a strict prohibition against extinguishing one's life.

If suicide is compatible with this life-based account of morality, this still leaves a further question: Can suicide ever be proper? Could it ever be rational or the right thing to do? The answer here is slightly more complicated.

Relative to an individual's values, suicide can be rational or irrational. It is or is not reasonable for a particular person to end his life under specific circumstances, given what his future will hold and its likely impact on the things that he cares most about—the reasons for which he embraces life in the first place. As we saw in chapter four, a person weighing the desirability of his life might commit any of the usual logical fallacies, drawing hasty conclusions, misconstruing causal relationships, omitting relevant facts, or exaggerating the significance of others, for example. He could miscalculate the probability of a political party's gaining power, misjudge how it would exercise that power, or underestimate the efficacy of opposing forces. A person might err in gauging the speed of a disease's progression, the severity of its effects, or the availability of corrective treatments. Thus, a decision to commit suicide could be irrational insofar as it is premised on false beliefs or faulty inferences about the attainability of one's ends.

By the same token, the decision to commit suicide could also be rational. Where the facts have been accurately identified and the inferences valid, the irreparable loss of what had made life worth living could provide reason for killing oneself. When life no longer offers the opportunity to attain the very things for which one lives, suicide would make sense. It is precisely because we do not live on bread alone—because our spiritual needs matter—that suicide can sometimes be the appropriate course despite a person's ability to satisfy his most basic physical needs.[25]

At a broader level, however, the decision of whether to embrace ends is not a question of rationality. Remember that the choice to live is prerational. Suicide is simply a more negative framing of that same basic choice. Whether a person finds life worth living is not the conclusion of a logical argument. After all the reckoning about likely future scenarios and effects on a person's ends has been completed, a person reaches a picture of what his life might be. The decision of whether to pursue this stands beyond the reach of reason. How a person arrived at his image of his future could be rational or irrational; whether he wants that future can be neither.

Thus, a decision to commit suicide could be "proper" in the narrow sense that it is logical *relative to* the person's ends. Since the ultimate end of whether to live or die is not itself subject to reason, however, suicide could never be "proper" in some more comprehensive or definitive manner.

FLOURISHING IS OBJECTIVE

Having explained what flourishing is and why flourishing is the proper end of value, we can turn to a final issue: flourishing's objectivity. If the moral code grounded in this account of value's foundations is to be objective, it is obviously important to retain objectivity in the end that morality aims to serve. Yet here again, conventional connotations are misleading. Flourishing is likely to strike some as too variable a phenomenon to be objective. Different things make different people happy. Who is to say which of these people are truly flourishing and which of them are deluded?

Given the account of flourishing presented thus far, however, it should not be difficult to appreciate that flourishing is an objective phenomenon. That a person thinks that he is flourishing is no guarantee that he is. Whether he is depends on the relationship of his activities to the promotion of his life. A few observations should secure this implication.

First, flourishing is contextual. What constitutes the flourishing of a given individual depends on his particular abilities, knowledge, and circumstances. A person flourishes to the extent that he does his best at leading his life in a life-furthering manner, but one person's best may be different from another person's best, and a person's best today may be different from his best several years hence (when his knowledge or abilities are further developed). A person can flourish before being as good as he may later become.

The major function of normative ethics is identification of broad metavalues that are necessary in anyone's life. Since the overall impact of the particular choices that a person confronts on the extended and wide-ranging goal of his life is usually not apparent, and because feelings are not a reliable guide to life-promoting action, a moral code reminds a person of the fundamentals that he must pursue in order to flourish. But this leaves individuals considerable discretion in choosing more specific values that are consonant with those metavalues.

Correspondingly, flourishing's objectivity does not straitjacket people into rigid uniformity. To say that flourishing is objective is not to say that

it is the same *in detail* for everyone. Flourishing allows considerable variation in the specific values that individuals pursue. Recall the discussion of
optional values in chapter four. Taste and choices may legitimately vary
regarding a range of things. A person may choose from myriad legitimate
professions to make his living; he may choose from myriad legitimate pastimes to spend his weekend. Life remains the benchmark for determining
whether a given activity is legitimate. As long as a person's activities further his life, these may all be avenues of flourishing.[26]

It is easy to be confused about the status of flourishing because flourishing may seem a more appealing purpose than survival. At least in their
colloquial connotations, flourishing seems a far more motivating aim. This
should not lure us into supposing that flourishing is morality's end simply
because we like it or want it, however (which *would* render flourishing,
and morality, a subjective matter of preference). Flourishing is not the
proper end of morality because it is more coveted or more popular than
survival. While flourishing permits many attractive optional values,
whether an activity contributes to flourishing is not determined by individual tastes. The activity of flourishing, no less than breathing, imposes objective requirements. A life well led (flourishing) is defined by the factual
requirements of life. What contributes to a person's flourishing is what
contributes to his survival.[27]

A second point: Resistance to flourishing's objectivity tends to treat the
feeling of flourishing as proof of the activity of flourishing. It assumes that
because people's feelings of flourishing are prompted by different sources,
flourishing itself must be a variable, subjective phenomenon. While I have
argued that how a person feels can be relevant to his factual flourishing,
influencing his propensity to take life-furthering actions, feelings are not
in fact the arbiter of value. This is because life does not rely fundamentally
on feelings; life depends on proper actions.

When we observe that different things make different people happy, we
are usually talking about the way people feel. Individuals certainly do take
pleasure in a variety of objects and enterprises. We must not equate positive feelings with the activity of authentic flourishing, however.

The activities that promote life constitute the core of flourishing and are
the basis for the agreeable feeling that is their usual (though not invariable)
companion. We can say what flourishing is because we can identify those
types of activities and characteristics that advance a person's existence.
Thus, the objectivity of flourishing is a direct outgrowth of the account of
values' function presented in chapter four. Nothing added in this chapter
to elaborate the meaning of values' end alters that account.

The chief explanation of flourishing's objectivity, however, is the most
simple: the unity of life and flourishing. Skepticism toward flourishing's

objectivity relies on a false separation of life from flourishing, treating the two as distinct phenomena. As I have already emphasized, however, flourishing does not consist of doing anything other than fulfilling life's requirements. Flourishing is a process that consists of *living* in a pro-life way. Since objective standards determine what is pro-life, objective standards determine what constitutes living in a pro-life way. This is the heart of flourishing's objectivity. Nature sets the terms for objective flourishing just as it sets the terms for surviving.

If life and flourishing were truly distinct phenomena, we would need a completely new basis for claiming that a person was flourishing and that flourishing was objective. But flourishing is nothing other than the healthy development of the same basic activities that life requires. Thus, it is grounded in the purpose of life and measured by the standard of life. Just as the requirements of survival are objective—we face definite facts about what will and will not promote life—flourishing is objective because we face definite facts about what constitutes living well.

(It might also be worth noting a less weighty, more polemical point. Dismissals of the objectivity of flourishing often ring disingenuous, for most of us *do* routinely presume objectivity in distinguishing people doing well from those doing poorly. Consider a small child. He is [and, we think, should be] carefully monitored by his parents and pediatrician to ensure that he is growing, functioning [e.g., breathing, digesting, hearing], and acquiring abilities [crawling, walking, talking, reading] in a certain pace and fashion. We measure a child's progress and call for special tests or treatment according to a definite conception of what it is for a child to be doing well. We apply similarly objective standards to adults, returning from a wedding, for example, and commenting on relatives not seen in several years. One cousin seems to be doing well on the grounds that she has "finally left that creep" or started her own business, while another does not seem to be doing so well, given that he continues to drift through dead-end jobs or has just filed for his third divorce.

The immediate issue is not the bases that might license such conclusions. The point is that these evaluations [frequently made without a second's hesitation] rely on an objective yardstick of flourishing. In making such distinctions—in treating certain episodes as reason to have the baby's hearing examined or to recommend that a friend go into therapy—we are presuming that we can judge whether people are, in fact, flourishing; that is, we are presupposing flourishing's objectivity.)

To reiterate the principal point, since life and flourishing are truly one and the same end—since flourishing is nothing other than living in a life-advancing manner well—whether a person is flourishing is an objective matter of fact.

CONCLUSION

Chapter four argued that life establishes the standard of value and provides the purpose and foundation for morality. Here, I have amplified the account of this foundation, explaining that life refers not simply to minimal physical subsistence but to the condition of flourishing.

The activity of flourishing refers to a person's meeting life's demands well. The feeling of flourishing is the correlative satisfaction that such activity typically generates. Flourishing is not a distinct objective from life that "ups the ante" for conclusions about values or morality. Rather, living *is* flourishing. To live is to live well because one must live well in order to sustain one's life. A person cannot survive, long range, without flourishing.

The activity of flourishing is simply the process of abiding by life-furthering principles, consistently taking life's requisite actions. Thus, its necessity in a life-based morality is transparent. The feeling of flourishing is also necessary, however, because a person's will is pivotal to his actions. Since human beings consciously choose their actions, a person must desire certain ends in order to act to attain those ends. He must experience the satisfaction of flourishing if he is to maintain the motivation to act to advance his life. Thus, sustaining life requires enhancing life; maintaining the appetite for life is as important to survival as the actions taken to satisfy that appetite.

The end of value is flourishing, then, because life requires it. Flourishing is another name for the condition of living in the only way that one can live, if one is to survive. Flourishing is thus at once the means to value and the end of value. It is the reason to be moral.

NOTES

1. Ayn Rand, "The Objectivist Ethics," *The Virtue of Selfishness* (New York: New American Library, 1964), 23, 24.

2. One can imagine certain deontologists objecting along these lines. To think that flourishing is not a sufficiently weighty purpose to warrant morality seems to retain the image of ethics as inherently obligatory, independently of individuals' aims.

3. The exact signs of well-being will vary for different types of plants, of course.

4. Recall the discussion of Dan and Larry in chapter four.

5. I borrow the golf analogy from J. L. Ackrill, cited in Richard Kraut, *Aristotle on the Human Good* (Princeton, N.J.: Princeton University Press, 1989), 211.

6. Some people are reluctant to admit the role of external goods because they confuse flourishing with virtue. A person controls his reactions to external events

and thus can respond more or less well. External fortune is not necessary for a person to be morally virtuous; his actions determine the virtue of his character. A person's actions cannot single-handedly determine whether he flourishes, however. (Even a plant cannot flourish without enough nutrients.) Virtue is important insofar as it is indispensable for flourishing, but it is not, by itself, enough.

7. Notice that luck provides no ground for expectations of further prosperity. Good fortune leaves a person equally susceptible to bad fortune; in itself, it makes a person no more fit to succeed in the future. When a person's actions are the engine of his prosperity, on the other hand, this furnishes reason to expect further gains. Self-generated success provides a basis for confidence that the person will act as he should and thereby further enhance his life.

We sometimes suspect that good fortune comes to worthy people—and there is a certain amount of truth in this. But this is because what superficially appears to be a matter of fortune often is not actually random chance but a result (or partial result) of a person's own past efforts. The opportunity that "fell into one's lap," for example, is a true opportunity only for those who have prepared themselves in ways that allow a certain turn of events to constitute an opportunity. The injury to the starting quarterback poses a great opportunity for the backup who has studied the playbook, kept his passing skills sharp, stayed in shape, and so on but not for the backup who has frittered practice time, ignored the playbook, and not prepared himself to play. To the extent that "good fortune" results from a person's own actions, it is obviously not truly fortune at work.

8. John Cooper, *Reason and Human Good in Aristotle* (Indianapolis: Hackett, 1986), 124; Julia Annas, *The Morality of Happiness* (New York: Oxford University Press, 1993), 36–37. See also Richard Kraut, *Aristotle on the Human Good* (Princeton, N.J.: Princeton University Press, 1989), 119, 253ff., 278, and Aristotle, *Nicomachean Ethics,* trans. W. D. Ross, in *Basic Works of Aristotle,* ed. Richard McKeon (New York: Random House, 1941) 1099a 31–b8; 1099b 18–30; 1140b 7.

Rand writes that only a man's own virtue can achieve happiness (Rand, *Atlas Shrugged* [New York: Signet, 1992], 939). Joel Feinberg believes that the highest good is self-fulfillment and that this cannot be a gift (Feinberg, *Harm to Self,* vol. 3 of *The Moral Limits of the Criminal Law* [New York: Oxford University Press, 1986], 42). I discuss the self-generated character of *eudaimonia* further in *Moral Rights and Political Freedom* (Lanham, Md.: Rowman & Littlefield, 1995), 67–69. What I meant by *eudaimonia* there is essentially what I mean by flourishing in this work.

9. A person might flourish in certain areas and not in others—for example, in his profession, in his marriage, in his golf game, or in his quest for greater self-understanding or self-control. To flourish in any area means that one is living as one should and prospering in that area. Flourishing in one area does not entail flourishing in all, however. A person is flourishing overall when he is flourishing in the most significant areas of his life, those carrying the greatest impact on his existence.

10. Rand, "The Objectivist Ethics," 29.

11. Rand, "The Objectivist Ethics," 28.

12. See James G. Lennox, "Health as an Objective Value," *Journal of Medicine and Philosophy* 20 (1995): 499–511.

13. I provide some similar arguments concerning *eudaimonia* in *Moral Rights and Political Freedom,* 43–48.

14. Bear in mind that the fact that a person seeks a certain quality of life does not convert his image of a good life into the standard of value. The point of the argument in chapter four was that we have no way to make sense of a "good" anything without life as the standard. Correspondingly, a "good life" is meaningless apart from that standard. What is good is that which furthers life. The sheer fact of seeking a certain quality of life does not render that end good.

15. See Rand, "The Objectivist Ethics," 31.

16. This list of kinds of needs is not meant as an exhaustive inventory. For a fuller discussion of types of needs, see Garrett Thomson, *Needs* (New York: Routledge and Kegan Paul, 1987).

17. Daniel J. Boorstin, *Cleopatra's Nose* (New York: Vintage Books, 1994), 165. In the same vein, it has been said that invention is the mother of necessity.

In a store recently, I overheard a woman announce that she needed some expensive French face cream. After buying the gift that I needed(?) for my mother's birthday, I passed another shop advertising items "for all your gift-giving needs." Were we all misusing the language?

18. The link between actions and feelings is not foolproof because of the complex roots of feelings. Feelings are based on a person's beliefs and values, including subconscious and potentially mistaken ones. A person might feel angry or anxious or happy or dejected without good grounds or fail to feel angry or anxious or happy or dejected when those feelings would be eminently justified. Thus, living well cannot guarantee that a person will feel happy or satisfied; no course of action could ever ensure particular feelings. This is why feelings cannot serve as the standard of value.

19. David Schmidtz, *Rational Choice and Moral Agency* (Princeton, N.J.: Princeton University Press, 1995), 68. His larger discussion of this falls primarily on pages 61 to 72.

We might also observe that people typically enjoy purposeful action. When a person takes steps toward an objective, even if he achieves no immediate payoffs or encouragement, he will often reap satisfaction from knowing that he is moving in the right direction. This may also be part of why satisfaction from the achievement of a long-term goal does not usually last for very long. People seem restless to undertake new purposes.

20. Schmidtz, *Rational Choice and Moral Agency,* 68, 72. I might word the point slightly differently to stress that a life of specific purposes *is* the survival that one seeks (i.e., survival is not truly a "further" end).

The role and value of purpose is a vast subject, and my remarks here only scratch the surface. I hope to pursue the subject in much greater depth in future work.

21. Schmidtz expresses a somewhat similar view, writing that the goal of survival usually evolves into part of "an increasingly complex hierarchy of ends." As people find things to live for, survival becomes more a means to these ends. "[T]he end of bare survival is too thin to sustain itself as a corpus of ends. Unless survival acquires instrumental value, our commitment to it will decay." The initial goal of survival falls away as a driving force, replaced by a set of ends comprising a com-

mitment to survive in a particular way (*Rational Choice and Moral Agency*, 73, 76–77).

While the spirit of this seems correct, I would deny that we could ever embrace survival without that objective's having some content, that is, without thereby embracing some specific ends. Schmidtz's statement seems to reflect the false dichotomy between quantity and quality of life. In fact, we *always* choose specific ends, even at the earliest embrace of life, although what those ends are is likely to change over time.

Note that the thirst for flourishing may hold for other forms of life. Acquaintances reported the following story. While friends of theirs were away on an extended vacation, Sean and Pam visited the friends' home a few times daily to feed and play with the travelers' dog. As the press of time got to them over the weeks, they gradually shrank playtime until they attempted to eliminate it altogether and simply feed the dog. The dog, however, refused to eat unless they first played with him. Despite Sean's and Pam's resistance to this ploy, the dog would not eat, so in desperation they succumbed to the bribe and played with him first. Even for dogs, perhaps, the unfun life is not worth living. (I am preserving my sources' anonymity to shield them from the dog owners' possible dismay.)

22. See, for example, Joel Feinberg, *Social Philosophy* (Englewood Cliffs, N.J.: Prentice Hall, 1973), 21, and Edith Hamilton, *The Greek Way* (New York: Random House, 1942), 35.

23. In old age, of course, some needs may diminish, as for sleep or calories.

24. We sometimes lament a friend's not having outgrown certain pastimes that entertained the both of us fifteen years ago, regarding stunted growth not simply as reflecting different taste from our own but as regrettable because it limits a person's life.

25. The moral permissibility of suicide should not be confused with its political permissibility. A person possesses the right to commit suicide on any grounds, rational or irrational. Since it is his life, he may dispose of his life however he wishes (as long as he respects others' rights). Rights concern what a person should be free to do rather than the overall moral propriety of an action. For a fuller explanation of this distinction, see *Moral Rights and Political Freedom*, 21–23.

26. A person's activities would have to further his life no less than available alternatives in order to be most conducive to his flourishing. Also, the possibility of variety in particular values is not unique to the quest for a desirable "quality" of life; recall that even many basic survival needs can be met in a variety of ways. A person can obtain protein by eating fish or poultry or beans, for example; a person can exercise by swimming, bike riding, or running on a treadmill.

27. I suspect that many people are wary of the idea of objective flourishing because the only defenses of objectivity they have encountered are arbitrary or groundless. Trotting out certain lives as "self-evidently" flourishing does nothing to logically demonstrate flourishing's objectivity. Such Intuitionistic appeals only give the notion of objective flourishing a bad name.

6

Principled Egoism:
The Only Way to Live

We have now established that life is the root and reward of value. The translation of this foundation into specific moral prescriptions is, as a project in normative rather than metaethics, a subject for another book. Nonetheless, the reason to identify values is to gain instruction for how to live. Thus, to understand fully the account of morality's foundation that I have presented, we should observe the general character of the normative guidance that it would dictate.

The implications of Rand's explanation of value are emphatically egoistic. The end of ethics is individual flourishing; a person should pursue values and follow moral guidance for the sake of his own happiness.

Defenses of egoism have been unusual in the history of ethics. They have also been unpopular.[1] Egoism is typically an object of derision that most ethicists dismiss as unworthy of serious consideration. Indeed, philosophers widely assume that morality, by definition, is contrary to self-interest. Philippa Foot, for example, writes that "a moral man must be ready to go against his interests." William Galston considers a theory moral insofar as "it appeals to individual motivations other than self-interest." Kurt Baier speaks for many in describing moralities as "systems of principles whose acceptance by everyone as overruling the dictates of self-interest is in the interest of everyone alike." While this overruling of interest is allegedly in a person's interest, Baier further contends that "[t]he best possible life for everyone is possible only by everyone's following the rules of morality, that is, rules which quite frequently may require individuals to make genuine sacrifices."[2]

These attitudes are undoubtedly familiar to most readers. What I wish to call attention to is the offhand manner in which dismissals of egoism are made, the *equation* of the moral with the selfless. Characterizations of morality as antithetical to self-interest are typically treated as self-evident, noted merely as preliminaries to discussion of the meaty controversies within moral philosophy. The prevalence of such anti-egoistic assumptions is all the more reason to address the egoistic implications of Rand's account.

My purpose in this chapter is to clarify morality's egoism more than to defend it. The heart of egoism's defense rests in the argument given in chapter four, and the remainder of a full defense would demand the complete specification of morality's normative code, along with arguments for each of its prescriptions—which is, again, beyond the scope of this project. Since principled egoism is the proper path for living and flourishing, however, it is important to dispel prevalent misconceptions that prevent a just appraisal of egoism.

To do this, I will proceed in three stages. First, I will explain why a life-based moral code must prescribe actions aimed at the agent's own well-being. (I will use "well-being" interchangeably with "survival," "life," and "flourishing.") Second, since the propriety of egoism depends largely on the nature of interest, I will elaborate on what self-interest is and demands, highlighting the role of spiritual values and the necessity of principled action to promote a person's survival. Finally, I will explain two of the more controversial implications of this account: the pursuit of interest is not a zero-sum game, and individuals' rational interests do not conflict. The upshot should be a clearer base for understanding the propriety of egoism.[3]

THE NECESSITY OF EGOISM

Ethical egoism is the thesis that a person should act to promote his own self-interest.[4] Rand holds that selfishness means "concern with one's own interest," and she advocates "rational selfishness"—the pursuit of "the values required for man's survival *qua* man."[5]

> Just as life is an end in itself, so every living human being is an end in himself, not the means to the ends or the welfare of others . . . man must live for his own sake, neither sacrificing himself to others nor sacrificing others to himself.[6]

The propriety of egoism is a direct outgrowth of the need for values that I traced in chapter four. What emerges from value's origin in life is a code of moral prescriptions designed to promote the agent's own flourishing.

Recall the central conclusions of that discussion. Life makes values possible and necessary. Distinctions between things as good or bad (and, derivatively, between actions as right or wrong) are intelligible only in relation to the quest for life. No purported value that does not benefit an organism's life would be a genuine value. The conditional nature of value—the fact that a person must seek his life in order to be subject to morality's authority—underscores that the point of living morally is to benefit oneself. The life that is pivotal is not life per se, the life of mankind or of all flora and fauna. Rather, value is contingent on the aim of serving one's own life. The fact that life makes values necessary means that the person who seeks his life must act morally in order to achieve values to sustain his life. That is the foundation for moral obligation.

As such, morality is egoistic through and through. Egoism concerns not merely one corner of a broader moral code that addresses many independent questions. Egoism is infused in morality from the outset, in the very nature of value and the logic of its pursuit. There is not one argument for morality and another argument for egoism.[7] Rather, the selfish purpose of securing one's life establishes the answers to all of morality's more particular questions concerning what constitute virtues and vices and how a person should act. What are the stakes of living morally? A person's own life. The reason to follow any specific moral principle is that doing so is in one's interest.

At root, the case for egoism *is* the case for morality. It rests in the fact that if a person does not nourish his existence, he will die. Human beings survive by acting *for their own benefit.* Egoism simply is the policy of living—of wanting to live and acting to live, of having that purpose and deliberately pursuing it.

The necessity of egoism is corroborated by several pockets of egoism in popular practices. For all the attacks on selfishness and lip service to serving others that we routinely encounter, we also find ample areas in which people consider it perfectly appropriate to seek one's own prosperity. "Charity begins at home" is a familiar justification for refusing to deny oneself for the benefit of others. "Don't be a doormat," friends counsel one another; "don't allow yourself to be taken advantage of"; "stand up for yourself." Few parents have qualms about doing all they can for the good of their children; a woman who devotes more energy to other people's children is condemned as a neglectful mother far more than she is praised as a moral ideal. Yet the devotion to one's children is selfish insofar as it is based on one's love for them. One cares for these children as opposed to countless others because of their value *to the parent;* they are among the values that significantly contribute to the parent's flourishing.[8]

For that matter, consider a child's own actions. When an infant thirstily sucks its mother's milk or begins to crawl or walk and we react with encouraging exclamations of "good boy!," what are we celebrating but the fact that these activities are good *for him*? That he is acquiring the ability to do things that will help him become strong and self-sufficient—in short, the sorts of things necessary for him to flourish?

We could extend this list at length. Self-defense is hardly considered a sin; no one complains that a victim who defends herself from a rapist is being selfish. While profit is widely vilified, most people consider it perfectly reasonable to seek a raise or lucrative employment benefits. Similarly, most people think it reasonable to "vote their pocketbooks," supporting political policies and candidates that serve their interests. Indeed, people most often object to self-interested politics when they suspect that others' pursuit of their interests will prove costly to *them*.

Business is the realm most often treated as an enclave from altruistic demands, governed by rules of its own that permit self-interest. This stands to reason. As the realm of production and trade, business places people's survival most directly at stake. If a person does not make a living—enabling him to eat, pay the rent, and so on—he will die. In business, the failure to be egoistic carries obvious and dramatic consequences.

My point in observing these instances of egoism is not that people are all truly egoists at heart. People's practices and attitudes toward egoism tend to be confused and inconsistent. I wish simply to indicate the considerable regions in which people do, unapologetically, endorse and engage in self-interested action. The reason for this is the fact that we must practice egoism. We "tolerate" egoism because we depend on egoism. Living requires that a person act to promote his own interest. A consistently practiced renunciation of self-interest would be utterly impossible. No one could survive on such a policy.

Assessments of egoism have usually been skewed by assumptions that egoism's structure is parallel to altruism's. Altruism is the view that moral goodness "consists in always denying oneself for the sake of others."[9] The contention that a person should sacrifice himself for others places primary significance on the identity of the beneficiary of a person's actions. The fact that altruism poses a "me or you" choice leads people to presume that egoism must also center around this choice. Thus, egoism is typically portrayed as an answer to the question: Who should a person place first, himself or others?

The history of moral philosophy testifies to the influence of altruism on our image of egoism. For the classical Greeks, "self-concern was not only considered acceptable, but the foundation of the moral life."[10] Yet many scholars resist interpreting the Greeks as egoists—in large part, I suspect, because their egoism was not elaborated in terms of a contest with altruism. Aristotle's egoism, for example, did not consist in an explicit renunciation of altruism as much as in counseling the achievement of personal excellence by developing qualities most conducive to the agent's *eudaimonia*. Indeed, egoism was not a keen issue in moral philosophy until the widespread preaching of service to others. According to Alasdair MacIntyre, the debate between egoism and altruism did not appear in full-fledged form until the seventeenth and eighteenth centuries.[11]

However entrenched it may be, the "me or you" alternative is a misleading framework for understanding egoism. The mandate for egoism emerges from considering the basis of all moral instruction, not merely the question of how to treat others. Egoism is the course prescribed in order for anyone to live. Everyone is an end in himself; no one is born under an obligation to place others' lives above his own. Each person should pursue his own flourishing, and no alternatives to self-interested action can achieve this end. While the injunction to pursue one's own interest carries the implication that one should not treat others' interests as weightier than one's own, one's relationship to others is not what egoism is *about*. Egoism would be equally imperative if a person were alone on a deserted island, for the fact that necessitates egoism is not other people but one's own nature. Whether a person is situated all by himself or in a city of millions, his life depends on life-promoting (i.e., self-interested) action.

Prudence

Many people might agree that life demands a quotient of self-interest yet deny that this renders ethics egoistic. Rather, they would maintain, looking after one's own well-being is a matter of prudence, a distinct province of human affairs. Morality is reserved for loftier concerns. William Frankena's claim that "morality must be contrasted with prudence" expresses the reigning contemporary view.[12]

This distinction is unwarranted, however. Accustomed as today's ethicists may be to distinguishing morality from prudence, historically, prudence and morality were inseparable. As one scholar has observed, "[O]pposition between prudence and virtue was unthinkable within the traditional conception."[13] For centuries, prudence was regarded as the virtue that perfected reasoning about human action. Many of the Greeks regarded prudence as a major moral and intellectual virtue. Epicurus, for example, held that "the greatest good is prudence," regarding prudence as "the source of all the virtues."[14] For Aristotle, prudence was primarily an intellectual virtue yet intimately linked with morality by being required for moral virtue. Indeed, in Aristotle's view, one could not be virtuous without being prudent, and one could not be prudent without being virtuous.[15]

Centuries later, Aquinas saw prudence as not merely one among the cardinal virtues; it was central. "The whole matter of moral virtue falls under the direction of prudence," Aquinas wrote. In contrast to the contemporary conception of prudence as clever self-seeking often practiced at the expense of morality, Aquinas considered prudence an integral part of the good.[16]

More important than the distance between contemporary and historical conceptions of prudence, of course, is the basis for these disparate conceptions and any possible basis for distinguishing morality from prudence. We have uncovered no ground for "shoulds" other than an individual's life, however. In chapters two and three, I demonstrated the failure of several traditional attempts to provide the grounds of moral obligation. In chapter four, we found that an organism's life is the only phenomenon that could explain value. No other foundation exists for value or derivative obligations. "Shoulds" make sense only in relation to the quest for life.[17]

Given this fact, we have no justification for excluding self-interest from the realm of morality. On the contrary, we must recognize that self-interest stands at the heart of morality. Every decision that a person makes potentially carries impact on his life. Correspondingly, a life-based ethics means that every decision carries potential moral significance.

All moral choices do not carry the same degree of significance; significance depends on the degree of actions' impact on a person's survival. Yet all decisions are potentially moral insofar as they affect the object of ethics. The important point is that prudence and morality are coextensive; both prescribe self-interested, life-furthering actions. The same actions that are prudent are moral, and the same actions that are moral are prudent.[18]

Recognizing the coincidence of morality and prudence helps to prevent ethics from being filled with anti-egoistic prescriptions. That is, relegating self-interest to the "subordinate" status of prudence would allow morality to command actions directly antithetical to an individual's self-interest. Any deference to such policies would impede the kind of action that is necessary for life. The recognition that morality itself is egoistic is thus crucial to the unequivocal endorsement of individuals' pursuit of their own lives.

The upshot is that the dismissal of self-interest as "mere prudence" is unwarranted. It suggests that morality is concerned with weightier matters than a person's life. Since value arises from the struggle for life, however, there are no weightier matters.

Thus far, then, we have seen that egoism is the logical implication of chapter four's argument that life requires values. If value and all derivative "shoulds" are intelligible only in light of the purpose of achieving one's life and if egoism is the path to that end, then egoism is not merely permissible—it is indispensable. Egoism is proper because it is the only way to live.

WHAT SELF-INTEREST IS AND DEMANDS

One of the greatest obstacles to acceptance of egoism rests in misconceptions concerning the nature of self-interest. Correcting these and fleshing out a proper image of self-interest thus go a long way toward demonstrating the logic of egoism.[19]

The most common grounds of resistance to egoism are the beliefs that egoism is hedonistic, materialistic, or subjective.[20] The egoism that emerges from Rand's account of the basis of morality, however, has none of these characteristics. Interest must be gauged rationally rather than emotionally. More fundamentally, interest must be measured by the same standard as all value: life. Doing so disentangles egoism from the unsavory characteristics with which it is often associated.

We have previously seen that life, as the purpose and standard of morality, means long-term survival, the comprehensive condition of flourishing. Correspondingly, something is valuable to a person, or in his interest, insofar as it contributes to this end. This means that interest is itself a long-range, full-compass phenomenon. Judgments of interest pertain to the whole of a person's life. Interest does not designate any little thing that feels good or seems attractive to a person. Something must be life sustaining in order to be in a person's interest. What is life sustaining cannot be gauged by isolating a particular development from its full impact on a person's life, however. To ignore that larger impact is to ignore the fact that life is the standard of value.

The claim that something is in a person's interest marks a sophisticated judgment, guided by the standard of life, which takes into account all the person's life-promoting ends and all the ways in which the event in question affects those ends. "Interest" refers not to any momentary gratification or isolated segment of a person's experience but to the long-term, all-things-considered ramifications that an event carries on a person's ongoing flourishing.

Contrary to common assumptions, then, a person's interest is reducible neither to the satisfaction of his desires nor to his material condition. These, alone, offer too narrow a basis for conclusions about a thing's impact on a person's well-being. Nor does self-interest, in its most basic requirements, vary for different individuals. Rather, what is in a person's interest is what advances his life. We have no basis justifying the claim that anything is in a person's interest other than that thing's net impact on the person's survival. This central end offers the only objective yardstick by which to measure interest.

In order to completely dispose of damaging misconceptions of self-interest, I particularly wish to emphasize two of its features that are rarely recognized: self-interest's spiritual dimension and self-interest's rigorous demands.

Self-Interest's Spiritual Dimension

As we saw in the last chapter, a person has spiritual as well as material needs. Nonmaterial goods, such as an inspiring friend, a rational philosophy, intelligence, hope, self-respect, or self-confidence, can all significantly contribute to an individual's survival. Such things can play a constructive role in a person's enjoyment of life, will to live, and ability to act as life requires.

Because a human life is a many-faceted enterprise, self-interest encompasses anything capable of affecting that enterprise's various constituent values. The point here is that interest refers to a wider range of goods than one's material condition. Since a person is more than a body, physical fitness and material resources are not the whole of well-being. The condition of a person's consciousness is a crucial component of his overall welfare. Spiritual well-being is a function of all those aspects of consciousness capable of affecting a person's acting in life-promoting ways. It thus encompasses a person's intellectual and emotional states and activities. In more colloquial terms, spiritual well-being encompasses what and how a person thinks as well as what and how a person feels.

We saw in the discussion of flourishing that psychological well-being affects a person's broader well-being. Bread alone cannot sustain us. People's desires for spiritual ends—the desire for a sense of efficacy or of purpose or for knowledge or camaraderie, for example—are not frivolous cravings for inconsequential luxuries. Neglect of such desires brings destructive repercussions. (Recall the deleterious effects of depression.) A person's self-interest is spiritual as well as material because a person's state of mind matters to his survival.

The reason that a person's spiritual condition matters is that we rely on the mind to live. Life depends on taking actions that promote one's life. What identifies the appropriate actions is a person's rational faculty. A person must exercise his mind both to choose life-furthering ends and to determine how best to achieve those ends.

Survival depends, in part, on the sharpness of a person's thinking skills. It depends on his ability to focus, concentrate, accurately identify relevant phenomena, and trace logical relationships. How a person thinks is crucial to the validity of his conclusions and the actions that he takes on the basis of those conclusions. A person's mental habits directly influence his flourishing. How vividly does a person tie abstract concepts to their referents in reality? When questions cloud a person's grasp of some new item of information, does he persevere in addressing those questions, or does he push them aside without attempting to resolve them? Does chronic self-doubt prompt him to substitute others' judgment for his own? These sorts of tendencies will affect the quality of his thinking and the prudence of his action.

The point is, rationality is critical to the maintenance of any individual's life.[21] Consequently, the condition of a person's rational capacity is of tremendous selfish value.[22] Insofar as a person's mind is his tool of survival, it is in his interest to keep that instrument in peak working condition.

The spiritual aspect of interest does not refer exclusively to a person's rational acumen, however. A person's basic outlook on life also affects his well-being. His answers to certain fundamental questions are pivotal to the sorts of goals that he will pursue and the actions that he will take. Whether a person's characteristic outlook is optimistic or pessimistic, for example, or whether he is by and large contented or dissatisfied, at peace or uneasy, all influence his actions. Does he believe that effort is likely to pay off and that projects can succeed, or does he believe that ambitions are doomed to fail? Is fear or confidence his daily companion? Does he view life as worthwhile, or as "one damned thing after another"?

A further element of a person's spiritual condition is his evaluation of himself. Does a person consider himself basically fit or unfit to attain happiness? Is he the sort who chronically breaks New Year's resolutions such that he regards himself as full of empty promises? Or has he earned his own trust and confidence? Such basic attitudes about one's prospects and worthiness tangibly affect a person's will to live, the goals that he pursues, and the degree of commitment that he exerts in seeking those goals—all of which, again, exert an impact on a person's overall flourishing.

While mental aptitudes and attitudes are vital to a person's physical survival, the mind is valuable not strictly as a means to material ends, as if those were the only truly worthy ends. Human beings are integrated organisms whose lives are both physical and psychological; neither dimension is more real or naturally superior to the other. (Remember that a person must choose to live in order for his existence to generate values.) A person's spiritual condition is also critical to his interest because it affects his enjoyment of life. Consciousness affords many of life's most sublime satisfactions. For many people, it is not exclusively physical pleasures—the prospect of another bowl of cereal or a warm fire (or even of fine champagne or terrific sex)—that animate the will to live. It is the drive to create, to understand, to solve challenging problems, to experience beauty, love, passion—in short, to engage and savor intellectually and emotionally.

Particular motivations and pleasures obviously vary among different individuals. The point is simply that some of a person's deepest satisfactions and most life-enhancing experiences may be nonmaterial. We do not apply our intellects simply to enable ourselves to eat and dress. We also eat and dress to enable ourselves to pursue activities of consciousness.[23] Material and spiritual goods are mutually reinforcing: achieving material values can aid spiritual well-being just as achieving spiritual values can aid material well-being. Neither is simply a means to the other.

All of this testifies to the spiritual dimension of self-interest. Numerous nonmaterial goods—for example, friends, music, education, pride, purpose, or enjoying one's work—can be in a person's interest. Such things are not bread or clothes or roofs or medicine; they are not even jobs through which a person earns the money to obtain bread or clothes or roofs or medicine. But they enhance a person's life by fostering the thirst for life and/or by strengthening his ability to satisfy that thirst. The realization that interest has a spiritual dimension significantly expands our understanding of egoism, indicating that the range of things that can be in one's interest and of actions that can be self-interested is much wider than is usually supposed. Correspondingly, it suggests ways in which certain actions that one might naturally assume are self-interested actually are not because they weaken one's position vis-à-vis spiritual values.

Since flourishing refers to more than physical survival, then, we should be able to appreciate that a person's interest encompasses more than the materialistic measure of the clothes in his closet, the food on his table, or the cost of the gifts under his Christmas tree.

Self-Interest's Demands

The second important feature of egoism that is rarely appreciated is the fact that egoism can be practiced only by a certain kind of person. Egoism is concerned not only with what a person does for himself; it also demands something *from* the self. Self-interest requires cultivation of a disciplined, virtuous character.

In the popular imagination, egoism represents the slackening, if not the complete abandonment, of all moral rigors. Egoism is seen as the easy way out, authorizing individuals to do whatever they feel like doing. The egoist does not fulfill responsibilities if he is not in the mood; the egoist does not tell the truth if it does not suit his purposes. People frequently picture the egoist as an insatiable consumer, a sort of Ms. PacMan gobbling up goods, raiding his surroundings for whatever strikes his fancy. Thus, egoism seems less an alternative moral code than a rejection of morality altogether. (Its frequent confusion with hedonism and subjectivism no doubt contributes to this.)

In fact, this portrait is completely erroneous. It bears no resemblance to the egoism entailed by the metaethics that I have defended. And at this stage, it should not be difficult to see why such policies would not be in a person's interest. Consider the sorts of things required in order for a person to accomplish a long-term goal, such as making a team, completing a degree, or running a profitable business. Success at these endeavors demands such qualities as initiative, industry, foresight, and perseverance. Successfully advancing one's interest (which is largely composed of such projects) similarly demands these and other virtues. As such, it imposes definite requirements.

The image of egoism as indulgent consumption belies the fact that a person's life is not sustained without effort. Consumption per se is not the measure of a person's interest because human beings do not live simply by consuming. Consumption depends on production. Human beings must produce life-promoting values; we must *make* value. Consequently, the means of doing that become vital to advancing one's interests. An egoist must cultivate qualities that generate the values that his survival depends on. Since an egoist is committed to his own life, he must strive to fulfill all its requirements, every kind and level of needs. A selfish person must thus be a source of values as much as a consumer of values.

Central among life's requirements is the fact that the selfish person must be rational. To achieve his flourishing, he must adopt ends that are life enhancing, attainable, and mutually compatible. He must adopt values and make choices by considering such questions as, How could I obtain this end? Do I possess the requisite skills or knowledge? Does this end hinge on things beyond my control? Would pursuing it interfere with any of my other ends? Are those ends more or less important? Could I try alternative, less costly routes to any of these?

In addition, of course, a person must determine whether an alleged value actually possesses the properties ascribed to it. Will achieving it truly advance the end it is expected to and not impede any more important aspect of the person's life? In short, the egoist's actions must be based on a reflective overview of his purposes and priorities and on a rational assessment of how particular actions would affect that hierarchy of ends.

A corollary requirement is that the egoist must be realistic—about his goals, his abilities, as well as the conditions necessary to achieve his ends. The flourishing person does not lightly retreat from his objectives, but nor does he pursue unattainable dreams. Rather, he takes concrete steps to enable himself to realize sometimes difficult (but reachable) goals. He does not permit his wishes concerning his needs to override the evidence of what his needs are and of what is required to fulfill them.

Still another requirement of egoism is discipline. Self-interest does not permit erratic fluctuations in a person's course, frequent reversals prompted by fleeting fears, moods, or external pressures. The wisely self-interested person refuses to allow passing inclinations to displace his logical strategy for pursuing carefully chosen ends.

My point is not that the egoist must remain aloof, failing to feel his emotions or to commit himself fully to his ends. On the contrary, I think that the healthy egoist will be intensely emotionally engaged, but that is a more psychological hypothesis than I should pursue here. The self-interested person is not *ruled* by his emotions, however. He has a mature appreciation of what his self-interest comprises and does not mistake the inclinations experienced on any isolated occasion for his overall flourishing. Clarity about his end and dedication to its achievement fortify his disposition to properly self-interested action.

Articulation of specific moral virtues would convey considerably more detail of what an egoistic character demands.[24] The point for present purposes is simply that advancing one's interest demands a great deal of a person. Something is in a person's interest when it contributes a net gain to that person's life. Since this end has many aspects, we must be sensitive to the numerous respects in which a given action might advance or detract from a person's interest. It is only in the framework established by that overarching aim, however, that we can identify what furthers a person's interest. The widespread assumption that egoism is easy relies on a simplistic, shallow understanding of what self-interest is.

The Egoist Needs Principles

One aspect of egoism's demands warrants special attention. The rational egoist must abide by principles. While the full rationale for principles is a complex, largely epistemological subject that I can only hint at here, even a brief sketch should considerably illuminate the character of life-based egoism.

The need for principles is a direct outgrowth of the nature of interest. Since the yardstick of interest, a person's life, is an intricate, multifaceted phenomenon that encompasses the entirety of a person's experience, we have no reason to expect the most effective means to its achievement to be transparent on every decision-making occasion. Life's sheer extension across time leaves it susceptible to many variables' effects. The longer the period between the start and finish of a project, the greater the number of intervening factors capable of influencing its success. Consider the numerous factors that enter into a single long-term project, such as financial independence. All sorts of expenditures—on housing, meals, clothes, health, studies, transportation, entertainment—must be meticulously managed to achieve one's ultimate goals. Or consider the Olympic aspirant who must subscribe to a prolonged regimen of training, exercise, and diet, repeatedly resisting counterproductive temptations.

Ambitious as these goals may be, they are far more modest than the pursuit of one's life itself. For life encompasses all such projects. Yet even these comparatively delimited goals demand considerable forethought and planning. A goal that seems to belong in one department of life has a natural tendency to seep into others. What seemed an athletic endeavor easily influences a person's leisure time, personal relationships, and finances, for instance.[25] Extrapolating to a person's entire life, including all the aims splashed across every day of it, we can see that a skillful orchestration of activities is essential if a person is to flourish. A person needs a systematic overview of his primary goal, of the status and relationships among subordinate goals, as well as of the best paths for attaining these ends.

To know how specific actions are likely to affect his goals, a person needs principles. Since a person's actions can carry many effects and since a person's ends can be affected by all sorts of events, rational decisions designed to promote one's interest demand that a tremendous volume of information be evaluated. If, each time he faced a decision, a person tried to recall every relevant fact and began, then and there, searching for their implications concerning how he should act, his calculations would short-circuit from the cognitive overload. Human beings cannot juggle that much data at once.[26]

Volume is not the only factor creating the need for principles' guidance. Navigating such information to identify the repercussions of various alternatives and reach correct conclusions about the best course of action often requires painstaking effort—recalling all of past experience's relevant lessons, identifying exactly what *is* relevant, attending to details, appreciating fine distinctions, and so on. Assessing actions' impact on all the ends that compose a person's interest is hard work.

Nonetheless, a person needs to take all relevant information into account if he is to reach the most life-promoting decisions. Ignoring an action's likely impact on the full gamut of his ends would recklessly endanger those ends. Thus, we need intellectual tools that sift through the abundance of information to help us identify the optimal life-furthering course.

In short, the complexity of a person's interest alongside the limits of his cognitive capacities create the need for guidance in the form of principles. Moral principles are fundamental prescriptive generalizations, such as the direction to be honest, or just, or courageous. These are inductive conclusions identifying the best means of sustaining and enhancing one's life. Principles are built by combing information, identifying relevant facts, and pinpointing their lessons for the propriety of different types of action. Principles rely on a long-range, wide-range perspective. As such, principles deliver the most fully informed and rationally considered guidance possible. The propriety of this form of guidance is based on recognition that a person cannot tell what is best for his life purely by superficial, case-by-case appearances.

It is crucial to recognize that principles' authority is rooted entirely in their practicality. Principles are not inherently compelling, reflecting an implicit belief in intrinsic value or devotion to deontological duties. Adherence to principles is not a penance that must be suffered at a cost to one's interest. On the contrary, adherence to principle is the most effective course for promoting one's interest since principles' instruction is based on the comprehensive assessment of myriad factors affecting one's flourishing. Moral principles are practical insofar as they report and prescribe the most effective means of advancing one's life.

To illustrate, consider the principle of honesty. My purpose here is not to prove that honesty is a proper moral principle (which would require a far more thorough examination) but to indicate the general manner in which adherence to principles serves a person's interest.[27]

The principle of honesty instructs us to be truthful in portraying the world. As Leonard Peikoff writes, honesty is the refusal to fake reality.[28] This injunction applies across all areas of life, for example, with one's friends, family, lovers, boss, clients, colleagues, therapist, and oneself; at work, in play, and in regard to one's finances, drinking habits, health, knowledge, emotions, desires, motivations, and philosophical premises. It is based on the recognition that misrepresenting reality does not change reality. Deceiving others or oneself does not alter the misrepresented facts. Consequently, it does not strengthen a person's ability to deal with those facts in the pursuit of his life.

The temptation to deceive may at times be intense (in order to enjoy an immediate pleasure and tune out its destructive repercussions, for instance, or to spare another person's feelings, or to "justify" a financial extravagance). The principle of honesty, however, serves as a reminder that deception cannot succeed. Dishonesty does not actually advance a person's survival. Dishonesty is impractical because misrepresenting reality does not transform reality. One is not, by mouthing deceptive words, catapulted into the imaginary world projected by one's lie, a make-believe realm in which the misrepresented fact does not obtain. Lying about what you can afford, for example, does not propel you into an alternate universe in which you can afford the car that you cannot. Dishonesty leaves the facts that were denied as real as ever—the bill to be paid, pounds to be lost, marital tensions to be resolved. In fact, dishonesty only worsens one's situation in at least a few significant respects.

First, dishonesty postpones addressing the underlying facts, however distasteful, that led a person to lie. It deters him from taking steps to try to change certain facts or to alleviate a problem (e.g., seeking a higher-paying job or taking measures to repair his marriage). Often, the longer one neglects the problems one denies, the more entrenched and more difficult to correct they become. (Obviously, the more critical the facts are to one's survival, the more damaging the deception will be. Lying to oneself about ominous symptoms of illness, for example, can result in a more threatening illness that honesty and early treatment might have prevented.)

Second, by lying, a person creates a new problem: the lie, which will have to be maintained or explained. Either is bound to prove costly. Maintaining a cover-up is a taxing, never-ending enterprise, achievable only through the most vigilant attentiveness. This naturally drains energy that might be more constructively directed to other activities. If the lie is disclosed, for whatever reasons, the revelation of this breach of trust may inflict permanent damage on what had been valuable relationships. The deceived individuals may well be hurt, angered, or resentful of the attitude toward them that the duplicity suggests.

Third, lying is likely to carry destructive effects on the liar's own psyche and ability to be honest in the future. Engaging in dishonesty encourages a habit of deceit, weakening one's inclination to truthfulness and nurturing an inclination to faking things. Since misrepresentation does not change facts, however, this is a self-destructive course; honesty remains the policy necessary for successful action in life. Further, as long as a liar tries to conceal his lie, he must engage in whatever further deceptions this requires. Thus, he must give his mind contradictory standing orders: seek the truth; conceal the truth. This schizophrenic prescription will hardly incline him toward more consistently honest action or nourish a healthy self-respect. The attempt to obey conflicting instructions is a recipe for self-loathing. Every action that a person takes, honest or dishonest, is ripe for criticism insofar as it violates one of the two instructions that he is allegedly trying to uphold.

What all of this indicates is that the propriety of honesty is grounded in its practical, pro-life benefits. Faking facts does not change facts and deters a person from addressing those facts in ways that could further his survival. Engaging in make-believe is a self-defeating course. The same holds for all well-founded moral principles. Properly, such principles are identified by the standard of life and intended to assist a person's drive for life—which makes adherence to those principles completely egoistic.[29]

The Status of Ill-Begotten Gains

The proposal that an egoist should adhere to principles chafes against customary expectations. If the egoist seeks his own best interest above all, shouldn't he take advantage of opportunities to violate principles whenever they present themselves? Wouldn't a person be better off abiding by principles sometimes but cheating when he can get away with it? (This sort of question is familiar from consideration of Contractarianism, in which individuals' motivation is also allegedly self-interest.)

This reasoning rests on significant confusions, however. Understanding these should help us appreciate that "ill-begotten" gains—goods acquired through violation of moral principles—are not truly gains.

First of all, the supposition that something obtained by circumventing life-promoting principles could serve a person's interest ignores the interlocking layers of a person's life and the sophisticated evaluation that a verdict about interest represents. Something is in a person's interest only if it offers a net benefit to the person's life. Since a person's life is not reducible to any isolated element of his condition, we cannot fasten on such elements to draw valid conclusions about what truly serves a person's interest. Focusing exclusively on the "reward" that a moral shortcut seems to offer (such as money, power, or prestige) neglects an action's full repercussions on a person's life.

Further, remember that value is relational. A thing's value cannot be appraised independently of its role in a given individual's life. The value of money, for example, does not inhere in a fifty-dollar bill. Whether a particular object is in a person's interest depends on the role that it plays in that individual's life. Its role, in turn, depends in part on how he obtained it. The money obtained by fraud does not carry the value of money obtained by productive work; the victory secured by cheating does not carry the value of the victory won by skill.

Productive work and skill are valuable not only for the immediate money or victory they can deliver but also because they nourish a person's broader, ongoing ability to act in the manner appropriate for all value seeking. In any judgment of a person's interest, it is imperative to employ the proper standard of value: long-term survival. Although a person may get what he wants through a particular incident of cheating or fraud, what a person wants is not the objective measure of what is good for him. Short-range gratification is not the test of long-range flourishing.

A person's means of promoting his life are an important determinant of whether a given event truly serves his interest. One's means sometimes carry effects beyond the immediate or obvious. Thus, it is important to ascertain that the means of obtaining an apparent benefit do not inflict countervailing damage. Because a person has ongoing needs, his capacity to fulfill needs is as important (if not more important) than their fulfillment on any one occasion. Given the ongoing need for food, for instance, a person must be concerned both with obtaining food for tonight's dinner and with his ability to secure future meals. Given the ongoing need for rational decision making, a person must be alert to activities' potential impact on that capacity. In short, we cannot accept apparent gains at face value without ensuring that the sources of such gains are themselves conducive to one's survival.

Everyday examples reflect commonplace recognition of this point. Remedies that only treat an illness's symptoms do not alleviate our concern for the friend who is suffering from those symptoms. While we welcome news that his symptoms have subsided, that is not nearly as welcome as the diagnosis that their source was benign. As long as the underlying causes remain unknown or untreated, we cannot be sure that our friend is truly better off. (Indeed, if the alleviation of his symptoms discourages him from further investigating their cause and something *is* seriously amiss, he may be worse off by being lulled into ignoring the problem.)

Similarly, enthusiasm over a friend's dramatic weight loss is usually dimmed on hearing that he accomplished it through a liquid protein diet. This news is deflating because this is not the healthiest course and because that artificial a regimen is unlikely to be sustained beyond a few months. This sort of quick-fix does not address the underlying causes of his weight problem, so the gains (or, in this case, loss) do not necessarily mark a genuine enhancement of his well-being.

It is not difficult to recognize that shortcuts are self-defeating when an apparent gain weakens a person's long-term fitness. That is precisely what occurs with ill-begotten gains. Ill-begotten gains are not gains because, by the method of their acquisition, they weaken a person's means of furthering his life. My point is not that the gain is outweighed by a greater loss. The point is that the apparent gain is not genuine because it does not enhance the person's long-term survival—and *that* is the standard of value and interest.

My thesis about ill-begotten gains may be best illustrated by considering a couple of cases in which the violation of principles is widely thought to be in the agent's interest. In fact, when a person's principle is rational and life promoting, this assumption cannot withstand scrutiny.

First, consider the person who misrepresents his qualifications in order to obtain a job (knowing that his actual qualifications would be inadequate). Assume that this person (call him Bill) fools the employer and is hired as a structural engineer. Since Bill landed the position he sought, isn't he better off? Hasn't he advanced his life? Before we can say, we need to think through what he is in for.

Since Bill does not have the experience or expertise necessary to perform the work, he is not likely to be very good at it. Indeed, he may have to struggle mightily to be able to satisfy the job's minimal demands. To the extent that he is able to meet some of its demands, they will require far more effort than they would from a truly qualified engineer. This overly taxing work will leave him less time and energy to devote to other parts of his job, so even if he fulfills some of the job's demands, the effort required will leave him ill-equipped to fulfill all of them. The continual strain of this too-demanding work will exact a toll on Bill's performance as well as on his enjoyment of the job—on the satisfaction and sense of competence that he reaps from it.[30]

Moreover, the strain is unlikely to be lost on Bill's bosses. His employers' dissatisfaction with Bill's struggle to complete his work will naturally affect their treatment of Bill—coloring everything from how cordial office life is to Bill's chances for plum assignments, greater responsibility, raises, or advancement. Indeed, his subpar performance makes him vulnerable to replacement. Far from landing him in a desirable position, Bill's deception sets him up for twin failures: frustrating himself and alienating his superiors.

Imagine that on a couple of early assignments, through some fluke, Bill does perform as desired and is given greater responsibilities as a result. This would only intensify the pressure on him. Somewhere along the line, he will face work that he cannot do (but that he can reasonably be expected to do, given the experience that he claimed to have). Saying that he has certain qualifications does not give him those qualifications or their substantive value: the genuine ability to perform the relevant work. Thus, the lie is bound to catch up with him. Even if Bill does "get away with it" for a while, reality has not yielded to his misrepresentation of the facts. Because he does not have the abilities that he claims to, he cannot achieve the goals or reap the satisfaction from the work that a person who actually had those abilities could. (Bill also risks committing a major blunder, as in a faulty design, with catastrophic consequences.)

In addition to these problems emanating directly from his deficient qualifications, Bill must worry about his deception being discovered. Will the company check on the accuracy of his resume? Particularly since his job performance fails to meet expectations, suspicions may be aroused, increasing the likelihood that employers will inquire to see whether he is what he claimed to be. Bill will realize that if his employers are unhappy with his work, they would feel more secure in dismissing him if they caught him in a lie. So he will naturally worry: "Even though they haven't checked up on me yet, they did ask for references and phone numbers. . . ."

To maintain his pretense, Bill must remain constantly on guard, poised to lie when fellow workers inquire about his background. He must be careful even in making claims about his personal life since where he has lived, gone to school, and the like are naturally related to his professional experience. As a result, Bill cannot relax with fellow workers; he cannot develop worthwhile friendships built on authentic, unedited responses. Bill can maintain only distant relations with these people, filtered through the constant monitoring of his every move's impact on preserving the fraud. Colleagues will regard him as stiff, aloof, or just plain weird. As such, he is also unlikely to win their professional confidence (which might have helped him gain more of the work-related knowledge that he lacks). Bill will also have to remain wary of people outside the company since he can never be sure who might know someone at the office and where a slip-up might come back to trap him. In short, no realm of his life is exempt from the continual calculation: If I say this, what effect will it have on the charade? Might it in any way blow my cover?

Bill's life must thus be organized in a defensive crouch against what other people might discover. Others become enemies because of their potential power to expose his fraud. If he had a job for which he were qualified and that he obtained without fraud, of course, his fate would depend on his job performance. Having lied to secure a goal, however, Bill's "success" rests at the mercy of anyone who discovers his deceit. It will be extremely difficult to keep his lie hidden indefinitely since it is natural for co-workers to talk to people doing similar work at other companies and to mention the new guy who supposedly formerly worked with them.

Thus we can ask, Even for the time that the lie is undetected, however brief or extended, what does Bill gain? A tense, anxious existence: He is sweating to do the work that he is not truly capable of and sweating to keep the lid on the lie. Bill is not reaping satisfaction from the work that he is ill-equipped to do; he is not promoting his career (since his work is not impressing anyone); and he is risking his career's complete implosion, should the fraud be discovered.

Finally, consider why Bill might have wanted this job in the first place. If he sought the job as a stepping-stone to other positions, deceit is a foolish strategy. Since he is not equipped to do the job, his superiors are unlikely to promote him or recommend him to others, and he is depriving himself of the opportunity to learn the necessary skills in a suitable environment. If he sought the position to impress other people, his precarious grip on it creates the prospect of his losing it—anything but impressive. (It is a further question what impressing others would give him, of course.) If Bill thought that he would enjoy the work, that is hardly the result, given that he is unable to competently complete it and is consumed by the need to preserve his pretense. Being in over one's head—particularly when it is due to one's own deception—is hardly a pleasant position.

In brief, on just a little reflection, we can see that this violation of the principle of honesty does not advance Bill's interest. Only a most superficial snapshot—detaching the fact that he got the job he wanted from whether it was rational to want it, from how he got it, and from the role that it plays in the larger scheme of life-promoting values—could tempt one to conclude otherwise. Bill would be better off honestly starting with a lower-level job, acquiring the appropriate training and experience, and earning his way to higher positions. The end run around principle is not a shortcut to a truly desirable result.

Now imagine a different sort of case, one in which a person's devotion to principle is portrayed as contrary to his interest. Consider the diplomat who resigns because he refuses to carry out a policy that he deems unjust.

Frequently, people applaud such action as moral but imprudent. They hail it as an admirable display of selflessness. While such an action could be motivated by selflessness, we can easily imagine circumstances in which the diplomat's action is thoroughly selfish.

Consider why a diplomat would take such action. Presumably, the conduct of just policies is more important to him than retaining his position. He refuses to view the execution of the unjust policy in isolation from his primary goal, namely, to practice a certain kind of diplomacy, that which is faithful to certain ideals. If he accepted the compromised course, however, he would not be practicing diplomacy as he sought. He would be changing his goal, which was to make his living as a diplomat *dedicated to certain principles.*

The diplomat's attitude seems to be that if he cannot make his living practicing that type of diplomacy, he will move on to something else. What he will not do is pretend that by enacting policies that he abhors, he would be gaining the value that he originally sought. By following that course, he would retain his position in name only. This was not what he was after.

Notice, also, what an impoverished view of self-interest the selfless interpretation of the diplomat's action stands on. Is it prudent to squander one's self-respect? Or the values for which one joined the diplomatic corps in the first place? If a man keeps his job at the expense of the work's any longer serving the purpose for which it was originally valued, what would he gain? He would continue to draw a salary, but doubtless he might find other means of doing that if that were the paramount goal.

Observe that the exclusion of spiritual values helps underwrite this selfless interpretation of the diplomat's action. If self-interest must mean immediate material interests, the selfishness of the diplomat's devotion to other values is mysterious.

It is important to recognize that, in fact, the diplomat is not choosing *between* practicality and principles. The rationale behind his action is not "there's something higher, more important than my values that is at stake here." Rather, he recognizes that his self-interest consists of more than a job today. He is pursuing what will truly best advance his flourishing.

To be selfish requires being true to oneself. To be true to oneself requires honoring one's values. It demands fidelity in action to one's rational hierarchy of values. If the diplomat were to acquiesce, he would be betraying his considered priorities.

When a person refuses a job because he is looking after his long-term well-being or more significant aspects of his well-being, then, he is not being selfless. He is not placing virtue above self-interest. He is simply pursuing an enlightened, mature conception of what his self-interest consists in.

What both of these examples illustrate is that "ill-begotten gains" are not truly gains. Fidelity to life-promoting principle is selfish. Deviation from correct principles works against a person's interest.

To determine whether to sell out and violate principles, the egoist must ascertain, What will it buy me? What can I gain that way? The answer is, not a genuine enhancement of one's interest. Selling out is a bad trade; it means surrendering a higher value for a lesser one (e.g., Bill's sabotaging his chances for professional success by rushing to satisfy the immediate desire for a particular job or the diplomat's jettisoning the values for which he sought a position so as to retain that position when it is devoid of those values). Thus, the problem with violating principles is not that the agent gains but that morality loses. Rather, the agent loses; it hurts *him*. Refusing to sell out is thoroughly, thoughtfully selfish.

The belief that a person can best advance his interest by sporadic adherence to principles—complying sometimes, cheating sometimes—rests on an equivocation over what self-interest is. It alternates between a holistic, integrated conception of interest that includes all the relevant elements and effects of a person's actions and a fragmented conception of interest that treats discrete elements as if they were the whole of it. Only this sort of indeterminacy about what a person's interest is can sustain the appeal of violating principles that are designed to advance a person's life.[31]

My proposal about principles' practicality is not that adherence to principle unfailingly delivers instant, visible rewards or that a violation of principle will be immediately fatal. The idea is not that one dishonest act assures a visit from the grim reaper by sundown.[32] Rather, my claim is that principles prescribe the types of actions that will promote a person's long-term survival. The fact that a person might occasionally "get away" with cheating does not render violations of principles an equally efficacious course any more than the fact that a person might cross a street blindfolded and emerge unscathed on the other side makes that a prudent street-crossing policy.[33]

The violation of moral principles represents a reversal of course. It is an interruption of a person's progress along a life-promoting path. Since life requires actions along that path, such departures are taken at tremendous risk. Recognizing certain principles as the best guidance for promoting one's life and then violating those principles is comparable to following a trail in the woods to a specific destination and then abruptly abandoning it. It is not simply a matter of taking a lengthier detour to one's destination, nor is it taking a side excursion, a path in a different direction for a temporary change of surroundings. Rather, the violation of a life-promoting principle is a complete about-face; it is turning directly backward and heading in the opposite direction, moving away from life and toward death.

In order to remain on a life-propelling track, the egoist committed to advancing his life must adhere to principles.

IMPLICATIONS FOR THE RELATIONSHIP BETWEEN INDIVIDUALS' INTERESTS

This elaboration of what self-interest is and demands should dispel most of the usual reservations about egoism. The relationship between different people's interests may still cloud a complete understanding of egoism's logic, however. Thus, we should consider two significant implications of this portrait for that relationship. Since both contravene conventional beliefs, understanding them is crucial to understanding the egoism that this metaethical theory prescribes.

Pursuit of Self-Interest Is Not a Zero-Sum Game

The first implication denies the prevalent presumption that egoism is predatory. People typically assume that different individuals' interests are naturally antagonistic and that the only way to promote one's own interest is by injuring others (or, less directly, by taking from the world's finite goods and thereby leaving others worse off).[34] This belief assumes that the pursuit of interest is a zero-sum game: Gains for some necessarily entail losses for others. One individual can advance his interest only at a cost to other individuals. The conclusion is that a policy of egoism recommends hurting other people.[35]

On such a model, hostility toward egoism is understandable. This model is fundamentally mistaken, however. Since the zero-sum hypothesis is a widely taken-for-granted, often unspoken source of opposition to egoism, it is important to show that its assumptions about value are unwarranted.[36]

Fortunately, what we have learned about value to this stage steers us to a proper understanding of this issue. First, the fact that a thing's value depends on its position in a given individual's life means that value is contextual. Value is not a static, one-size-fits-all commodity into which anyone can tap to equal benefit. Second, the fact that value is not intrinsic means that values are created rather than found. Furthering one's interest is not a matter of getting one's hands on some inherently worthwhile stuff, of which only a fixed quantity is available. No such ready-made values await our acquisition. These two points expose the errors in the zero-sum picture. Let me elaborate on each of them.

Value Is Contextual

Value is inextricably dependent on a given individual's context. We have already seen that the value of anything depends on its function in a particular person's life—it depends on such things as his abilities, tastes, purposes, possessions, and knowledge. To determine whether a given thing is valuable to a particular person, we must ascertain its role relative to *his* position and ends. The fact that an object may be valuable to most people does not ensure that it is valuable to him, nor, if it is valuable to him, does it ensure that it occupies the same degree of value for him that it does for other people. For many professors, for example, becoming a dean might be a significant advance. While Allan might be able make more money and enjoy greater prestige as a dean than as a philosophy professor, however, he might find the work considerably less rewarding. Turning down a deanship may not be best for his bank account, but it might be very good for his relish for waking up in the morning and going to work.

We can embroider such examples to highlight an assortment of factors potentially relevant to a person's overall flourishing. The point is simply that values are not interchangeable goods that automatically confer the same benefits in anyone's hands. Declarations of what is in a person's interest must respect this. Those accepting a zero-sum model are typically too quick to conclude that a given thing is in a person's interest.

A second, related observation indicating the contextual character of value is the fact that a person normally embraces many different ends, all of which may contribute to his flourishing. At any given time, a person typically pursues a variety of goals of differing significance, complexity, difficulty, and duration. To determine whether any particular object, activity, event, or condition advances a person's interest, we must understand the totality of this network. We must know the person's overarching objective, his major subordinate goals, their subordinate goals, as well as the rationality, compatibility, and relative status of each. What are the person's priorities? What is the rational hierarchy of his assorted objectives? Is his career more important than his golf game? Would more free time or a higher income be better for him? Does his friendship with an employee outweigh the significance of the friend's lackluster job performance?

Since a single action frequently carries multiple effects, we must heed all these effects on all of a person's ends in order to reach an accurate evaluation of the action's impact on his interest. Such evaluations require knowledge of how effects on one segment of a person's life are likely to bear on others. Accepting a job offer, for example, may be good for one's career but bad for one's marriage. Consequently, the self-interested agent must be ever mindful of his complete hierarchy of values. He cannot afford to kid himself about the relative weight of various goods or to allow momentary urges to distort his choices.

Note, further, that the more ends a person adopts, the greater the number of things that can affect his ends. The more engaged a person is in a variety of projects—professional, personal, social, aesthetic, athletic—the more likely it is that some of his concerns will be affected by a given event. This creates still further reason to measure interest carefully, seeking to ensure that a person is not acting in a way that is contrary to any of his values.

Finally, remember the importance of a person's means of promoting his values. While a thing's effects on a person's enduring capacity to promote his life are often not obvious, such effects are vital to his overall well-being. Satisfying a present need by means that cripple one's ability to satisfy future needs is not truly in a person's interest. Pronouncements of what is in a person's interest must respect these less obvious effects of a person's actions as well.[37]

In sum, interest is a phenomenon of enormous scope, composed of often complicated relationships. When we take into account the relational nature of value, the many ends that a person's life encompasses, and the importance of a person's means of achieving ends to his overall well-being, we realize that claims that things are in a person's interest are often unwarranted. Assessments of interest must be based on a grasp of the "big picture" for the given individual. We cannot treat a lone event's impact on a person or an isolated or temporary aspect of his condition as a decisive barometer of his flourishing. Correspondingly, the person trying to promote his interest must evaluate alternatives in relation to the whole of his life. He cannot detach events from the past or the future—from how they come about, their necessary conditions, or from what will take place afterward, the likely ramifications of his actions. He cannot compartmentalize the pursuit of some of his values from others. Yet this is exactly what glib assumptions about gains for some necessitating losses for others completely overlook. Hasty conclusions of what is in a person's interest feed the belief that one person's gains are costly to others. In fact, many of the "gains" that allegedly exact a toll on others are not truly gains at all.

Value Is Created

The second part of the explanation of why the pursuit of interest is not a zero-sum game is the fact that value is not intrinsic. Consequently, values are not simply found, to be taken. Values are created. This holds in a few significant respects.

First, people create value insofar as we choose our ends. No ends are preordained. In chapter four, I explained how life itself must be sought; we stand under no freestanding obligation to maintain our lives. It is only if one does wish to live that values arise. Values are those objects of a person's actions that contribute to the achievement of his life and its constituent, life-furthering ends. Absent such ends, nothing could bear that relationship, so nothing could be of value to him. Individuals choose their ends, however, deciding to pursue a particular career or sport or political cause, for example. The adoption of such ends is indispensable to anything's being valuable.

Further, we create value by acting to achieve our objectives. It is only by *applying* for the scholarship, *practicing* the piano, *writing* the speech, *saving* the vacation money, and so on that one attains values. Whatever the type of end—understanding quantum mechanics or deepening a friendship, skiing the Alps or running a gas station, attending the Super Bowl or perfecting a soufflé—our actions are our means to realizing them. Natural resources may seem naturally valuable to human beings without requiring any effort on our parts. Yet while such resources are potentially valuable, even these must be manipulated to advance anyone's interest. A person *makes* a fire or a tree or a hide or a rock useful by transforming it into energy or shelter or clothes or tools. Intellectual and physical labor convert what we find into life-advancing values.[38]

It is crucial to remember that a person's flourishing is a function primarily of how he leads his life. The core of flourishing rests in what a person does rather than in what he has. What a person does, however, does not depend on taking anything from others. Because a person's flourishing is a function of his own activity, what other people possess is fundamentally irrelevant. The path for any individual to promote his interest is through acting in life-furthering ways. Such a course is not a means of attaining the "true" value that resides in certain external objects. Rather, such a course *is* what one's living and flourishing—and thus one's interest—consist of. Well-being resides in one's being having the character that only the proper leading of one's life can provide. A person creates value by acting in a way that advances his life.

Still a further way in which people create value is through the phenomenon of values begetting values. Purposes tend to reverberate throughout a person's experience: Once a person adopts certain goals, things that were formerly indifferent assume significance vis-à-vis his new ends. The means of advancing one's goals, as well as things that enhance a person's knowledge or enjoyment in regard to the new purpose, will become valuable. Once a person takes up golf or the guitar or gardening, for example, lessons from an experienced instructor or intelligent magazines on the subject or appropriate equipment become valuable to him. Once a person decides that he wants to practice medicine, his understanding of organic chemistry and admission into medical school become valuable to him. Once a person has a child, understanding infant nutrition and finding a good school become valuable. In short, individuals' ends themselves render certain things valuable that previously had not been.

Values beget values in a second sense as well. The achievement of some values often stimulates the pursuit of still others (which are not simply means to the first). Having definite values and acting to achieve objectives often heightens one's motivation to persist in the face of obstacles and to exert the extra effort that frequently brings success. Such success can fuel a person's enjoyment of values, his confidence in his ability to realize values, and his sense of worthiness to reach more challenging goals. Success and value expansion tend to be mutually reinforcing: The more a person pursues various ends, the more he is likely to do what is necessary to achieve those ends, and the more he achieves values, the more likely he is to adopt further ends to enjoy. This often propels a person's seeking still higher ends and enriching his life with ever more values.

The fact that people generate values through their choices and actions, then, further indicates that one does not promote one's interest by raiding a stock of prefabricated value. Since individuals must actively create values to promote their interest, self-interested action does not demand injury or expense to anyone else.

Even if I am right about the core of self-interest, one might suspect that this does not convey the whole story. Might not the component of a person's well-being that is out of his hands stand in an antagonistic relation to others' well-being? A person might work hard to equip himself for a certain job, for example, but he cannot ensure that he will be hired. There are just so many jobs. Thus, it may seem that, even if the core of interest is not zero sum, certain peripheral aspects are.

The mistake in this reasoning is its confusion of what is beyond a person's control with what is finite. In fact, the two bear no necessary connection; the inference from the first to the second is fallacious. This inference would be justified only on an erroneous assumption: that the world contains a fixed quantity of "good fortune." If it did, then another person's good fortune would be an impediment to my own.

In fact, good fortune is simply a name for the variety of beneficial circumstances that might arise in people's lives. It does not refer to the future's containing some preset number of "events beyond one's control," a certain proportion of which are destined to be favorable and a certain proportion unfavorable. The world is not stocked with a finite quantity of beneficial events sprinkled around by some cosmic overseer. Nor is the future like a deck of cards, such that enjoying some beneficial event is comparable to drawing an ace—which reduces others' prospects for aces (or for "good fortune").

Tomorrow, a man could wake up, decide to start a business, and hire ten people. Those people had not enjoyed that specific job opportunity a day earlier. This is a simple illustration of the fact that even the "good fortune" that stands out of one's own control is not a static quantity. The actions that other people might take that are capable of affecting a person are unbounded. We might easily imagine countless similar examples: A man decides to pursue a career composing music and proceeds to bring pleasure to millions; a woman pursues biomedical research that leads to pharmaceuticals relieving the ailments of millions; a partnership launches an electronics company whose innovations generate conveniences for millions. What is the limit on the number of people who can wake up and activate such plans? The population of the earth at any time. What is the limit on the number of beneficial plans they might initiate? Nothing.

Some might protest that job openings for ten are not enough to refute the zero-sum thesis since we can easily imagine fifty applicants for those ten positions. What about the forty who will be frustrated? Aren't all fifty in a classic zero-sum scenario?

No. And it is instructive to see why not. Assume that the applicants are sufficiently qualified to have a genuine chance of landing the job. In that respect, all fifty are better off because they now enjoy an opportunity that did not exist a day earlier. An occasion from which they might benefit has been created.

Only ten will be hired, of course, yet even after the jobs have been filled, the disappointed applicants are no worse off. Some of them may actually be better off, having benefited from the experience of preparing a résumé, being interviewed, making contacts, and so on. But even those who are not better off have not lost anything. It is not a person's loss to fail to obtain something that he seeks.

This exposes a further significant confusion fueling the zero-sum hypothesis. Earlier, I noted its advocates' too-ready inclination to consider certain developments in a person's interest. Here, we find that the zero-sum thesis also relies on an erroneous notion of what constitutes a loss. Since the concept of a loss is at the heart of the zero-sum thesis, it is worth considering with some care.

Just as gains represent forward progress or the strengthening of a person's fitness for living, losses are actual setbacks; they weaken a person's position. Failing to gain something is not the same as losing it, however. A setback is literally being set down or behind from one's previous position. If a person breaks his leg, wrecks his car, or loses his savings, for instance, he suffers a loss, being made worse off than he had been. Some of the energy that had been available for positive, life-furthering pursuits must now be redirected into repairing or recovering what has been damaged or lost. This person is no longer in as strong a position as he had been, pre-mishap, to engage in life-promoting activities.

Not obtaining a certain possible gain, by contrast, leaves the person in the same position that he was in initially. Disappointment per se does not weaken a person. Disappointment is an emotional reaction to unfulfilled desires. To have one's hopes dashed is not necessarily to suffer a loss, however, since emotions are not a reliable barometer of how a person's interest is faring. A person's desires might be ill-conceived, at odds with what is actually good for him. (Consider desires for unhealthy quantities of liquor or loafing.) When that is the case, failure to satisfy these desires can actually be more advantageous than satisfying them.

More important, even when a person's desires are rational and their fulfillment would enhance his life, the failure to satisfy them still does not mark a loss. A person cannot lose what he never had in the first place. Not getting the job you sought, the house you bid on, or the grant you applied for does not fire you from your current job, evict you from your current home, or reduce your current income. Such frustrations do not leave the person any worse off than he was beforehand. The benchmark for measuring loss is not a person's goals or wishes but his actual position. (If gains and losses were determined by an individual's desires, we would have no basis for judging whether a person would be better off having any particular desire satisfied since "gains" and "losses" would simply be disguised references to those desires themselves.)[39]

One might be tempted to protest that the time, energy, or money that a person invested in pursuing an opportunity that did not pan out *is* lost. He no longer has what he devoted to that failed enterprise. To conclude that this constitutes a setback to a person's life, however, reflects a seriously confused conception of our circumstances.

Achieving goals requires action. We do not know in advance which of our efforts will succeed. The fact that a person's goals are not always realized is not a loss, however. It is the natural condition of all human activity. Living requires energy. We burn calories, we spend time; we use our vital organs, some of which grow weaker for wear. The concepts of gain and loss do not refer to these unavoidable conditions of life. Rather, against the background of these conditions, "gains" and "losses" distinguish those events that fortify a person's life from those that weaken it. A loss must be an event other than what inevitably occurs in the normal course of events. Today was not a bad day because I aged, for example, in the way that it would be a bad day if I had wrecked my car or broken my leg. It is largely because losses are not unavoidable—because we can act to influence our gains and losses—that it is useful to distinguish these phenomena so as to guide our actions.[40]

The belief that time spent in an ultimately unsuccessful effort represents a loss treats a person's hypothetical or desired position as if it were already realized. It ignores life's actual conditions and measures gains and losses by the yardstick of some favored, imagined alternative. Correspondingly, it converts life into a losing proposition, discouraging a person from attempting very much. Why should a person bother attempting to achieve any objective with long odds? If only one in five grant proposals will win funding, for example, it seems irrational to apply. If the attempt to move ahead carried such a high probability of actual *loss,* a person would be better off simply maintaining the status quo. Given life's requirement that a person achieve values, however, a policy of coasting with the status quo would be suicidal.

My point, again, is that the failure to gain a desired end cannot be equated with a loss. The proper barometer of gains and losses is not fantasy but reality: a person's actual condition. Once we surrender the beliefs that disappointment signifies loss and that gains should be available either without effort or with efforts' success ensured, a more accurate picture of the relation between different individuals' interests can emerge.

The broader lesson is this: Value is not finite because the engine of value—the human mind and human action—is not finite. We find no limits on human ambition in conceiving new ends or on human ingenuity in actualizing them. A person confronts no bounds on the number of life-propelling purposes he might adopt or in the means he might devise for achieving them. Since we create values rather than find them, we can always create more; enjoying a value does not deplete a finite supply. Objections to egoism stemming from the belief that one person's promoting his interest is damaging to others' interest are thus wholly unjustified.

Indeed, suspicions about the zero-sum thesis might have been immediately aroused simply by contemplating its implications. If other people's prosperity truly is a threat to me, then I would be better off doing away with people. Extermination of others would be the egoistic course. This is not rhetorical exaggeration; on the zero-sum hypothesis, only when a person is dead is the chance of his gains (and my correlative losses) eliminated. If the zero-sum model accurately portrayed our relationship, extermination would be the sensible, self-interested policy.

Can anyone who thinks about it for ten seconds really believe that such a course *is* in one's interest? Is it altruism that restrains us from a campaign to kill? Imagine your life without scores of friends, family, colleagues, and acquaintances, without the people you like, love, learn from, or simply get a kick out of—let alone the anonymous millions whose efforts have created your favorite books, songs, movies, games, and the products and technologies that ease our lives every day. Is news of a birth cause for grief, representing a setback to one's prospects for happiness? Should a person track the newspaper's obituaries and birth notices to gauge his self-interest, celebrating the deaths and lamenting the births?

Any given individual might be a parasite who creates few values and meets his needs by draining others. Some people do grow up to be sponges and predators of various degrees, from the modestly irresponsible to thieves and murderers. But every person has the potential to bring benefits to others. A person need not offer historic achievements to offer positive contributions. In addition to the Aristotles, Leonardos, and Edisons, we gain from the lives of countless diligent clerks, dependable mechanics, dedicated teachers, tenacious researchers, graceful musicians, insightful writers, and innovative chefs or, again, from the paragon of integrity, the faithful friend, or the person whose sense of humor, sense of seriousness, counsel, charm, eyebrows, voice, or values you come to love. Far from gaining as a result of others' failures, a self-interested person has every reason to cheer others' success since it may ultimately enrich his own life.

RATIONAL INTERESTS DO NOT CONFLICT

Finally, we can appreciate a further unorthodox implication of this account of interest. We have just seen that self-interest is not promoted by injuring others. Along the same lines, it is a mistake to suppose that individuals' interests can conflict. Engrained as the assumption of such conflicts is, no such conflicts between rational interests exist.[41]

I say that "rational" interests cannot conflict because the irrational pursuit of self-interest can easily lead to conflicts. A person could be mistaken about whether something truly enhances his life, misjudging its efficacy as a means or its worthiness as an end, and consequently take actions that injure others. If I erroneously believe that misrepresenting my work experience will be in my interest, for example, the employer who I temporarily fool will suffer from my poor job performance. (I will suffer as well, as traced in the résumé-faker example.) The conflicts and harm caused in such cases stem from the person's miscalculation of what his interest is, however, rather than from the policy of pursuing one's interest.[42]

The belief that interests can conflict is the belief that a given event could enhance one person's life by damaging another person's life. The zero-sum thesis would be one basis for believing in conflicts between interests, but it is not the only possible basis. The zero-sum premise that one person's gain spells another person's loss entails that conflicts between interests are necessary. Conflicts need not be necessary in order to be possible, however. While the zero-sum model implies that every gain comes at another person's expense, the belief in conflicts between interests more modestly claims that gains sometimes come at another's expense. Thus, a person might believe that conflicts between interests can arise even after rejecting the zero-sum thesis.

While the two theses are distinct, they are closely related. The zero-sum model is the primary foundation for belief in conflicts between interests; thus, the failure of the zero-sum model substantially weakens the case for such conflicts. It should not take much further work to see where the belief in conflicts between individuals' interests goes wrong.

The key to appreciating that individuals' rational interests do not conflict rests in consistently employing the full, objective meaning of interest.

Life is the standard of value; a person's interest consists in the achievement of life-sustaining values. As long as we wrench egoism from the hedonism with which it is so frequently confused, recognizing that pleasure is not the measure of value and that interest cannot be equated with any feeling, desire, or short-range, superficial appearance of interest, the plausibility of conflicts between interests quickly evaporates.

Since what is in a person's interest is determined by what propels his life, conflicts between interests would mean conflicts between individuals' lives. As long as they are led rationally, however, people's lives do not conflict. Nothing that serves one person's long-term survival is naturally inimical to another person's long-term survival. Remember that a person's flourishing is fundamentally a function of how he leads his life. Any life can be led in a life-promoting manner regardless of how others conduct their lives. Living properly constitutes flourishing; the point and payoff of living properly reside in the living—not in a separate product that others might seize. Since flourishing must be self-generated through appropriate means, it is not vulnerable to others' expropriation. Anyone who attempts to enhance his life by injuring others is doomed to fail. A person advances his life by creating values rather than by extracting things from others. Cannibalism is not a policy that sustains human life.

One source of misunderstanding the relations between different individuals' interests may lie in confusing the optionality of certain values for the nonobjectivity of all values. As we observed in chapters four and five, ethics does not dictate every detail of what a person should and should not do; in ordinary circumstances, ethics does not tell him what music to listen to, what magazines to read, or what clothes to wear. Morality permits a person's taste to exert itself in many optional values.

If one lapsed into regarding all values as optional, the conflict-prone image of interests would be more plausible, for the belief that all values are optional would deny the objectivity of value, implying that we have no basis for discriminating genuine from artificial values. In that case, a value would represent nothing more than a person's assertion that something is valuable to him. Having rejected the basis for appraising such assertions, we could not challenge them. Thus, values would collapse into mere desires. And these certainly could conflict; I might well desire something at another's expense, seeking his car or his musical composition, for example.

In fact, however, not all values are optional. The fact that ethics does not dictate all of a person's values does not rescind the objectivity of values. Optional values must respect the parameters established by the standard of value; they must contribute to a life-promoting course. Optional values do not reflect a departure from objectivity but, rather, permissible variation in particular ways of pursuing objective values.

The principal point, again, is that clarity about the nature of interest dissolves the conflicts between interests that are commonly alleged. If one of two sisters (call them Lisa and Mary) stands to inherit grandpa's money, for example, the fact that one inherits it does not harm the other. While either woman may gain from an inheritance, neither stands to lose anything.[43] All that is truly in conflict are the two women's presumed desires, for nothing about Mary's inheriting the money would damage Lisa's life or impede Lisa's pursuit of her interest, and nothing about Lisa's inheriting the money would damage Mary's life or impede Mary's pursuit of her interest. Each remains as free and able as ever to act in a life-promoting manner. A conflict of desires does not signify a conflict between interests since desire is not the standard of value.

The same applies to examples from business, usually considered the arena of "dog eat dog" competition where conflicting interests are the order of the day. Losing out to a competitor is not the self-evident disaster that people routinely presume.

Not being the most successful in some field does not entail not being able to run a profitable business. Where some company is "number one," others are numbers two, three, and four. Without succeeding as much as certain competitors, a company could often remain in a field, prospering sufficiently to make that a rational, life-promoting course. Many are content—and flourish—in exactly this role.[44]

Further, if one's competitors' success reaches such proportions that it is no longer profitable for a person to keep his business operating, it is good for him to exit. To cling to his business rather than admit its failure simply because he really wants to make his career in this way may gratify certain desires, but it does not advance his life. Facing facts is a prerequisite for truly self-interested action. If a person is not able to offer as desirable a product as his competitor or to turn a satisfactory profit, he would be better off in another line of work.[45]

Disappointment stings, and the higher the stakes, the greater the hurt. Changing career tracks brings disruption and uncertainty. To think that these indicate net damage to a person's interest, however, is to revert to hedonism, treating feelings as determinative of a person's interest. It is to suppose that a person should be able to indulge his desire regardless of his actual abilities, competitors' abilities, and the prevalent demands in that market.

The lesson is, interest must be identified realistically. In this context, a person must recognize that commercial success depends on one's own performance as well as on others' evaluation of it and their consequent willingness to trade. Remember that a person's interest is grounded in all the relevant aspects of his circumstances, including the conditions necessary for the achievement of his values. In the business realm, those conditions include competition and the necessity of performing to the satisfaction of one's customers. A person must accept the possibility of failing in such competition but recognize that the competition is necessary for efficient production, which itself is necessary for any business to earn a profit and continue to function.[46]

It is only if one sets such realistic factors aside that one is tempted to view dashed expectations as the barometer of harm. "Losing" in business can be beneficial insofar as it steers a person away from an unsuccessful enterprise and toward using his energies more profitably. If a person does not perform as well as his competitors, it does not serve his life to pretend otherwise. Resistance to this conclusion stems from straddling the contradictory perspectives of fantasy and reality: "I want to stay open" (my fantasy); "I can't make my living this way" (my recognition of reality). Self-interest—living—depends on meeting the needs imposed by reality.

If we were to examine further examples, we would discover essentially the same mistake in all of them: a sloppy use of "interest" propping up the appearance of conflict. A thoughtful look at human relations, however, governed by life as the standard of value, reveals that far from chronic conflict, we actually encounter countless situations in which one person's prosperity enhances others'. The rise of the computer industry, for instance, has benefited not only its stars (e.g., Bill Gates and Michael Dell) but millions of individuals who enjoy computer-generated conveniences and millions employed in computer-related work—programmers, Web page designers, repair specialists, convention organizers, journalists, and so on. A similar pattern holds in many fields: A few individuals may win a great deal of money for their work in supplying popular products, but numerous others gain as well. For that matter, any free business transaction, however mundane, is completed because both parties judge themselves better off by making it. A person buys whatever he buys and sells whatever he sells only because he has concluded that he will gain from having that good or payment instead of what he trades for it.

Once one pauses to notice, one finds that situations of mutual advantage are ubiquitous. The success of a professional sports team is good not only for the team's owners but also for its players, fans, broadcasters, local hotels, restaurants, and souvenir shops. A successful film or play benefits not only its producers but also the company's employees and the audiences who enjoy the production. A best-selling author may take home a lot of money, but his agent, publisher, bookstores, and readers gain as well. When a university hires a celebrated scholar, presumably this is in his interest (which is why he accepts the position) and in the school's as well (upgrading its intellectual climate, strengthening its ability to draw other distinguished professors, enhancing its appeal to students).

Even competition from others, far from being a threat to a person's interest, often works to the advantage of all the competing parties. A popular innovation from one company may temporarily draw customers from competitors, but that often subsides when those competitors respond by offering a similar enticement or introducing a different one. Competitive efforts to provide a more appealing product often heighten interest in that product per se and increase business for all competitors in that market. IBM's popular personal computers created opportunity for numerous manufacturers of IBM clones, for example. Commonly, the success of one of a new sort of establishment (e.g., a cigar bar or supermarket offering ready-to-heat meals) sparks demand for others. As these demands are met, more businesses prosper, and customers enjoy an elevated caliber of options.

I am not claiming that competitive relationships invariably work out to all parties' advantage. All sorts of irrational decisions and clumsy performances can prevent this. The point is that competitive relationships *can* be mutually advantageous. Nothing inherent in the nature of value pits individuals' interests in conflict.

Nor am I adopting the Panglossian position that everything happens for the best or that bad things never happen to people. My contention is that the promotion of one person's interest cannot *make* another person suffer; when one individual's interest suffers, it is never because of another individual's gain. (By rejecting the zero-sum hypothesis, I denied that interests always conflict. Here, I am denying that rational interests ever conflict.) Interests sometimes appear to conflict only because we lapse into superficial, subjective notions of what a person's interest is.

CONCLUSION

In chapter four, I argued that life is the inescapable foundation of value and thus of all morality. Chapter five elaborated on the meaning of life as the end of value. Here, I have indicated the general character of the practical ethical guidance that follows from these metaethical foundations. A policy of egoism—acting to promote one's own interest—is the path to attaining a person's ultimate value. Since a person cannot advance his life by failing to meet its conditions—let alone through actions that directly subvert his life—egoism is the only way to live.

A full-fledged specification of an egoistic normative theory, with a corresponding defense of its prescriptions, is the subject of another book. Yet the egoistic implications of the metaethics defended here are too integral to Rand's theory and too significant to ignore. Thus, I have attempted to indicate the sort of egoism that I embrace primarily by correcting common misconceptions. A realistic understanding of interest, governed by the standard of life, confutes entrenched assumptions about how to promote one's interest. Contrary to conventional wisdom, self-interest is neither hedonistic, subjective, nor purely materialistic. Egoism demands disciplined adherence to farsighted principles rather than the indulgence of passing impulses. "Ill-begotten gains" are not truly gains, the pursuit of value is not a zero-sum game, and rational interests cannot conflict. The correction of these confusions eliminates many of the usual objections to egoism.

Much remains to be said to explain exactly which principles and virtues rational egoism prescribes. The lesson for the present, however, is clear: Morality is for living. That aim is the sum of its claim on anyone. Life sets the standard of value, life is the goal of morality, life is the reward of morality. What stronger answer can one imagine to the question of why we should be moral?

NOTES

1. Much in Aristotle's *Nicomachean Ethics* commends egoism, but many scholars have been reluctant to regard Aristotle as an egoist. (I will comment a bit further on this later.) Benedict Spinoza's ethics contains strongly egoistic themes but is not much studied. Friedrich Nietzsche's more emotional brand of egoism wins greater attention, but many treat its nonrational roots as grounds to reject egoism itself. The approval of self-interest that we occasionally hear from moral philosophers is typically based on the belief that a modicum of self-interest is necessary to equip a person to fulfill moral duties rather than the belief that it is welcome for the person's own sake. See, for example, Immanuel Kant, *Foundations of the Metaphysics of Morals,* trans. Lewis White Beck (New York: Macmillan, 1990), 15; Academy Edition, 399. Self-interest has gained a bit more attention with the recent revival of virtue ethics. See, for example, *Social Philosophy and Policy* 14 (Winter 1997), an issue dedicated to self-interest, and Kelly Rogers, ed., *Self-Interest—an Anthology of Philosophical Perspectives* (New York: Routledge, 1997).

2. Philippa Foot, "Reasons for Action and Desires," *Virtues and Vices* (Berkeley and Los Angeles: University of California Press, 1978), 154; William Galston, *Liberal Purposes—Goods, Virtues and Diversity in the Liberal State* (New York: Cambridge University Press, 1991), 118 (see also 114); Kurt Baier, "Why Should We Be Moral?" in *Readings in Contemporary Ethical Theory,* ed. K. Pahel and M. Schiller (Englewood Cliffs, N.J.: Prentice Hall, 1970), 437–38. Similar assumptions are rife throughout the literature. In an introductory text, Robert Solomon links morality with disinterestedness and holds that "morality essentially involves consideration of interests other than one's own" (Solomon, *Ethics—a Short Introduction* [Dubuque, Iowa: Brown and Benchmark, 1993], 13). Dan W. Brock explicates the nature of moral reasons by observing that they override judgments of self-interest (Brock, "The Justification of Morality," *American Philosophical Quarterly* 14 [January 1977]: 71).

3. Some of the material in this chapter is adapted from my "Reconsidering Zero-Sum Value: It's How You Play the Game," *Journal of Social Philosophy* 28

(Fall 1997): 128–39, and from "On Being *Really* Selfish" (paper presented to the Ayn Rand Society of the American Philosophical Association, Eastern Division Meetings, December 1996). Further discussion of egoism can be found in my "Rights, Friends, and Egoism," *Journal of Philosophy* 90 (March 1993): 144–48.

4. I harbor no sympathy for psychological egoism, the view that people in fact do always act to promote their own self-interest. Throughout, I will use "egoism" as a shorthand for "ethical egoism."

5. Ayn Rand, "Introduction," *The Virtue of Selfishness* (New York: New American Library, 1964), ix; "The Objectivist Ethics," *The Virtue of Selfishness,* 31.

6. Rand, "The Objectivist Ethics," 27.

7. See Rand, "Introduction," ix–x.

8. For more on the selfishness of love, see Rand, "The Objectivist Ethics," 31–32; "The Ethics of Emergencies," *The Virtue of Selfishness,* 43–46; and my "Why Do I Love Thee? A Response to Nozick's Account of Romantic Love," *Southwest Philosophy Review* 7, no. 1 (January 1991): 47–57. The idea that devotion to loved ones is selfless reveals a shallow notion of self-interest. My discussion of interest's spiritual dimension in the next section should make this more clear.

9. E. J. Bond, "Theories of the Good," in *Encyclopedia of Ethics,* vol. 1, ed. Lawrence C. Becker (New York: Garland, 1992), 410. Burton F. Porter characterizes altruism as "the position that one should always act for the welfare of others" (Porter, *The Good Life* [New York: Ardley House, 1995], 283). Lawrence Blum observes much confusion about altruism's definition but concedes that placing the interests of others ahead of one's own best reflects ordinary usage (Blum, "Altruism," in *Encyclopedia of Ethics,* 35).

10. Rogers, ed., *Self-Interest,* 5.

11. Alasdair MacIntyre, "Egoism and Altruism," in *Encyclopedia of Philosophy,* ed. Paul Edwards (New York: Macmillan, 1967), 462, 463. It is also noteworthy that the Greeks' conception of a good life as an integrated whole is antithetical to the compartmentalized conception of ethics that altruism both relies on and encourages. Altruism is more tenable when confined to narrow corners of life, demanded only in select realms. Such limited arenas for altruism allow the egoism in other arenas that a person's life requires. If ethics is conceived as all-encompassing, however, with the same basic principles governing all areas of activity, the consequences of the policies of altruism and egoism are more nakedly exposed. Altruism must be contained to limited spheres, in other words, because if it were conscientiously practiced across the board, it would result in self-destruction. (Another part of the reason for reluctance to consider Aristotle an egoist may simply be the assumption that "good guys" cannot be egoists.)

12. William Frankena, *Ethics* (Englewood Cliffs, N.J.: Prentice Hall, 1963), 6. For others either using or commenting on the prevalent meaning of prudence, see Daniel Mark Nelson, "Prudence," in *Encyclopedia of Ethics,* 1030–35; Philippa Foot, "Reasons for Action and Desires," 148–49; Thomas Nagel, "Desires, Prudential Motives, and the Present," in *Practical Reasoning,* ed. Joseph Raz (Oxford: Oxford University Press, 1978), 159; John McDowell, "Are Moral Requirements Hypothetical Imperatives?" *Proceedings of the Aristotelian Society* 52 (Suppl.

1978): 13–29; and Daniel Walker Howe, *Making the American Self* (Cambridge, Mass.: Harvard University Press, 1997), 12–13, 65.

13. Nelson, "Prudence," 1033.

14. Epicurus, *Letter to Menoeceus,* quoted in Rogers, ed., *Self-Interest,* 34, and Epicurus, "Principal Doctrines," *The Epicurus Reader,* trans. Brad Inwood and L. P. Gerson (Indianapolis: Hackett, 1994), 5.

15. MacIntyre, *Whose Justice? Which Rationality?* (Notre Dame, Ind.: University of Notre Dame Press, 1988), 128; see also 123.

16. Daniel Mark Nelson, *The Priority of Prudence* (University Park: Pennsylvania State University Press, 1992) ix; Aquinas, *Summa Theologica,* I–II, q 65, a 1, quoted in Nelson, *The Priority of Prudence,* 84. For further discussion of the Greeks' attitude toward prudence, see Nelson, "Prudence," and Ray Shelton, "A Life-Centered Metaethics: Ancient and Modern" (masters thesis, San Francisco State University, 1995). For a good discussion of prudence more generally, see John L. Treloar, "Moral Virtue and the Demise of Prudence in the Thought of Francis Suarez," *American Catholic Philosophical Quarterly* 65 (Summer 1991): 387–405. Treloar attributes the shift in understanding away from the moral character of prudence to the influence of Suarez, Hobbes, and Hume (404).

17. While my inquiry has focused on moral obligations, chapter four demonstrated that no "shoulds" are defensible apart from the overarching aim of a person's own life. That is, since the very concept of value depends on the quest for life, and since the concept of a "should" is derivative from the concept of value (that for the sake of which a person should do something), the validity of any "should" depends on its relation to the quest for life.

18. Certain decisions are not normally moral because a person's options would carry equal effects on his survival. Ordinarily, for example, whether a person washes his car on Saturday or Sunday, orders fish or fowl, or plays a Brahms or a Louis Armstrong disc is of no moral significance. Circumstances can arise in which such innocuous decisions do assume moral import, however—for instance, if Saturday is his only opportunity to tend to some more urgent task, if he is gravely allergic to fish, or if one type of music will distract his mind from important work that he must complete. Since morality prescribes living in a life-furthering way, anything that stands to enhance or impede one's life falls under morality's domain.

19. Just as a person might regard as valuable things that do not actually advance his life, a person might consider things in his interest that in fact are not. My references to interest are to those things that objectively serve a person's life.

20. Ethical egoism's frequent association with psychological egoism also engenders hostility to ethical egoism, but psychological egoism forms no part of my defense of ethical egoism.

21. For more on life's dependence on reason, see my *Moral Rights and Political Freedom* (Lanham, Md.: Rowman & Littlefield, 1995) chap. 2, and Rand, "The Objectivist Ethics," esp. 20–26.

22. I am using "selfish" interchangeably with "self-interested."

23. I am indebted to Darryl Wright for this point.

24. For a bit more on egoism's requiring an independent self, see my "On Being *Really* Selfish."

25. For testimony to this in a meditation on rowing, see Craig Lambert, *Mind over Water* (New York: Houghton Mifflin, 1998), 154.

26. Rand emphasizes human beings' limited perceptual capacity in explaining the cognitive role of concepts (Rand, *Introduction to Objectivist Epistemology*, 2nd ed. [New York: Penguin, 1990], chap. 7).

27. The metaethical foundations that I have presented are incompatible with certain conventionally accepted virtues and compatible with others (e.g., justice, honesty, and integrity). Even where we find apparent overlap, however, the meanings of some of these terms and the reasons for regarding them as virtues are not necessarily the same. Also, while much has been made of the differences between virtues and principles in recent moral philosophy, since those differences are tangential to my purposes here, I will leave them aside.

28. Leonard Peikoff, *Objectivism: The Philosophy of Ayn Rand* (New York: Dutton, 1991), 267.

29. For a fuller discussion of honesty and of how other virtues serve life, see Peikoff, *Objectivism*, chap. 8. I discuss some of the life-promoting payoffs of the virtues of justice and pride in "Justice as a Personal Virtue," *Social Theory and Practice* 25, no. 3 (Fall 1999), and "The Practice of Pride," *Social Philosophy and Policy* 15 (Winter 1998): 71–90. For an analysis of tolerance and forgiveness from this perspective, see my "Tolerance and Forgiveness: Virtues or Vices?" *Journal of Applied Philosophy* 14 (1997): 31–41.

30. Challenging work that represents a feasible stretch for a person is different from work that is beyond a person's ability. Bill has given himself the latter. A reasonable stretch is within what could be expected from a qualified worker but not from the unqualified.

31. Correspondingly, it lapses into the view that a person could know how best to serve his interest on a case-by-case basis. The reason for adopting principles, however, is the realization that principles' broader, deeper perspective on the ramifications of our actions is necessary to guide a person to take the course most conducive to his survival. We employ principles precisely to guard against moral myopia. If the self-interested course were always readily apparent, we would not need principles' guidance.

32. Peikoff discusses this (*Objectivism*, 216).

33. I am indebted to Peter Schwartz for this vivid analogy.

34. Jan Osterberg writes, "A person is said to act egoistically only if he ignores the interests of other people for the benefit of his own; it is possible to act egoistically only if one's interests conflict with those of other people" (Osterberg, *Self and Others* [Dordrecht: Kluwer Academic Publishers, 1988], 3).

35. My article "Reconsidering Zero-Sum Value: It's How You Play the Game" is devoted to this issue.

36. Rand rejects the idea that our alternatives are essentially masochism or sadism, self-sacrifice or domination of others (Rand, "The Soul of an Individualist," in *For the New Intellectual* [New York: Random House, 1961], 94–95). Those would be our alternatives, however, if the zero-sum thesis were true. If a gain for me meant a loss for others, egoism would require that I seek to sacrifice others to my interest. The only way to avoid such sacrifice would be to renounce the pursuit

of self-interest and thereby sacrifice myself to others. (Obviously, some who oppose egoism on the grounds of its negative effects on others are rebelling at the prospect of incursions on *their* self-interest—hardly a consistent basis for rejecting egoism.)

37. Rand emphasizes that a rational man "does not judge his interests by any particular defeat nor by the range of any particular moment. He lives and judges long-range" (Rand, "The 'Conflicts' of Men's Interests," in *The Virtue of Selfishness*, 53).

38. For more on the importance of people's mental and physical effort in producing values, see "Reconsidering Zero-Sum Value." In regard to various economic issues, see Julian Simon, *The Ultimate Resource 2* (Princeton, N.J.: Princeton University Press, 1996).

39. Rand observes, "To claim that a man's interests are sacrificed whenever a desire of his is frustrated—is to hold a subjectivist view of man's values and interests" ("The 'Conflicts' of Men's Interests," 50).

40. One might also observe gains and losses as a passive spectator, of course, but the concepts would have far less usefulness if we could not act to encourage gains and to resist or minimize losses. Note that the expression "a waste of time" designates foolish uses of time (in pursuit of irrational ends or in pursuit of rational ends by irrational means) rather than every expenditure of time that fails to accomplish the agent's purposes.

41. See Rand, "The 'Conflicts' of Men's Interests," 50–56. Spinoza also recognized the harmony of interests among people who live rationally. Spinoza held that nothing is more advantageous to a person than another person who is guided by reason and believed that "it is when each is most devoted to seeking his own advantage that men are of most advantage to one another" (Spinoza, *The Ethics and Selected Letters*, ed. Seymour Feldman, trans. Samuel Shirley [Indianapolis: Hackett, 1982], 198, 173). Proper relations between people are not only harmonious but positively beneficial.

Throughout this discussion, I am referring exclusively to conflicts between different individuals' interests rather than to conflicts that might arise from a single person's occupying roles designed to serve contrary purposes.

42. Rand writes, "The evil of a robber does *not* lie in the fact that he pursues his own interests, but in *what* he regards as to his own interest; *not* in the fact that he pursues his values, but in *what* he chose to value" ("Introduction," ix, emphasis in the original). Subsequent references to interest should be understood as referring to a person's rational interest unless I indicate otherwise.

43. In light of what I have said about measuring interest as impact on a person's overall well-being, one cannot assume that inheriting money is automatically in a person's interest. For simplicity here, however, let's assume both that the inheritance would be in the recipient's interest and that the estate cannot be divided between them or given to anyone else.

44. The fact that one company attracts more customers than a competitor does not deprive the competitor of anything to which it is entitled. We do not start in business with a claim to a particular share of the market, such that failure to achieve that volume of business constitutes a loss.

45. The same basic analysis applies to owning a business, making a living through a certain type of work, or holding a particular job.

46. See Rand, "The 'Conflicts' of Men's Interests," 53, 56.

Selected List of
Works Consulted

Anderson, Elizabeth. *Value in Ethics and Economics.* Cambridge, Mass.: Harvard University Press, 1993.

Annas, Julia. "The Good Life and the Good Lives of Others." *Social Philosophy and Policy* 9 (Summer 1992): 133–48.

————. *The Morality of Happiness.* New York: Oxford University Press, 1993.

Aristotle. *Nicomachean Ethics.* In *Basic Works of Aristotle,* ed. Richard McKeon. New York: Random House, 1941.

Attfield, Robin. *The Ethics of Environmental Concern.* Oxford: Basil Blackwell, 1983.

Audi, Robert. "Ethical Reflectionism." *The Monist* 76, no. 3 (1993): 295–315.

————. *Moral Knowledge and Ethical Character.* New York: Oxford University Press, 1997.

Baier, Kurt. *The Moral Point of View.* New York: Random House, 1958.

————. "Why Should We Be Moral?" In *Readings in Contemporary Ethical Theory,* ed. K. Pahel and M. Schiller. Englewood Cliffs, N.J.: Prentice Hall, 1970.

Beardsley, Monroe. "Intrinsic Value." *Philosophy and Phenomenological Research* 26 (1965): 1–17.

Binswanger, Harry. *The Biological Basis of Teleological Concepts.* Marina del Rey, Calif.: Ayn Rand Institute Press, 1990.

————. "The Is–Ought Dichotomy—How Morality Can Be Derived from Facts." Unpublished lecture.

————. "Life-Based Teleology and the Foundations of Ethics." *The Monist* 75 (January 1992): 84–103.

Blum, Lawrence. "Altruism." In *Encyclopedia of Ethics,* ed. Lawrence C. Becker. New York: Garland, 1992.

Bond, E. J. "Theories of the Good." In *Encyclopedia of Ethics,* ed. Lawrence C. Becker. New York: Garland, 1992.

Bradley, F. H. "Why Should I Be Moral?" *Ethical Studies.* G. E. Stechert, 1911.

Brandt, Richard. *Ethical Theory.* Englewood Cliffs, N.J.: Prentice Hall, 1959.

———. *Value and Obligation.* New York: Harcourt, Brace and World, 1963.

Brock, Dan W. "The Justification of Morality." *American Philosophical Quarterly* 14, no. 1 (January 1977): 71–78.

Butchvarov, Panayot. "That Simple, Indefinable, Nonnatural Property *Good.*" *Review of Metaphysics* 36 (September 1982): 51–75.

Butler, Joseph. *Five Sermons,* ed. Stephen L. Darwall. Indianapolis: Hackett, 1983.

Cheney, Jim. "Intrinsic Value in Environmental Ethics: Beyond Subjectivism and Objectivism." *The Monist* 75, no. 2 (April 1992): 227–35.

Clarke, Samuel. "A Discourse of Natural Religion." In *British Moralists 1650–1800,* ed. D. D. Raphael. Oxford: Oxford University Press, 1969.

Cooper, John. *Reason and Human Good in Aristotle.* Indianapolis: Hackett, 1986.

Darwall, Stephen L. "Pleasure as Ultimate Good in Sidgwick's Ethics." *The Monist* 58 (July 1974): 475–89.

———. "Reasons, Motives, and the Demands of Morality." In *Moral Discourse and Practice,* ed. Stephen Darwall, Allan Gibbard, and Peter Railton. New York: Oxford University Press, 1997.

Darwall, Stephen, Allan Gibbard, and Peter Railton. "Toward *Fin de Siecle* Ethics: Some Trends." In *Moral Discourse and Practice,* ed. Stephen Darwall, Allan Gibbard, and Peter Railton. New York: Oxford University Press, 1997.

Dworkin, Ronald. *Life's Dominion.* New York: Knopf, 1993.

Edel, Abraham. "The Concept of Value and Its Travels in Twentieth Century America." In *Values and Value Theory in Twentieth Century America,* ed. Murray G. Murphey and Ivar Berg. Philadelphia: Temple University Press, 1988.

Epicurus. "Principal Doctrines." *The Epicurus Reader,* trans. Brad Inwood and L. P. Gerson. Indianapolis: Hackett, 1994.

Feldman, Fred. "On the Intrinsic Value of Pleasures." *Ethics* 107 (April 1997): 448–66.

Finnis, John. *Natural Law and Natural Rights.* Oxford: Clarendon Press, 1980.

Foot, Philippa. "Are Moral Considerations Overriding?" *Virtues and Vices.* Berkeley and Los Angeles: University of California Press, 1978.

———. "Morality as a System of Hypothetical Imperatives." *Virtues and Vices.* Berkeley and Los Angeles: University of California Press, 1978.

———. "Reasons for Action and Desire." *Virtues and Vices.* Berkeley and Los Angeles: University of California Press, 1978.

Frankena, William. *Ethics.* Englewood Cliffs, N.J.: Prentice Hall, 1963.

———. "Value and Valuation." In *Encyclopedia of Philosophy,* ed. Paul Edwards. New York: Macmillan, 1967.

Galston, William A. "Cosmopolitan Altruism." *Social Philosophy and Policy* 10, no. 1 (Winter 1993): 118–34.

Gauthier, David. *Morals by Agreement.* New York: Oxford University Press, 1986.

Gewirth, Alan. *Reason and Morality.* Chicago: University of Chicago Press, 1978.

Hampton, Jean. "Selflessness and the Loss of Self." *Social Philosophy and Policy* 10, no. 1 (Winter 1993): 135–65.

Harman, Gilbert. "Toward a Theory of Intrinsic Value." *Journal of Philosophy* 64 (December 1967): 792–804.

Hospers, John. "Why Be Moral?" In *Readings in Ethical Theory,* 2nd ed., ed. Wilfred Sellars and John Hospers. Englewood Cliffs, N.J.: Prentice Hall, 1970.

Howe, Daniel Walker. *Making the American Self.* Cambridge, Mass.: Harvard University Press, 1997.

Hudson, W. D. *Modern Moral Philosophy.* New York: Macmillan, 1970.

Irwin, Terence. *Aristotle's First Principles.* Oxford: Clarendon Press, 1988.

Kagan, Shelley. "The Limits of Well-Being." *Social Philosophy and Policy* 9 (Summer 1992): 169–89.

Kant, Immanuel. *The Doctrine of Virtue,* trans. Mary Gregor. Philadelphia: University of Pennsylvania Press, 1964.

———. *Foundations of the Metaphysics of Morals,* trans. Lewis White Beck. New York: Macmillan, 1990.

———. *Lectures on Ethics,* trans. Louis Infield. Indianapolis: Hackett, 1963.

Korsgaard, Christine M. "Two Distinctions in Goodness." *The Philosophical Review* 92 (April 1983): 169–95.

Kraut, Richard. *Aristotle on the Human Good.* Princeton, N.J.: Princeton University Press, 1989.

LaFollette, Hugh. *Personal Relationships—Love, Identity and Morality.* Cambridge, Mass.: Blackwell, 1996.

Laird, John. *The Idea of Value.* New York: August M. Kelley, 1969.

Lemos, Noah. *Intrinsic Value.* New York: Cambridge University Press, 1994.

Lennox, James G. "Health as an Objective Value." *Journal of Medicine and Philosophy* 20 (1995): 499–511.

Lepley, Ray, ed. *Value: A Cooperative Inquiry.* New York: Columbia University Press, 1949.

MacDonald, Scott. "Ultimate Ends in Practical Reasoning: Aquinas' Aristotelian Moral Psychology and Anscombe's Fallacy." *Philosophical Review* 100, no. 1 (January 1991): 31–66.

MacIntyre, Alasdair. "Egoism and Altruism." In *Encyclopedia of Philosophy,* ed. Paul Edwards. New York: Macmillan, 1967.

———. *A Short History of Ethics.* New York: Macmillan, 1966.

———. *Whose Justice? Which Rationality?* Notre Dame, Ind.: University of Notre Dame Press, 1988.

Martinich, Aloysius. *The Two Gods of Leviathan.* New York: Cambridge University Press, 1992.

McDowell, John. "Are Moral Requirements Hypothetical Imperatives?" *Proceedings of the Aristotelian Society* 52 (Suppl. 1978): 13–29.

Medlin, Brian. "Ultimate Principles and Ethical Egoism." *Australasian Journal of Philosophy* 35, no. 2 (August 1957): 111–18.

Moore, G. E. "The Conception of Intrinsic Value." *Philosophical Studies.* London: Routledge and Kegan Paul, 1922.

———. *Ethics.* New York: Henry Holt, 1912.

———. *Principia Ethica.* New York: Cambridge University Press, 1903.

Nagel, Thomas. *The View from Nowhere.* New York: Oxford University Press, 1986.

Nelson, Daniel Mark. *The Priority of Prudence.* University Park: Pennsylvania State University Press, 1992.

———. "Prudence." In *Encyclopedia of Ethics,* ed. Lawrence C. Becker. New York: Garland, 1992.

Nielsen, Kai. *Why Be Moral?* Buffalo, N.Y.: Prometheus, 1989.

Nozick, Robert. *The Examined Life—Philosophical Meditations.* New York: Simon and Schuster, 1989.

———. *Philosophical Explanations.* Cambridge, Mass.: Harvard University Press, 1981.

O'Neill, John. "The Varieties of Intrinsic Value." *The Monist* 75, no. 2 (April 1992): 119–37.

Osterberg, Jan. *Self and Others.* Dordrecht: Kluwer Academic Publishers, 1988.

Overvold, Mark Carl. "Morality, Self-Interest, and Reasons for Being Moral." *Philosophy and Phenomenological Research* 44, no. 4 (June 1984): 493–507.

Peikoff, Leonard. *Objectivism: The Philosophy of Ayn Rand.* New York: Dutton, 1991.

Perry, Ralph Barton. *General Theory of Value.* New York: Longmans, Green, 1926.

Prichard, H. A. "Does Moral Philosophy Rest on a Mistake?" In *Readings in Ethical Theory,* ed. Wilfred Sellars and John Hospers. New York: Appleton-Century-Croft, 1952.

———. "Duty and Interest." *Moral Obligation and Duty and Interest.* New York: Oxford University Press, 1968.

Railton, Peter. "Facts and Values." *Philosophical Topics* 14 (Fall 1986): 5–31.

Rand, Ayn. "Causality versus Duty." *Philosophy: Who Needs It.* New York: Bobbs-Merrill, 1982.

———. *Introduction to Objectivist Epistemology.* 2nd ed. New York: Penguin, 1990.

———. "The Metaphysical versus the Man-Made." *Philosophy: Who Needs It.* New York: Bobbs-Merrill, 1982.

———. "The Soul of an Individualist." *For the New Intellectual.* New York: Random House, 1961.

———. *The Virtue of Selfishness.* New York: New American Library, 1964.

Rawls, John. "Kantian Constructivism in Moral Theory: The Dewey Lectures 1980." *Journal of Philosophy* 77, no. 9 (September 1980): 515–72.

———. *A Theory of Justice.* Cambridge, Mass.: Belknap Press, 1971.

Raz, Joseph, ed. *Practical Reasoning.* Oxford: Oxford University Press, 1978.

Rogers, Kelly, ed. *Self-Interest—an Anthology of Philosophical Perspectives.* New York: Routledge, 1997.

Ross, W. D. *The Right and the Good.* Indianapolis: Hackett, 1988.

———. "What Makes Right Actions Right?" In *Readings in Ethical Theory,* ed. Wilfred Sellars and John Hospers. New York: Appleton-Century-Croft, 1952.

Schmidtz, David. *Rational Choice and Moral Agency.* Princeton, N.J.: Princeton University Press, 1995.

Shelton, Ray. "A Life-Centered Metaethics: Ancient and Modern." Masters thesis, San Francisco State University, 1995.

Sherman, Nancy. *The Fabric of Character.* Oxford: Clarendon University Press, 1989.

Sidgwick, Henry. *The Methods of Ethics.* 7th ed. Indianapolis: Hackett, 1981.

Smith, Tara. "Intrinsic Value: Look–Say Ethics." *Journal of Value Inquiry* 32 (1998): 539–53.

———. *Moral Rights and Political Freedom.* Lanham, Md.: Rowman & Little-field, 1995.

———. "On Being *Really* Selfish." Unpublished lecture.

———. "Reconsidering Zero-Sum Value: It's How You Play the Game." *Journal of Social Philosophy* 28 (Fall 1997): 128–39.

———. "Rights, Friends, and Egoism." *Journal of Philosophy* 90 (March 1993): 144–48.

———. "Why Do I Love Thee? A Response to Nozick's Account of Romantic Love." *Southwest Philosophy Review* 7, no. 1 (January 1991): 47–57.

Social Philosophy and Policy 14, no. 1 (Winter 1997).

Spinoza, Benedict. *The Ethics and Selected Letters,* ed. Seymour Feldman, trans. Samuel Shirley. Indianapolis: Hackett, 1982.

Sumner, L. W. "Two Theories of the Good." *Social Philosophy and Policy* 9, no. 2 (Summer 1992): 1–14.

Thomson, Garrett. *Needs.* New York: Routledge and Kegan Paul, 1987.

Thomson, Judith Jarvis. "On Some Ways in Which a Thing Can Be Good." *Social Philosophy and Policy* 9 (Summer 1992): 96–117.

Thornton, J. C. "Can the Moral Point of View Be Justified?" In *Readings in Contemporary Ethical Theory,* ed. K. Pahel and M. Schiller. Englewood Cliffs, N.J.: Prentice Hall, 1970.

Toulmin, Stephen. *Reason in Ethics.* Cambridge: Cambridge University Press, 1964.

Treloar, John L. "Moral Virtue and the Demise of Prudence in the Thought of Francis Suarez." *American Catholic Philosophical Quarterly* 65 (Summer 1991): 387–405.

Urmson, J. O. "A Defense of Intuitionism." *Proceedings of the Aristotelian Society* 75 (1974–75): 111–19.

Vallentyne, Peter, ed. *Contractarianism and Rational Choice.* New York: Cambridge University Press, 1991.

von Wright, G. H. *The Varieties of Goodness.* London: Routledge and Kegan Paul, 1963.

Wiggins, David. "Truth, Invention, and the Meaning of Life." *Proceedings of the British Academy* 62 (1976): 331–78.

Williams, Bernard. *Making Sense of Humanity and Other Philosophical Papers.* New York: Cambridge University Press, 1995.

———. "The Makropulos Case: Reflections on the Tedium of Immortality." *Problems of the Self.* New York: Cambridge University Press, 1973.

Index